Garfield
SINGS FOR HIS SUPPER

BY JIM DAVIS

Ballantine Books • New York

A Ballantine Books Trade Paperback Original

Copyright © 2013 by PAWS, Inc. All Rights Reserved.
"GARFIELD" and the GARFIELD characters are trademarks of PAWS, Inc.

Published in the United States by Ballantine Books, an imprint of The Random House Publishing Group,
a division of Random House, Inc., New York.

BALLANTINE and colophon are registered trademarks of Random House, Inc.

ISBN 978-0-345-52593-2
eBook ISBN 978-0-345-53777-5

Printed in the United States of America

www.ballantinebooks.com

9 8 7 6 5 4 3 2 1

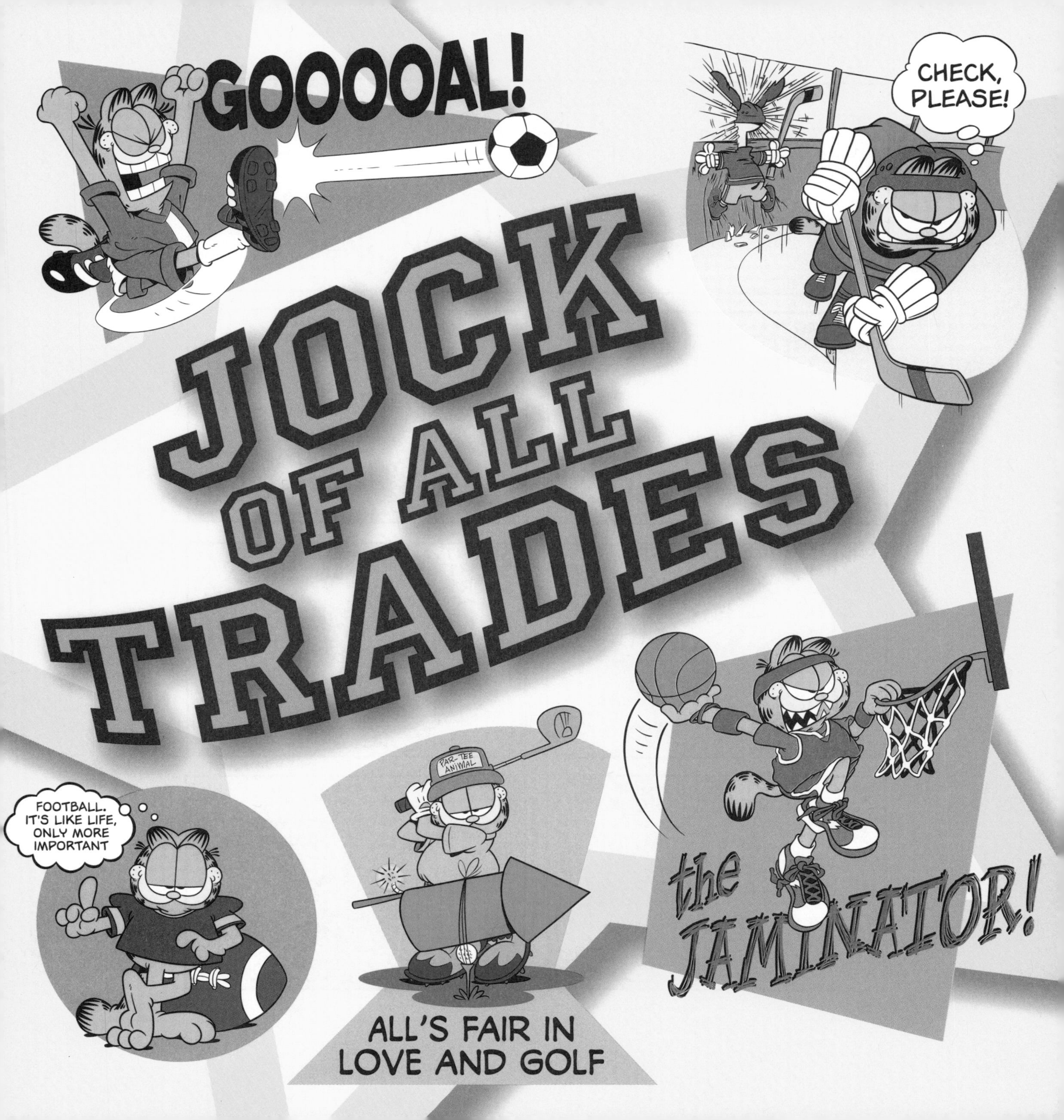
GOOOOAL!
CHECK, PLEASE!
JOCK OF ALL TRADES
PAR-TEE ANIMAL
FOOTBALL. IT'S LIKE LIFE, ONLY MORE IMPORTANT
the JAMINATOR!
ALL'S FAIR IN LOVE AND GOLF

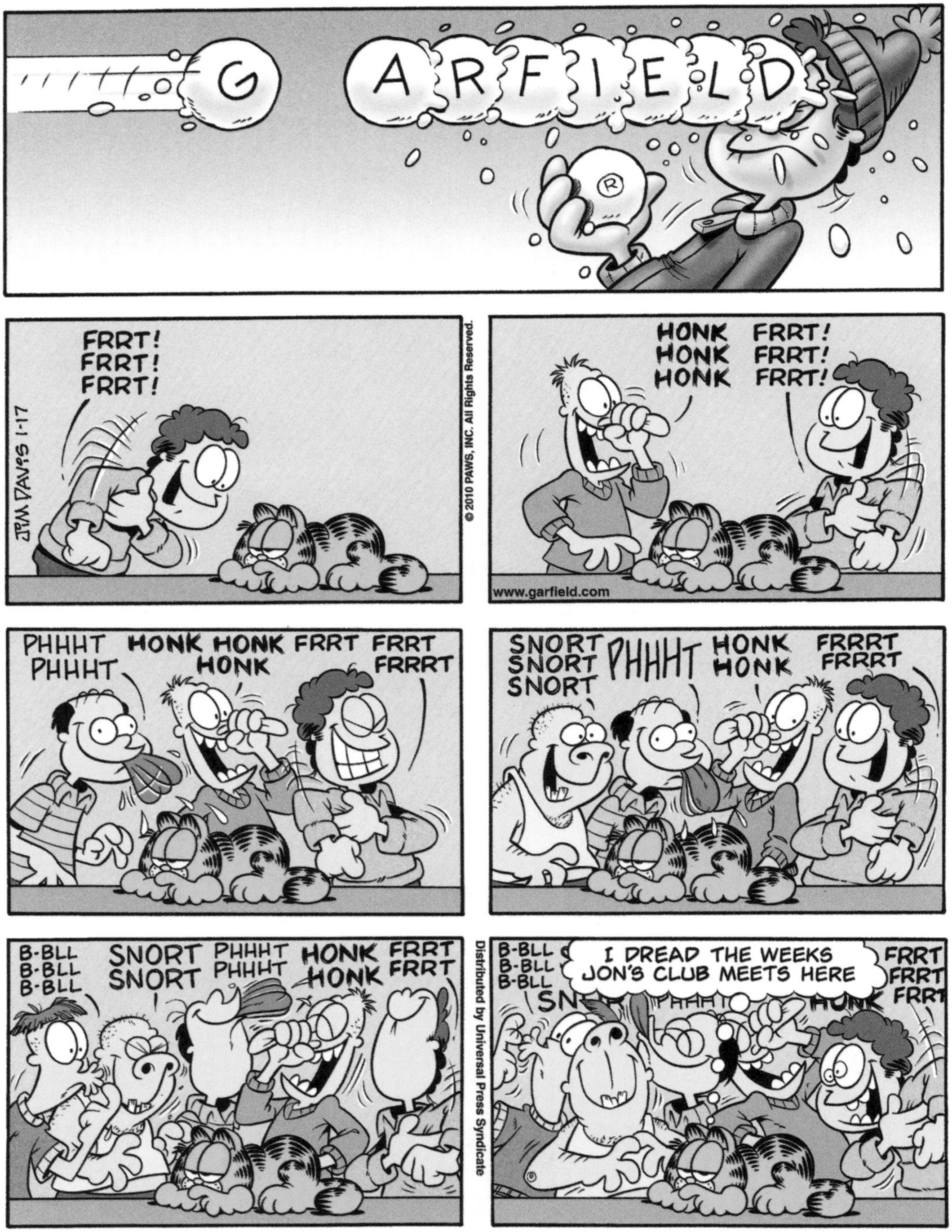
GARFIELD
®
FRRT!
FRRT!
FRRT!
JPM DAVIS 1-17
© 2010 PAWS, INC. All Rights Reserved.
HONK
HONK
HONK
FRRT!
FRRT!
FRRT!
www.garfield.com
PHHHT
PHHHT
HONK HONK
HONK
FRRT FRRT
FRRRT
SNORT
SNORT
SNORT
PHHHT
HONK
HONK
FRRRT
FRRRT
B-BLL
B-BLL
B-BLL
SNORT
SNORT
PHHHT
PHHHT
HONK
HONK
FRRT
FRRT
Distributed by Universal Press Syndicate
B-BLL
B-BLL
B-BLL
I DREAD THE WEEKS
JON'S CLUB MEETS HERE
FRRT
FRRT
FRRT

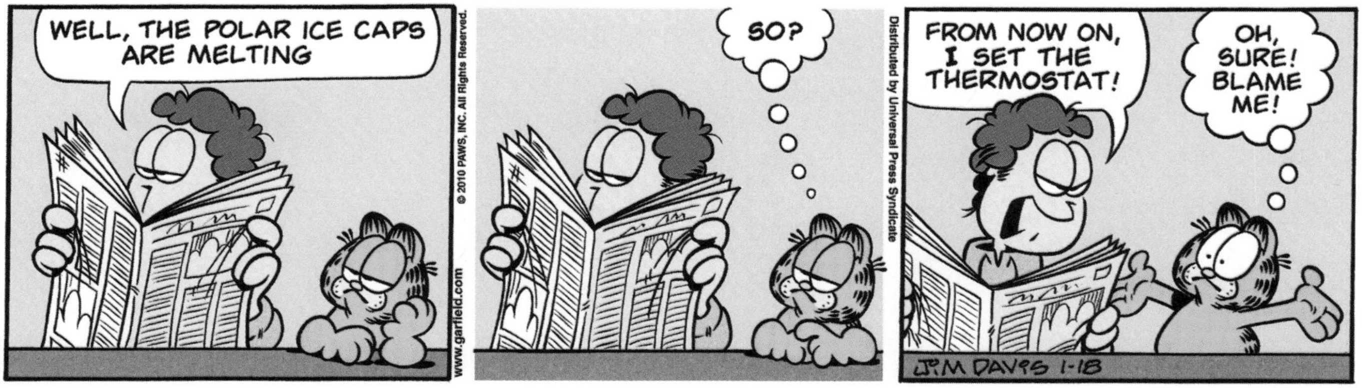
WELL, THE POLAR ICE CAPS ARE MELTING
SO?
FROM NOW ON, I SET THE THERMOSTAT!
OH, SURE! BLAME ME!
JIM DAVIS 1-18
© 2010 PAWS, INC. All Rights Reserved.
www.garfield.com
Distributed by Universal Press Syndicate

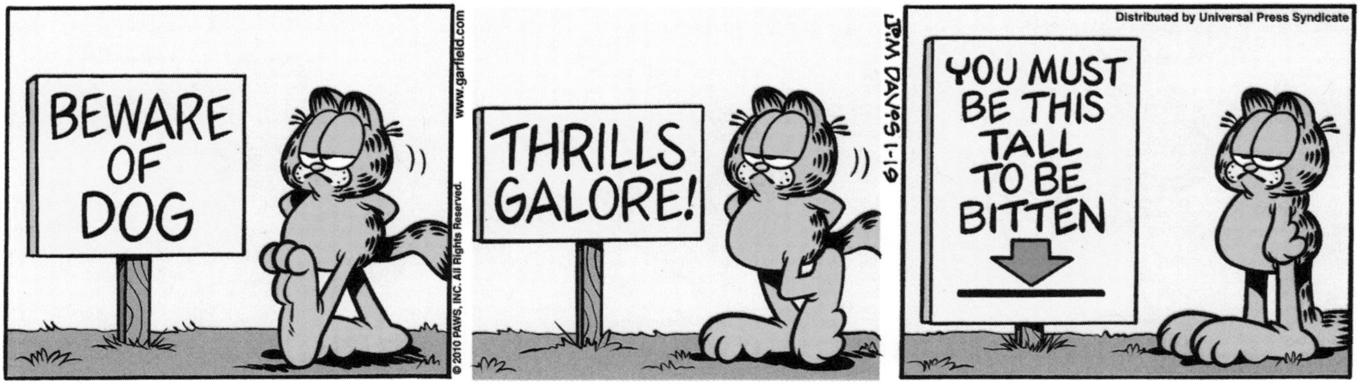
BEWARE OF DOG
THRILLS GALORE!
YOU MUST BE THIS TALL TO BE BITTEN
JIM DAVIS 1-19
© 2010 PAWS, INC. All Rights Reserved.
www.garfield.com
Distributed by Universal Press Syndicate

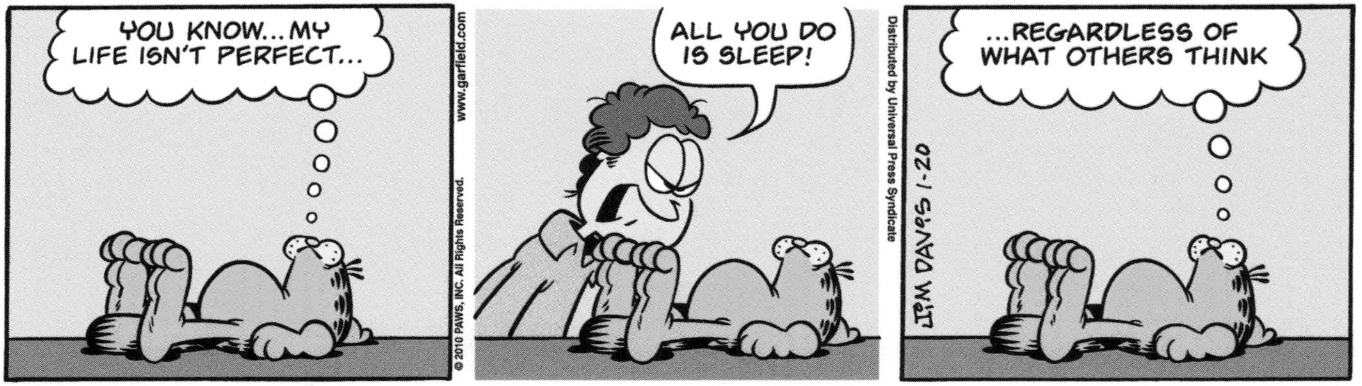
YOU KNOW... MY LIFE ISN'T PERFECT...
ALL YOU DO IS SLEEP!
...REGARDLESS OF WHAT OTHERS THINK
JIM DAVIS 1-20
© 2010 PAWS, INC. All Rights Reserved.
www.garfield.com
Distributed by Universal Press Syndicate

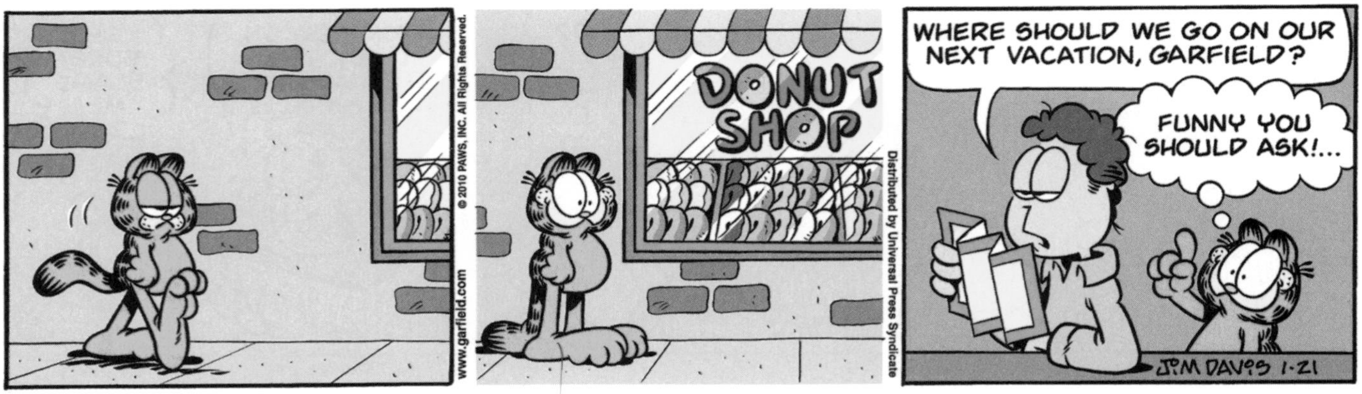
DONUT SHOP
WHERE SHOULD WE GO ON OUR NEXT VACATION, GARFIELD?
FUNNY YOU SHOULD ASK!...
JIM DAVIS 1-21

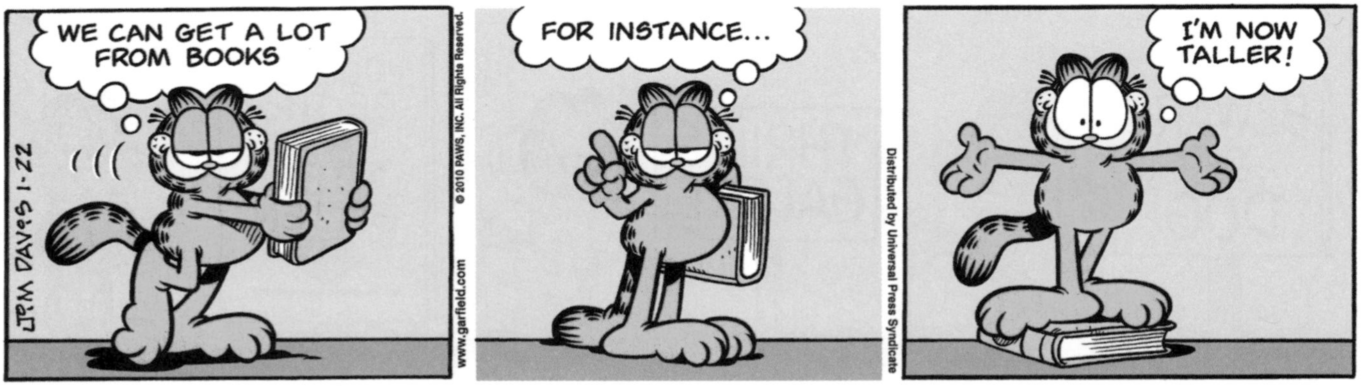
WE CAN GET A LOT FROM BOOKS
JIM DAVIS 1-22
FOR INSTANCE...
I'M NOW TALLER!

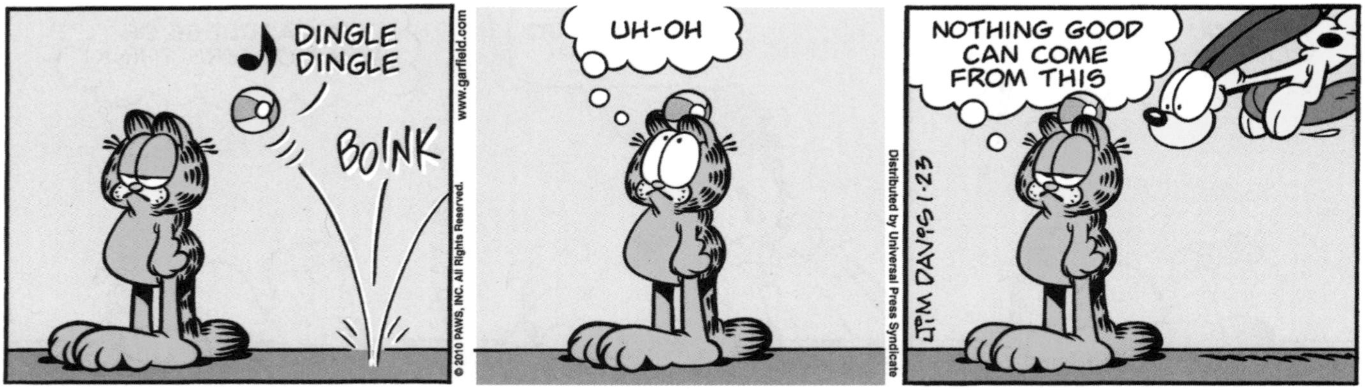
DINGLE DINGLE
BOINK
UH-OH
NOTHING GOOD CAN COME FROM THIS
JIM DAVIS 1-23

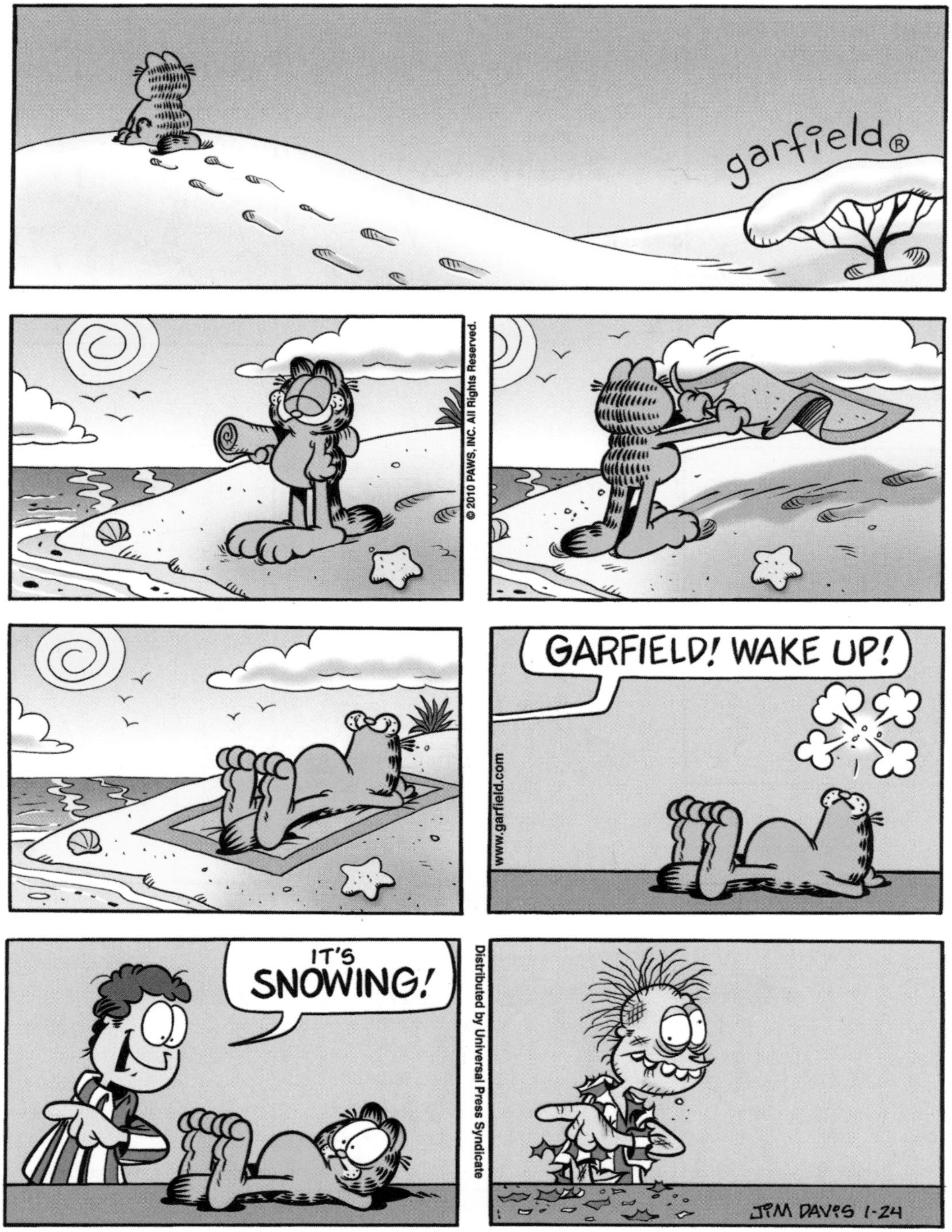
garfield®
© 2010 PAWS, INC. All Rights Reserved.
GARFIELD! WAKE UP!
www.garfield.com
IT'S SNOWING!
Distributed by Universal Press Syndicate
JIM DAVIS 1-24

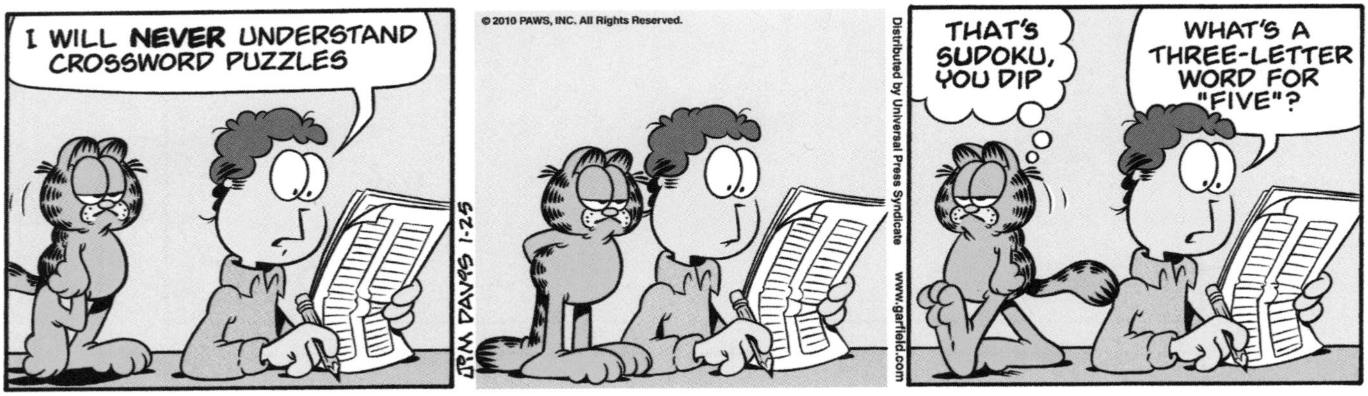
I WILL NEVER UNDERSTAND CROSSWORD PUZZLES
JIM DAVIS 1-25
© 2010 PAWS, INC. All Rights Reserved.
Distributed by Universal Press Syndicate www.garfield.com
THAT'S SUDOKU, YOU DIP
WHAT'S A THREE-LETTER WORD FOR "FIVE"?

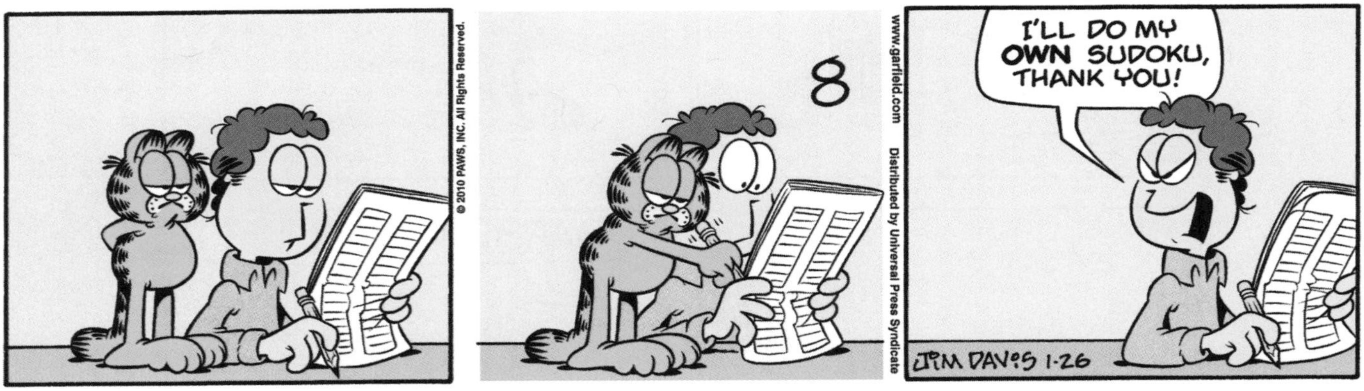
© 2010 PAWS, INC. All Rights Reserved.
8
www.garfield.com Distributed by Universal Press Syndicate
I'LL DO MY OWN SUDOKU, THANK YOU!
JIM DAVIS 1-26

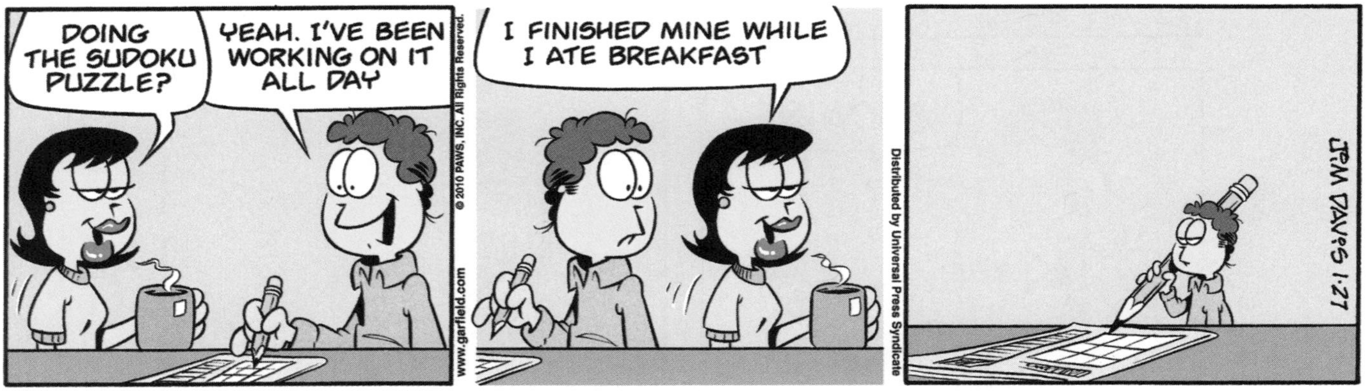
DOING THE SUDOKU PUZZLE?
YEAH. I'VE BEEN WORKING ON IT ALL DAY
© 2010 PAWS, INC. All Rights Reserved. www.garfield.com
I FINISHED MINE WHILE I ATE BREAKFAST
Distributed by Universal Press Syndicate
JIM DAVIS 1-27

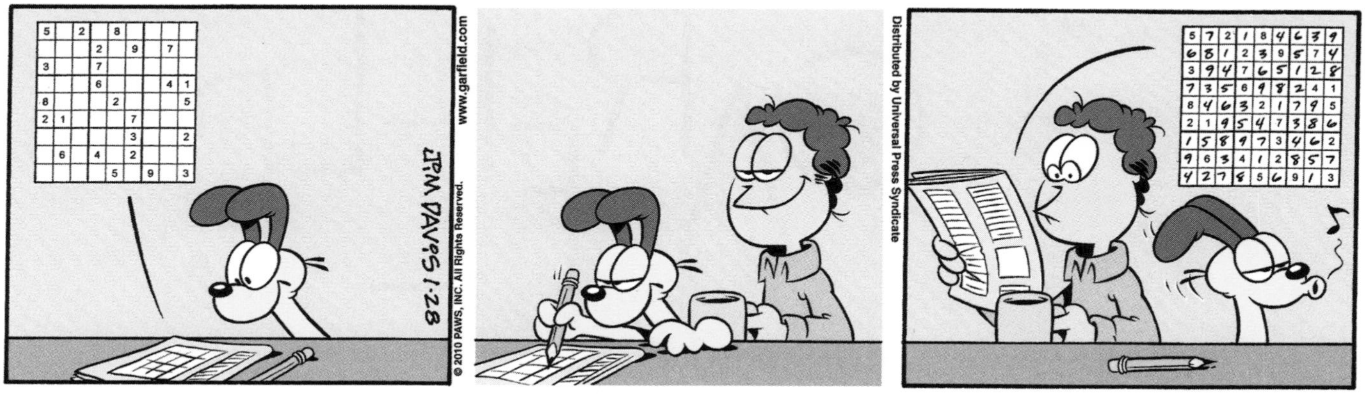
JIM DAVIS 1-28
© 2010 PAWS, INC. All Rights Reserved.
www.garfield.com
Distributed by Universal Press Syndicate

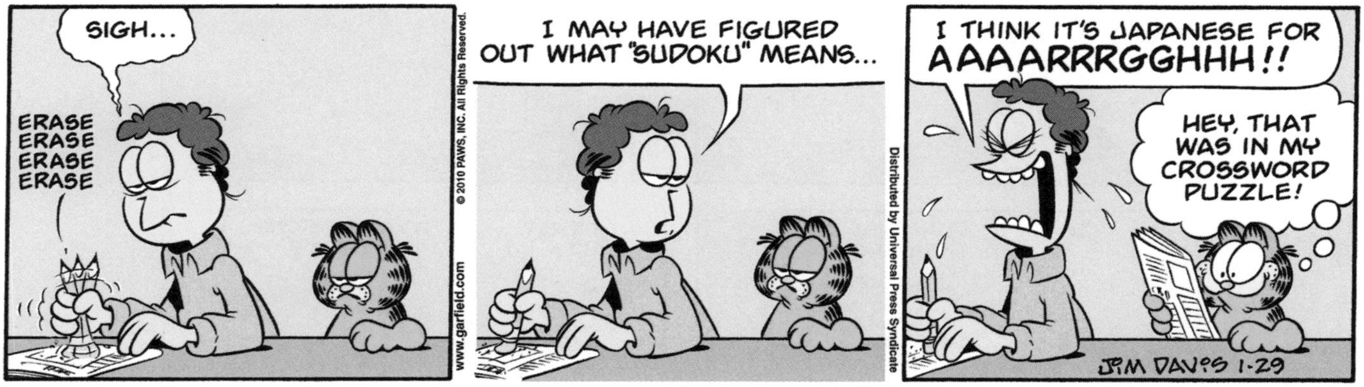
SIGH...
ERASE ERASE ERASE ERASE
© 2010 PAWS, INC. All Rights Reserved.
www.garfield.com
I MAY HAVE FIGURED OUT WHAT "SUDOKU" MEANS...
Distributed by Universal Press Syndicate
I THINK IT'S JAPANESE FOR AAAARRRGHHH!!
HEY, THAT WAS IN MY CROSSWORD PUZZLE!
JIM DAVIS 1-29

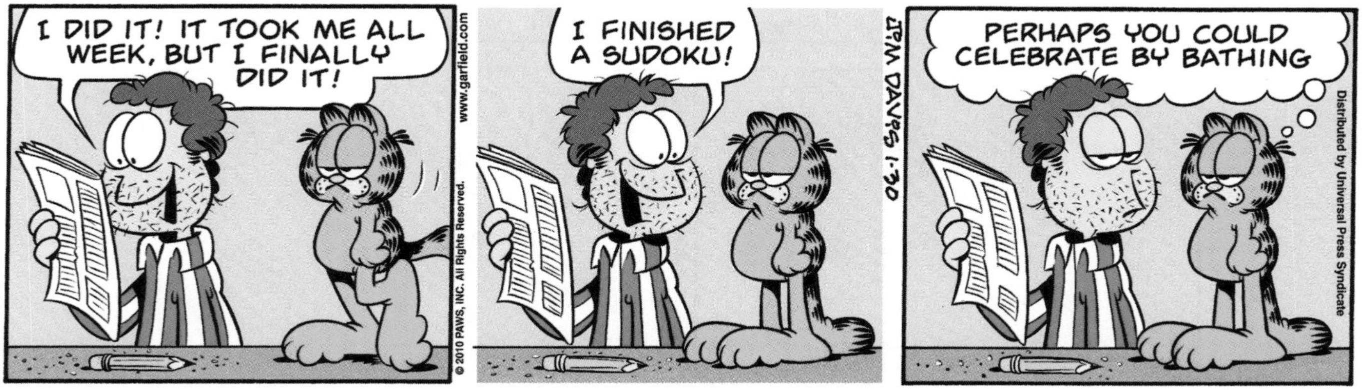
I DID IT! IT TOOK ME ALL WEEK, BUT I FINALLY DID IT!
www.garfield.com
© 2010 PAWS, INC. All Rights Reserved.
I FINISHED A SUDOKU!
JIM DAVIS 1-30
PERHAPS YOU COULD CELEBRATE BY BATHING
Distributed by Universal Press Syndicate

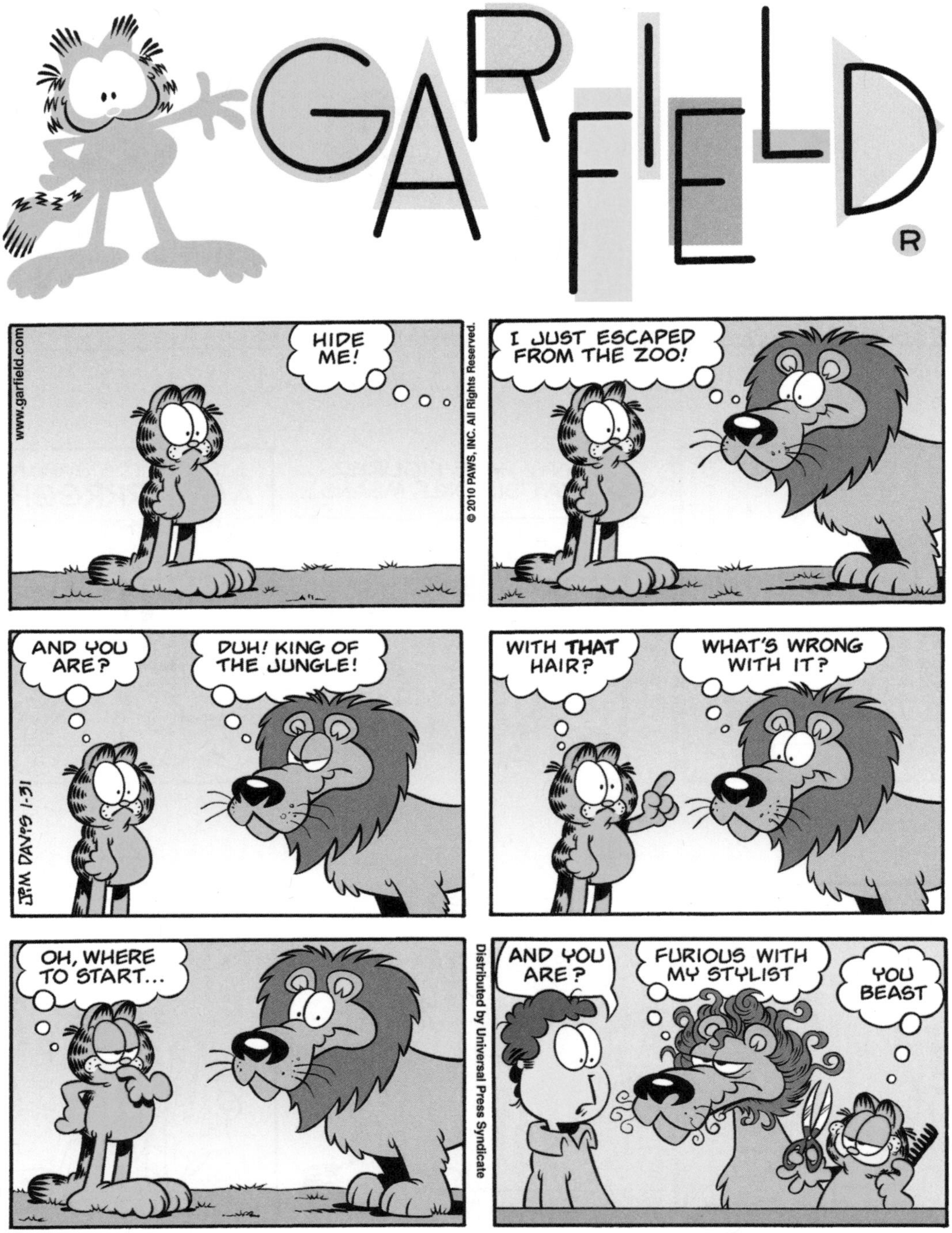
GARFIELD®
www.garfield.com
HIDE ME!
© 2010 PAWS, INC. All Rights Reserved.
I JUST ESCAPED FROM THE ZOO!
AND YOU ARE?
DUH! KING OF THE JUNGLE!
JPM DAVPS 1-31
WITH THAT HAIR?
WHAT'S WRONG WITH IT?
OH, WHERE TO START...
Distributed by Universal Press Syndicate
AND YOU ARE?
FURIOUS WITH MY STYLIST
YOU BEAST

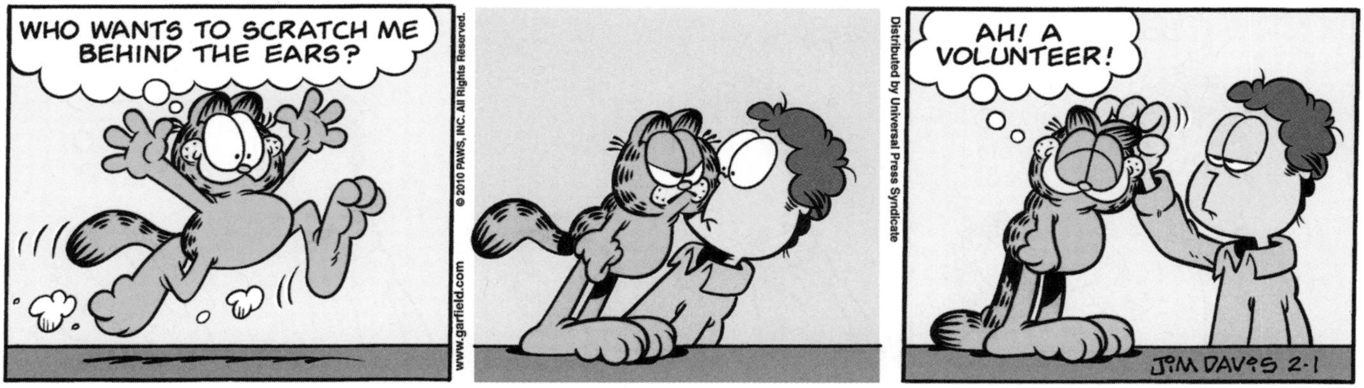
WHO WANTS TO SCRATCH ME BEHIND THE EARS?
© 2010 PAWS, INC. All Rights Reserved.
www.garfield.com
Distributed by Universal Press Syndicate
AH! A VOLUNTEER!
JIM DAVIS 2-1

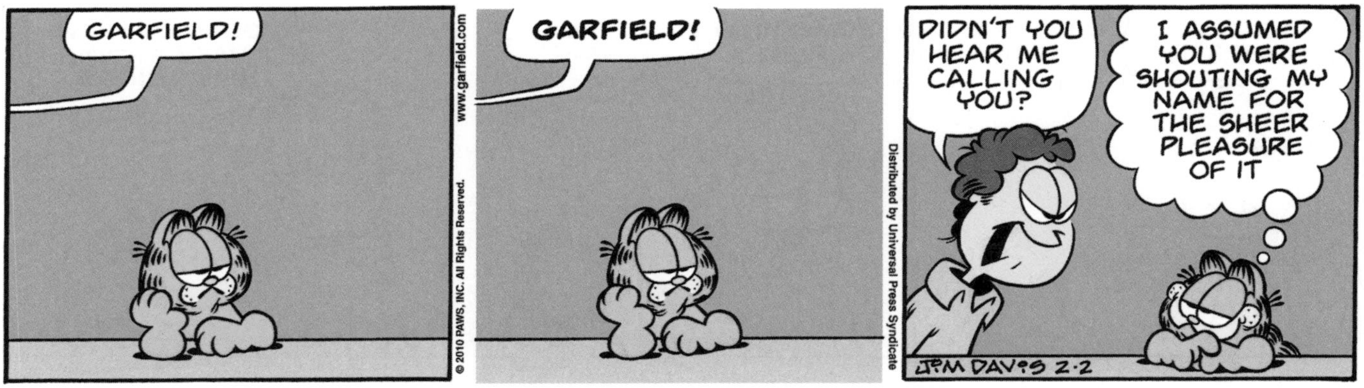
GARFIELD!
www.garfield.com
© 2010 PAWS, INC. All Rights Reserved.
GARFIELD!
Distributed by Universal Press Syndicate
DIDN'T YOU HEAR ME CALLING YOU?
I ASSUMED YOU WERE SHOUTING MY NAME FOR THE SHEER PLEASURE OF IT
JIM DAVIS 2-2

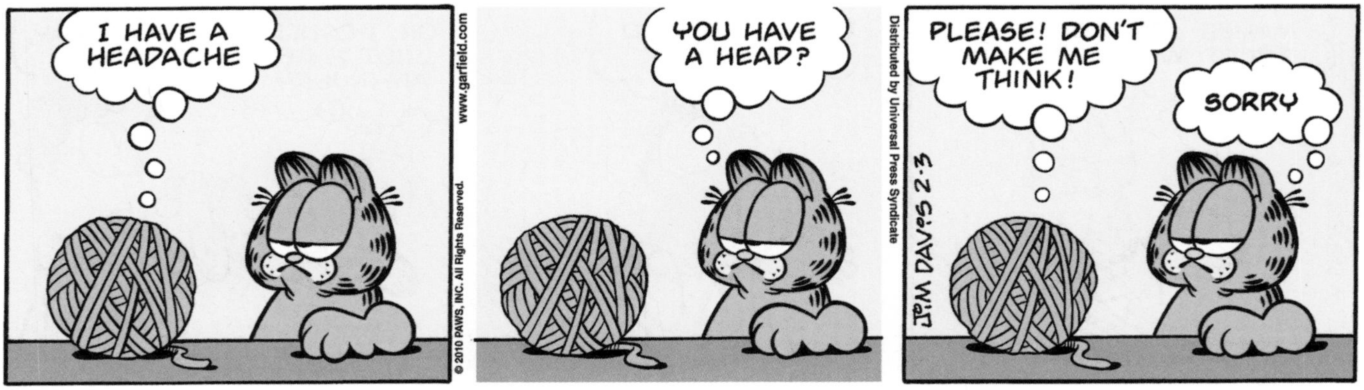
I HAVE A HEADACHE
www.garfield.com
© 2010 PAWS, INC. All Rights Reserved.
YOU HAVE A HEAD?
Distributed by Universal Press Syndicate
PLEASE! DON'T MAKE ME THINK!
SORRY
JIM DAVIS 2-3

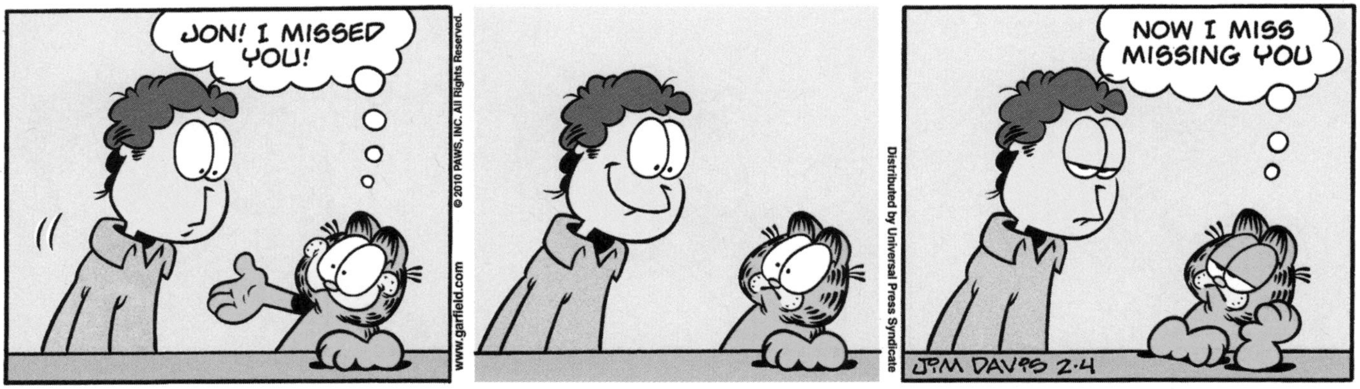
JON! I MISSED YOU!
NOW I MISS MISSING YOU
© 2010 PAWS, INC. All Rights Reserved.
www.garfield.com
Distributed by Universal Press Syndicate
JIM DAVIS 2-4

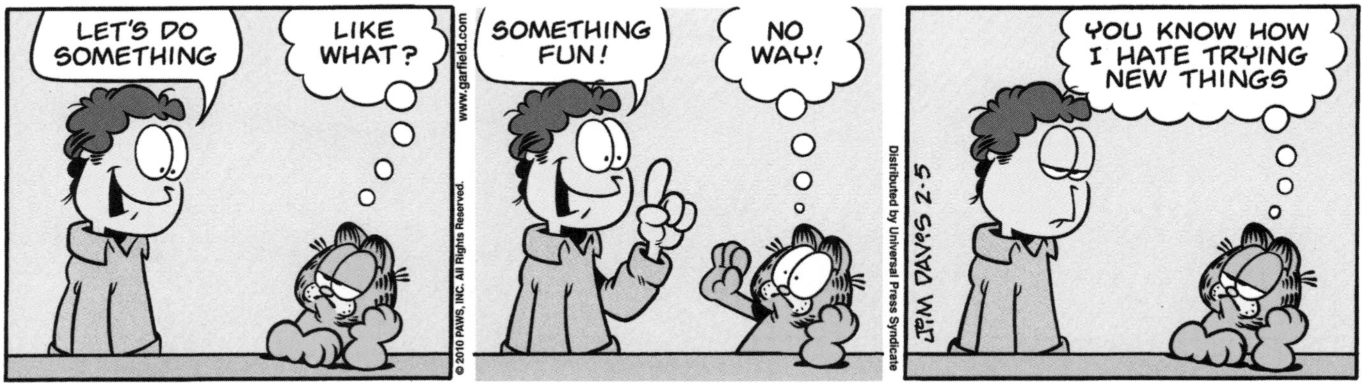
LET'S DO SOMETHING
LIKE WHAT?
SOMETHING FUN!
NO WAY!
YOU KNOW HOW I HATE TRYING NEW THINGS
© 2010 PAWS, INC. All Rights Reserved.
www.garfield.com
Distributed by Universal Press Syndicate
JIM DAVIS 2-5

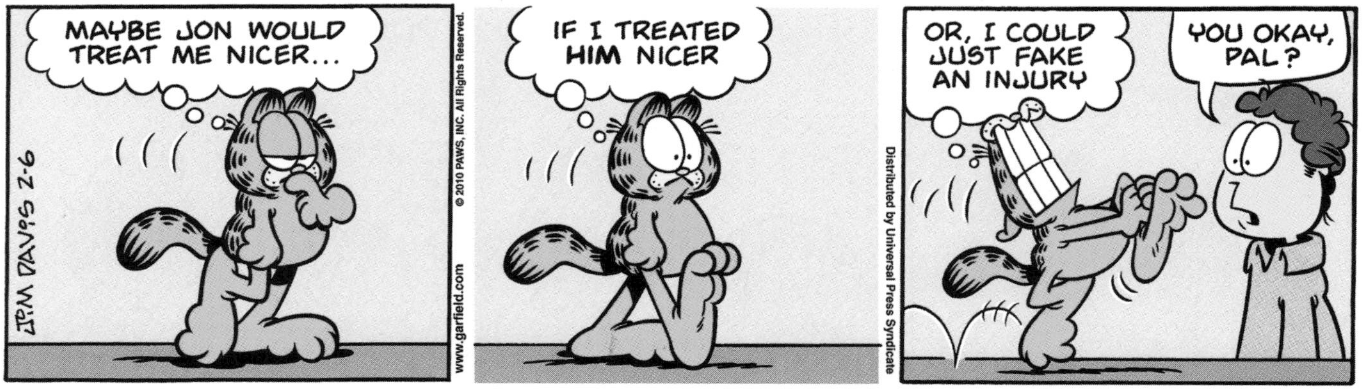
MAYBE JON WOULD TREAT ME NICER...
IF I TREATED HIM NICER
OR, I COULD JUST FAKE AN INJURY
YOU OKAY, PAL?
JIM DAVIS 2-6
© 2010 PAWS, INC. All Rights Reserved.
www.garfield.com
Distributed by Universal Press Syndicate

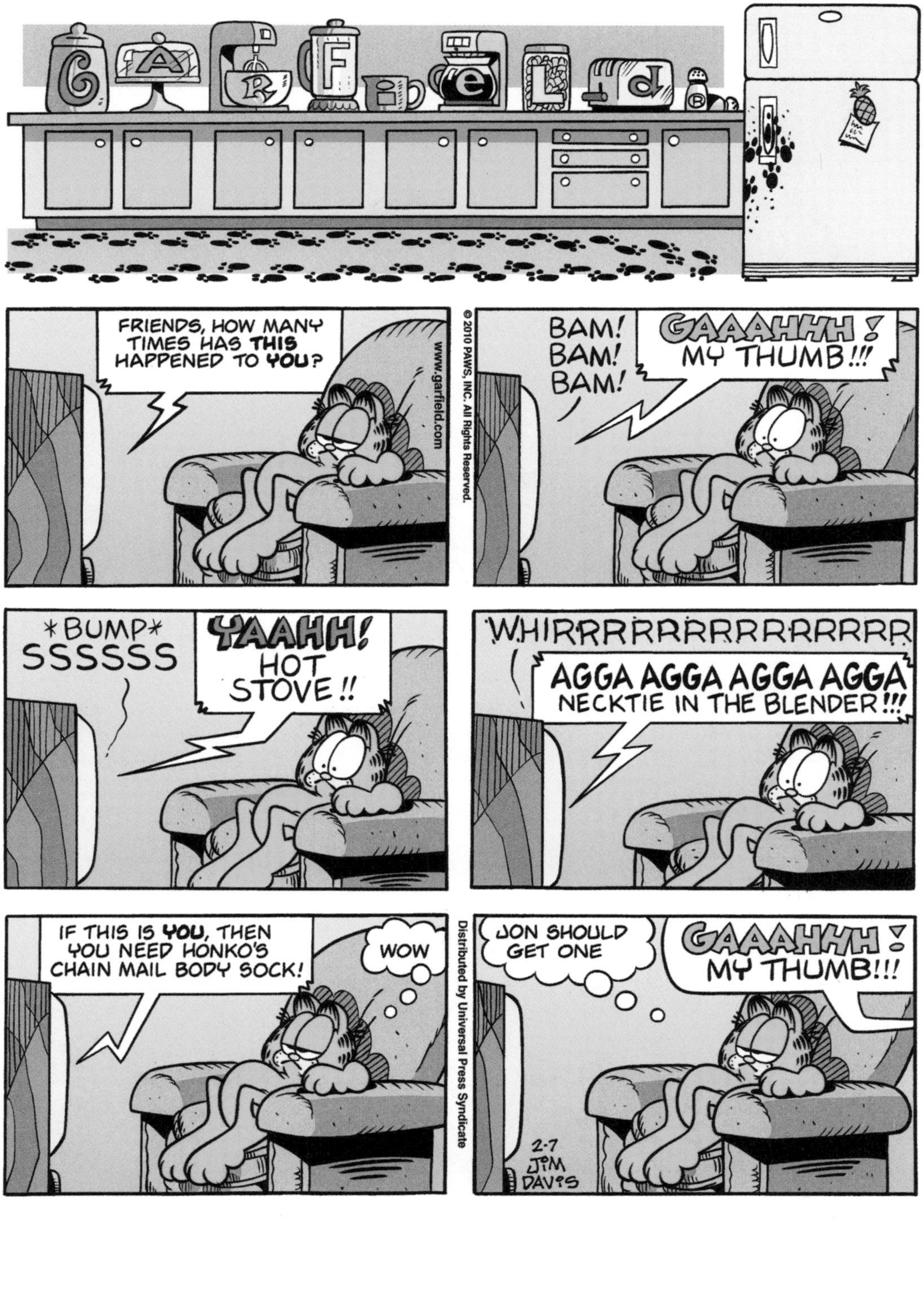
GARFIELD
FRIENDS, HOW MANY TIMES HAS THIS HAPPENED TO YOU?
BAM! BAM! BAM!
GAAAHHH! MY THUMB!!!
BUMP SSSSSS
YAAHH! HOT STOVE!!
WHIRRRRRRRRRRRRRR
AGGA AGGA AGGA AGGA NECKTIE IN THE BLENDER!!!
IF THIS IS YOU, THEN YOU NEED HONKO'S CHAIN MAIL BODY SOCK!
WOW
JON SHOULD GET ONE
GAAAHHH! MY THUMB!!!
© 2010 PAWS, INC. All Rights Reserved.
www.garfield.com
Distributed by Universal Press Syndicate
2-7 JIM DAVIS

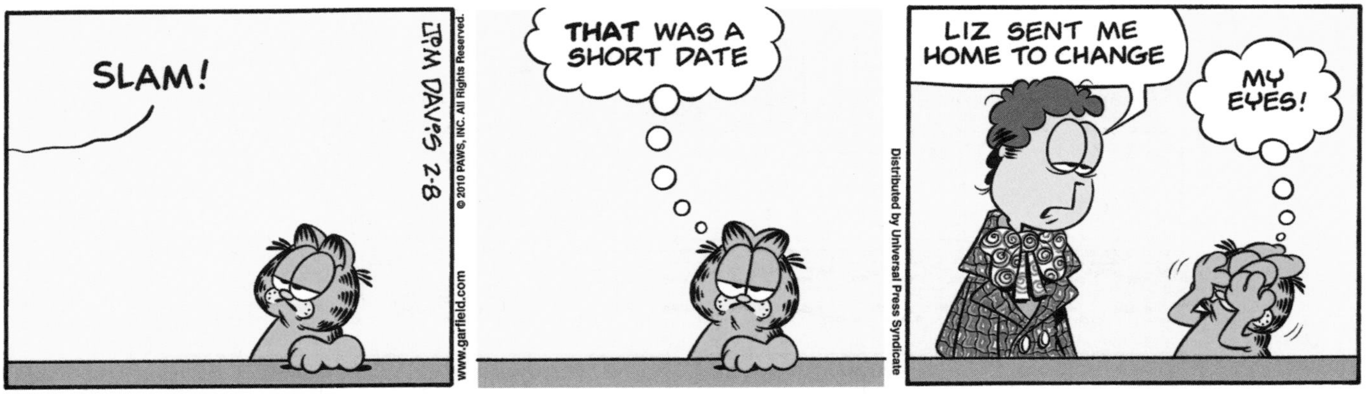
SLAM!
JIM DAVIS 2-8
© 2010 PAWS, INC. All Rights Reserved.
www.garfield.com
THAT WAS A SHORT DATE
Distributed by Universal Press Syndicate
LIZ SENT ME HOME TO CHANGE
MY EYES!

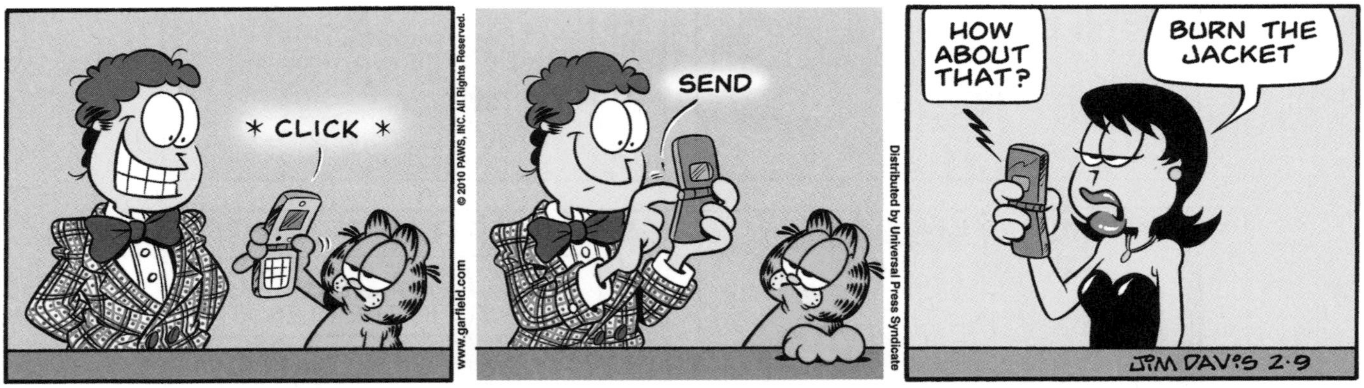
* CLICK *
© 2010 PAWS, INC. All Rights Reserved.
www.garfield.com
SEND
Distributed by Universal Press Syndicate
HOW ABOUT THAT?
BURN THE JACKET
JIM DAVIS 2-9

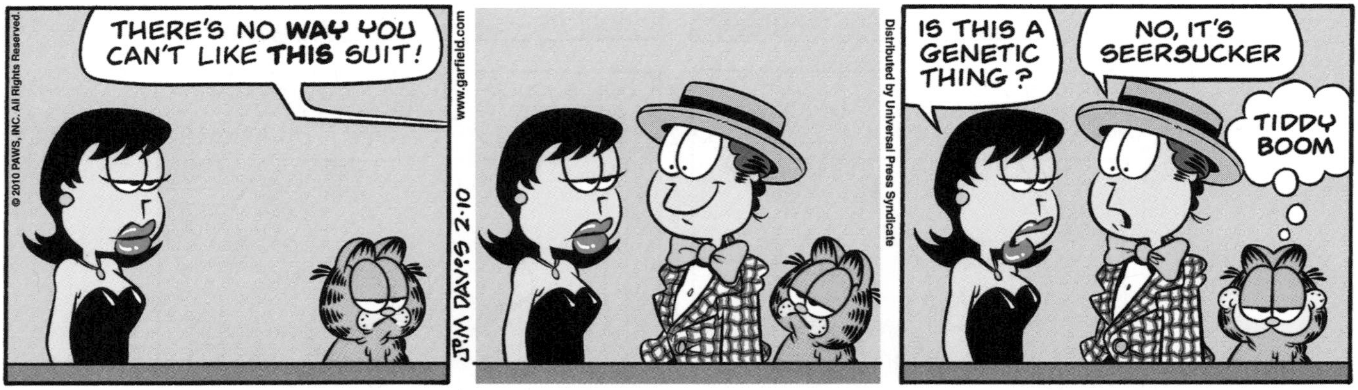
© 2010 PAWS, INC. All Rights Reserved.
THERE'S NO WAY YOU CAN'T LIKE THIS SUIT!
www.garfield.com
JIM DAVIS 2-10
Distributed by Universal Press Syndicate
IS THIS A GENETIC THING?
NO, IT'S SEERSUCKER
TIDDY BOOM

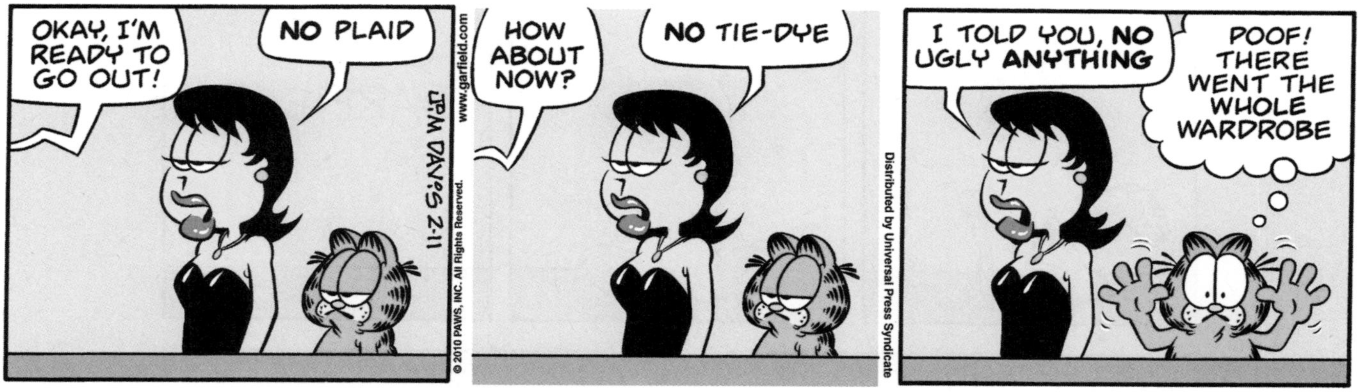
OKAY, I'M READY TO GO OUT!
NO PLAID
JIM DAVIS 2-11
www.garfield.com
© 2010 PAWS, INC. All Rights Reserved.
HOW ABOUT NOW?
NO TIE-DYE
Distributed by Universal Press Syndicate
I TOLD YOU, NO UGLY ANYTHING
POOF! THERE WENT THE WHOLE WARDROBE

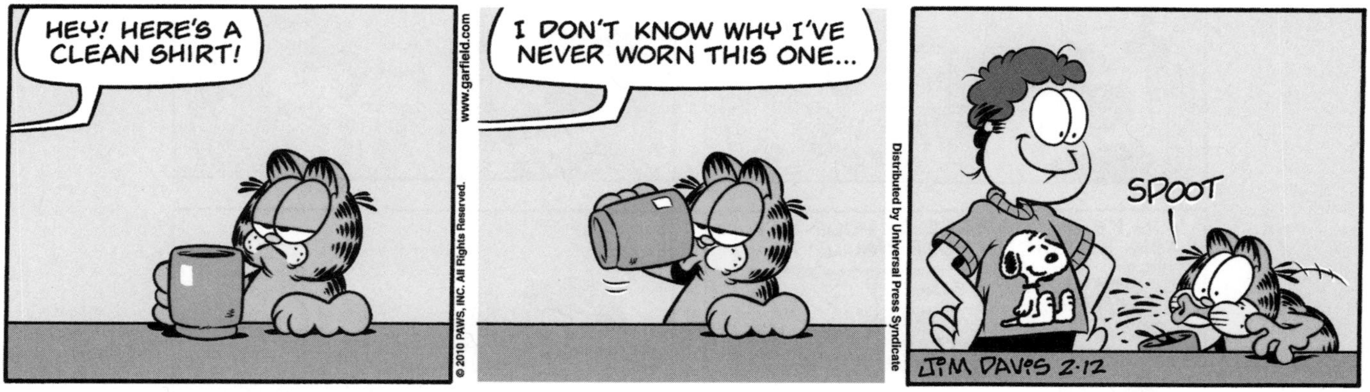
HEY! HERE'S A CLEAN SHIRT!
www.garfield.com
© 2010 PAWS, INC. All Rights Reserved.
I DON'T KNOW WHY I'VE NEVER WORN THIS ONE...
Distributed by Universal Press Syndicate
SPOOT
JIM DAVIS 2-12

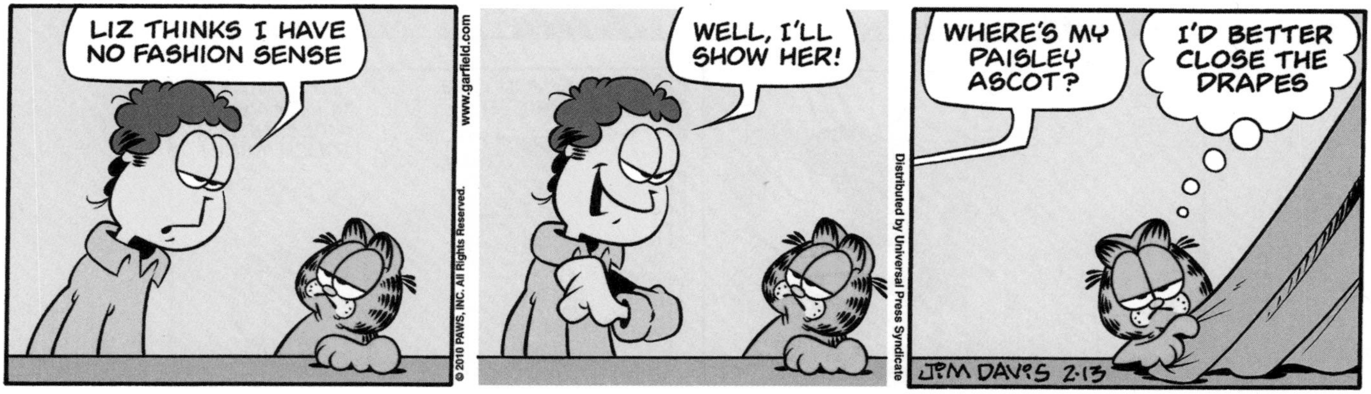
LIZ THINKS I HAVE NO FASHION SENSE
www.garfield.com
© 2010 PAWS, INC. All Rights Reserved.
WELL, I'LL SHOW HER!
Distributed by Universal Press Syndicate
WHERE'S MY PAISLEY ASCOT?
I'D BETTER CLOSE THE DRAPES
JIM DAVIS 2-13

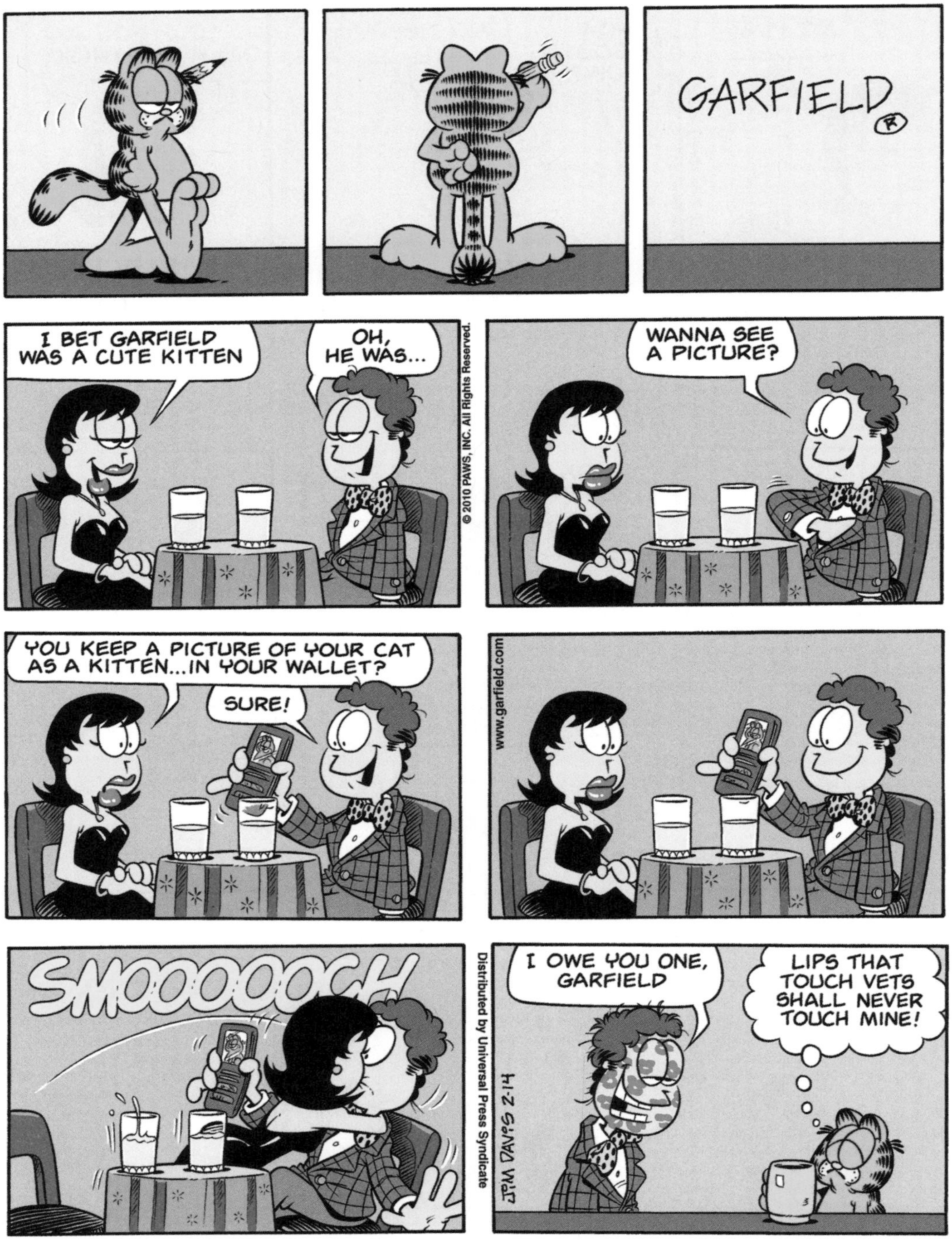
GARFIELD®
I BET GARFIELD WAS A CUTE KITTEN
OH, HE WAS...
© 2010 PAWS, INC. All Rights Reserved.
WANNA SEE A PICTURE?
YOU KEEP A PICTURE OF YOUR CAT AS A KITTEN...IN YOUR WALLET?
SURE!
www.garfield.com
SMOOOOOCH
JPM DAVIS 2-14
Distributed by Universal Press Syndicate
I OWE YOU ONE, GARFIELD
LIPS THAT TOUCH VETS SHALL NEVER TOUCH MINE!

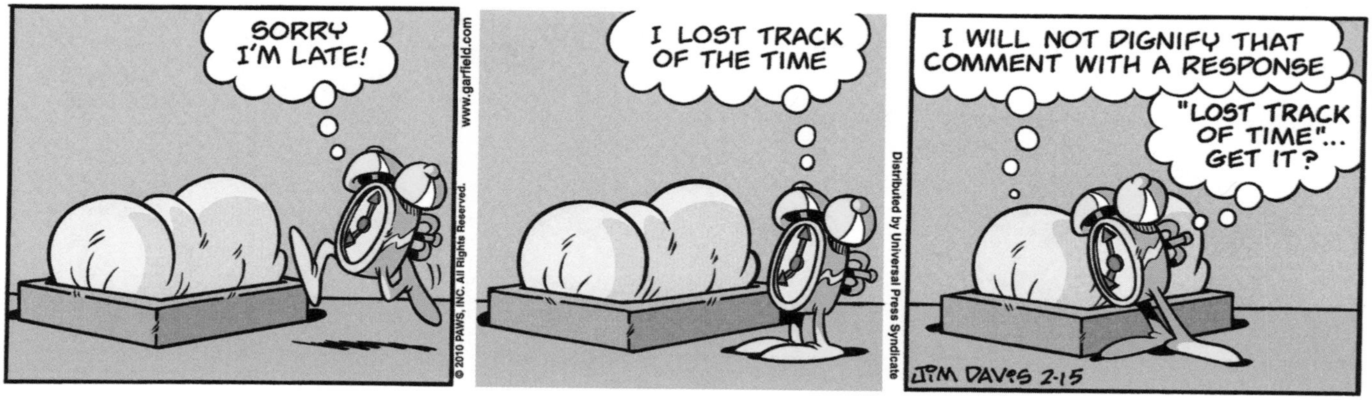
SORRY I'M LATE!
www.garfield.com
© 2010 PAWS, INC. All Rights Reserved.
I LOST TRACK OF THE TIME
Distributed by Universal Press Syndicate
I WILL NOT DIGNIFY THAT COMMENT WITH A RESPONSE
"LOST TRACK OF TIME"... GET IT?
JIM DAVIS 2-15

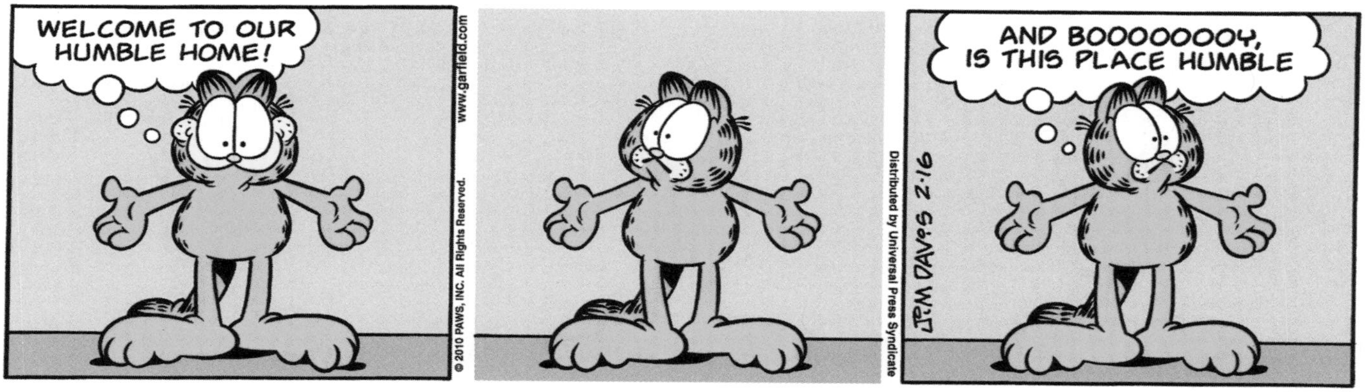
WELCOME TO OUR HUMBLE HOME!
www.garfield.com
© 2010 PAWS, INC. All Rights Reserved.
Distributed by Universal Press Syndicate
JIM DAVIS 2-16
AND BOOOOOOOY, IS THIS PLACE HUMBLE

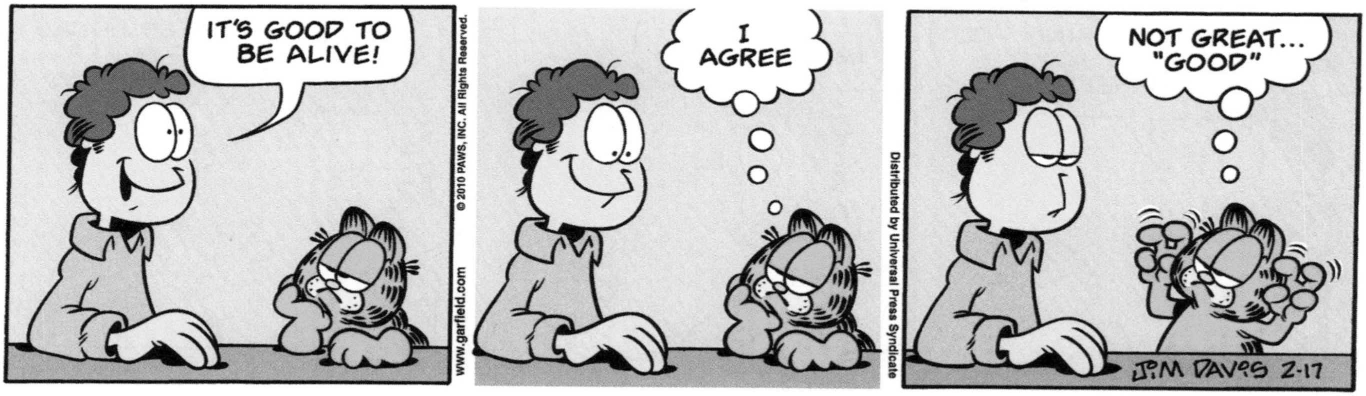
IT'S GOOD TO BE ALIVE!
© 2010 PAWS, INC. All Rights Reserved.
www.garfield.com
I AGREE
Distributed by Universal Press Syndicate
NOT GREAT... "GOOD"
JIM DAVIS 2-17

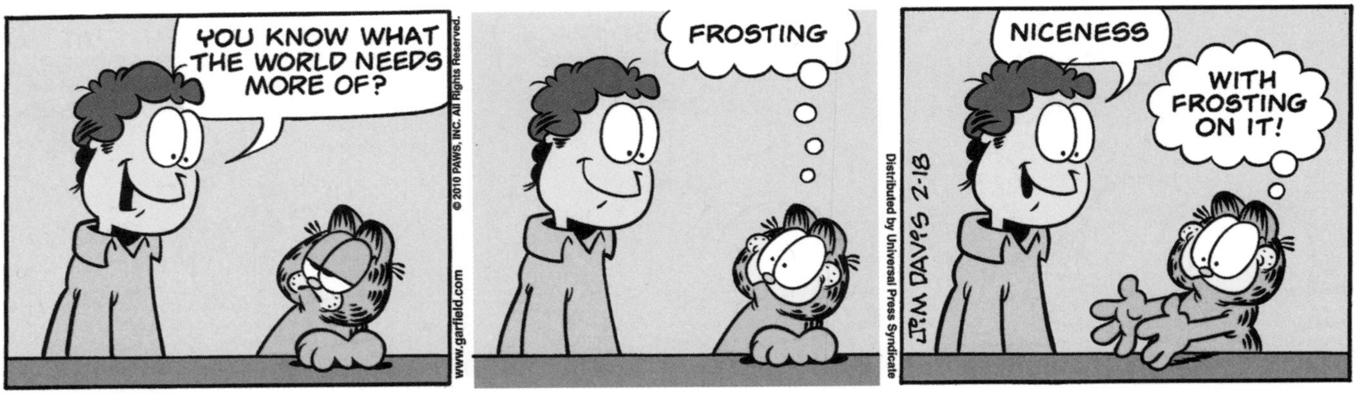
YOU KNOW WHAT THE WORLD NEEDS MORE OF?
FROSTING
NICENESS
WITH FROSTING ON IT!
JIM DAVIS 2-18
© 2010 PAWS, INC. All Rights Reserved. www.garfield.com
Distributed by Universal Press Syndicate

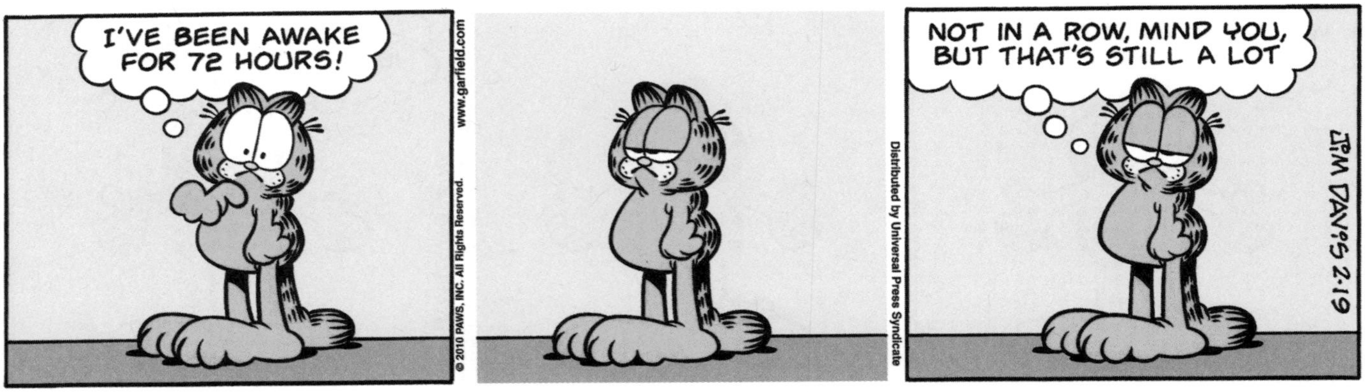
I'VE BEEN AWAKE FOR 72 HOURS!
NOT IN A ROW, MIND YOU, BUT THAT'S STILL A LOT
JIM DAVIS 2-19
© 2010 PAWS, INC. All Rights Reserved. www.garfield.com
Distributed by Universal Press Syndicate

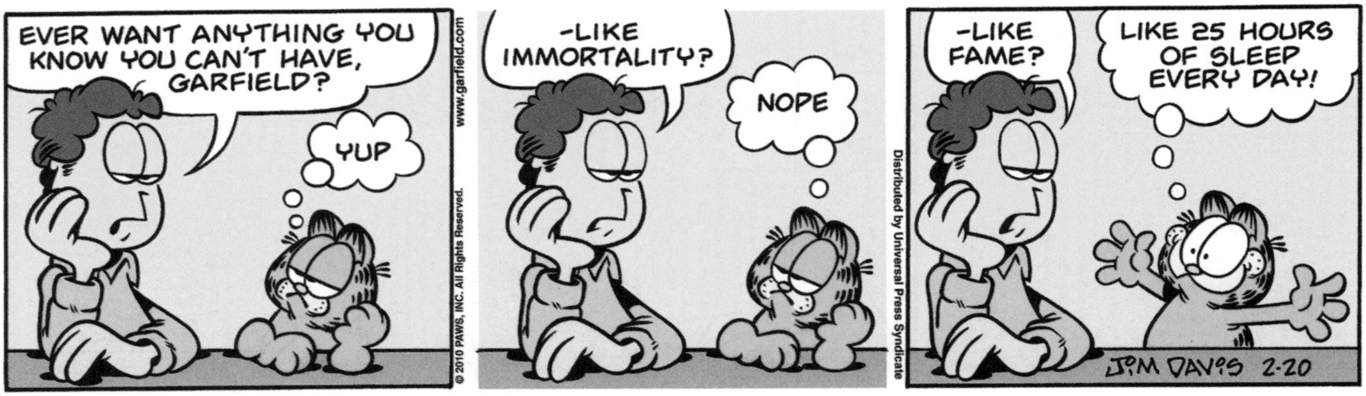
EVER WANT ANYTHING YOU KNOW YOU CAN'T HAVE, GARFIELD?
YUP
-LIKE IMMORTALITY?
NOPE
-LIKE FAME?
LIKE 25 HOURS OF SLEEP EVERY DAY!
JIM DAVIS 2-20
© 2010 PAWS, INC. All Rights Reserved. www.garfield.com
Distributed by Universal Press Syndicate

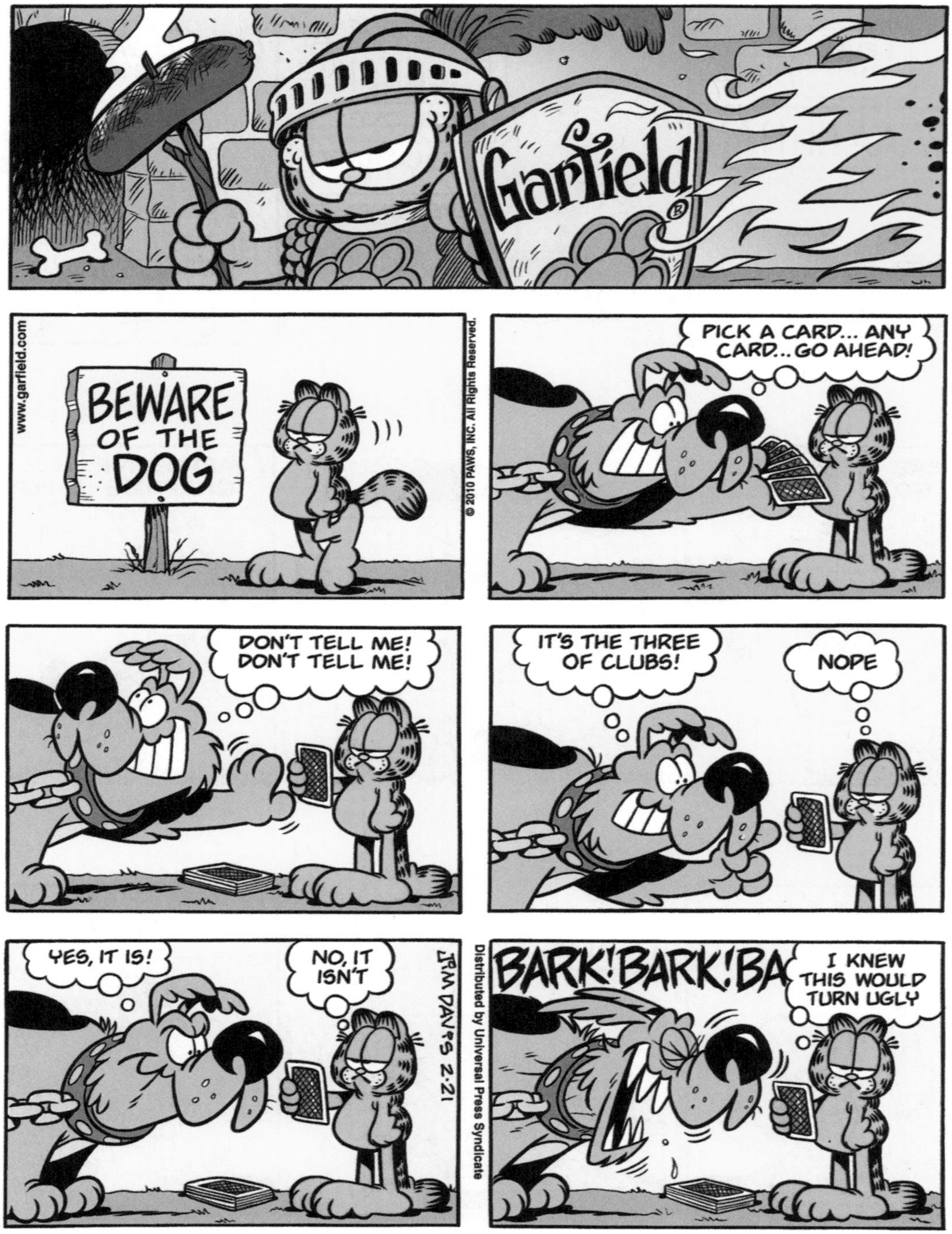

Garfield®
www.garfield.com
BEWARE OF THE DOG
© 2010 PAWS, INC. All Rights Reserved.
PICK A CARD... ANY CARD...GO AHEAD!
DON'T TELL ME! DON'T TELL ME!
IT'S THE THREE OF CLUBS!
NOPE
YES, IT IS!
NO, IT ISN'T
JIM DAVIS 2-21
Distributed by Universal Press Syndicate
BARK! BARK! BA
I KNEW THIS WOULD TURN UGLY

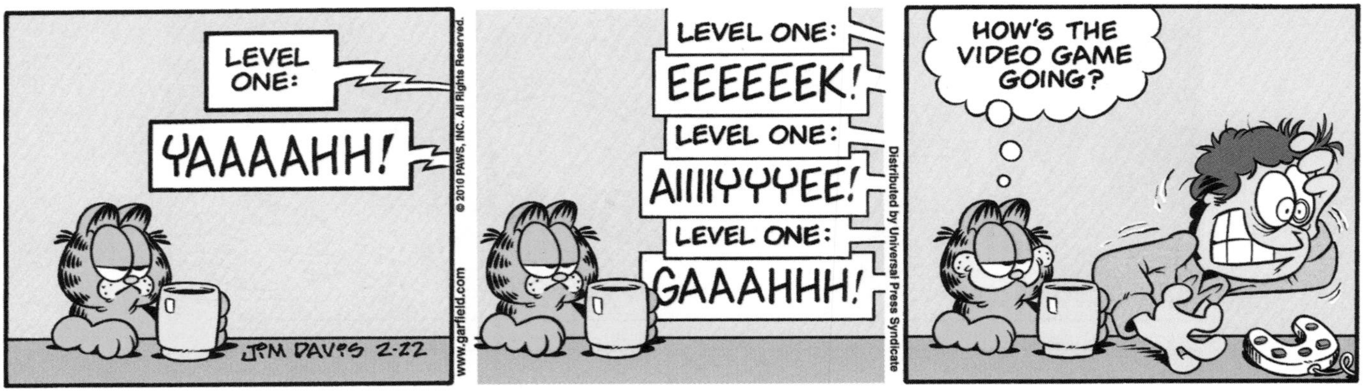
LEVEL ONE:
YAAAAHH!
JIM DAVIS 2-22
© 2010 PAWS, INC. All Rights Reserved.
www.garfield.com
LEVEL ONE:
EEEEEEK!
LEVEL ONE:
AIIIIYYYEE!
LEVEL ONE:
GAAAHHH!
Distributed by Universal Press Syndicate
HOW'S THE VIDEO GAME GOING?

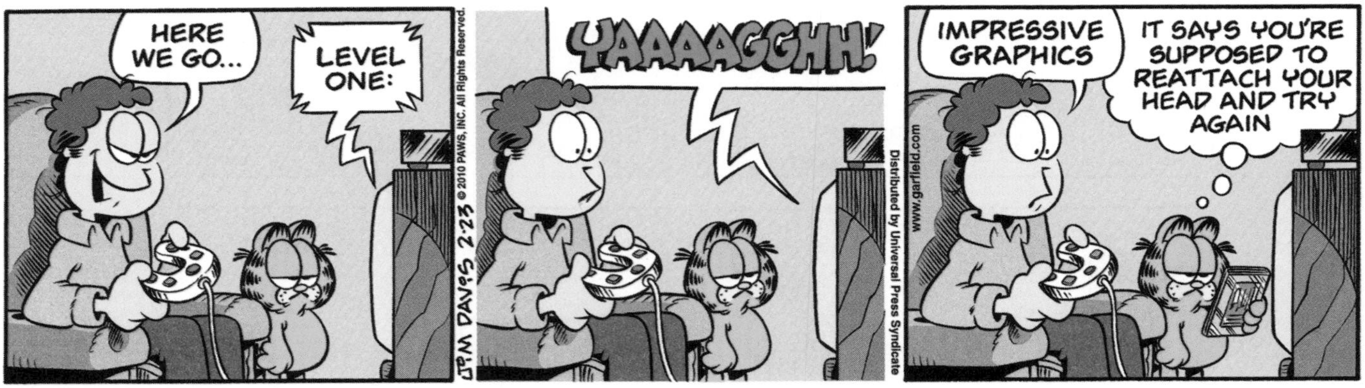
HERE WE GO...
LEVEL ONE:
JIM DAVIS 2-23
© 2010 PAWS, INC. All Rights Reserved.
YAAAAGGHH!
www.garfield.com
Distributed by Universal Press Syndicate
IMPRESSIVE GRAPHICS
IT SAYS YOU'RE SUPPOSED TO REATTACH YOUR HEAD AND TRY AGAIN

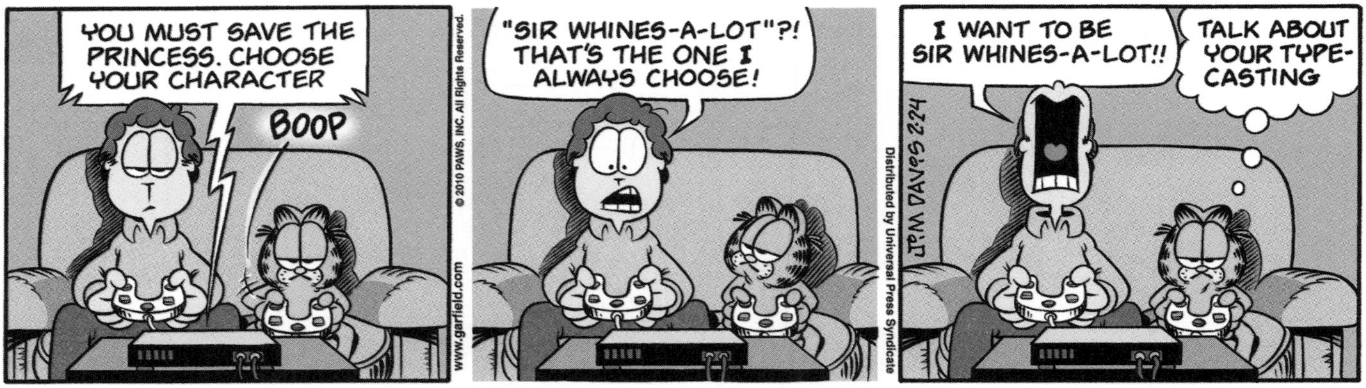
YOU MUST SAVE THE PRINCESS. CHOOSE YOUR CHARACTER
BOOP
© 2010 PAWS, INC. All Rights Reserved.
www.garfield.com
"SIR WHINES-A-LOT"?! THAT'S THE ONE I ALWAYS CHOOSE!
Distributed by Universal Press Syndicate
JIM DAVIS 2-24
I WANT TO BE SIR WHINES-A-LOT!!
TALK ABOUT YOUR TYPE-CASTING

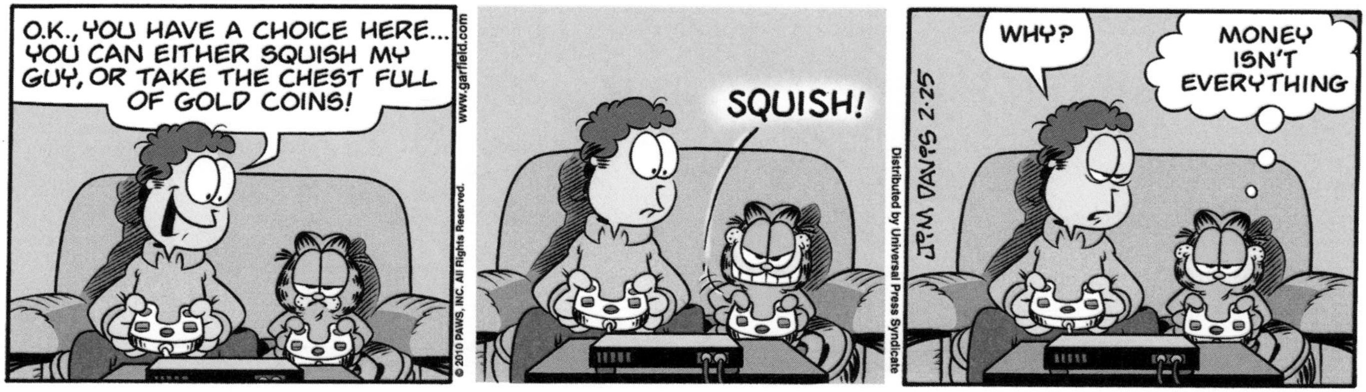
O.K., YOU HAVE A CHOICE HERE... YOU CAN EITHER SQUISH MY GUY, OR TAKE THE CHEST FULL OF GOLD COINS!
© 2010 PAWS, INC. All Rights Reserved.
www.garfield.com
SQUISH!
Distributed by Universal Press Syndicate
JIM DAVIS 2-25
WHY?
MONEY ISN'T EVERYTHING

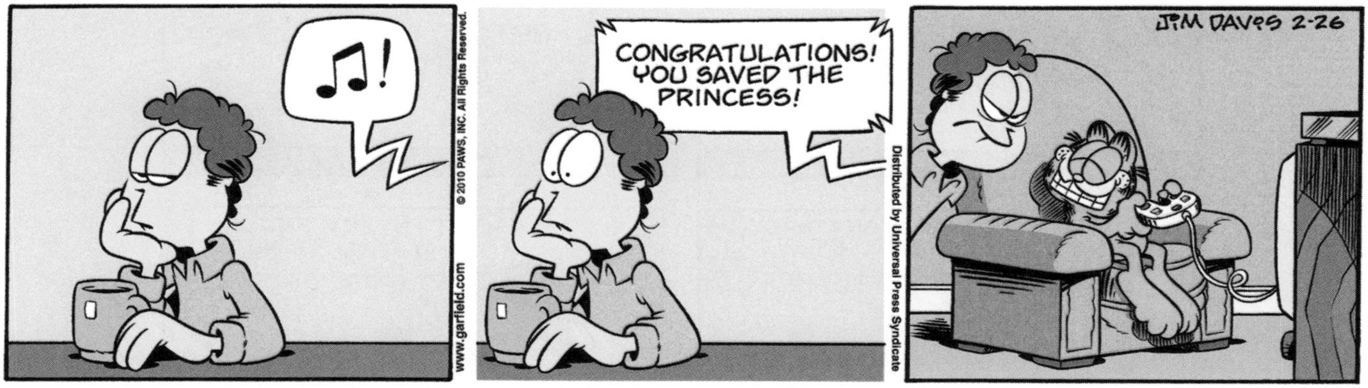
♫!
www.garfield.com
© 2010 PAWS, INC. All Rights Reserved.
CONGRATULATIONS! YOU SAVED THE PRINCESS!
Distributed by Universal Press Syndicate
JIM DAVIS 2-26

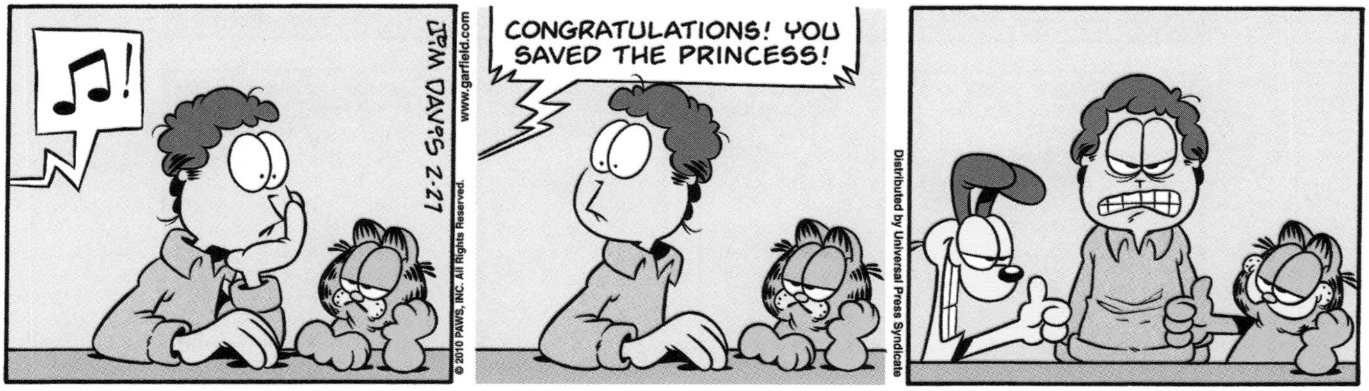
♫!
JIM DAVIS 2-27
www.garfield.com
© 2010 PAWS, INC. All Rights Reserved.
CONGRATULATIONS! YOU SAVED THE PRINCESS!
Distributed by Universal Press Syndicate

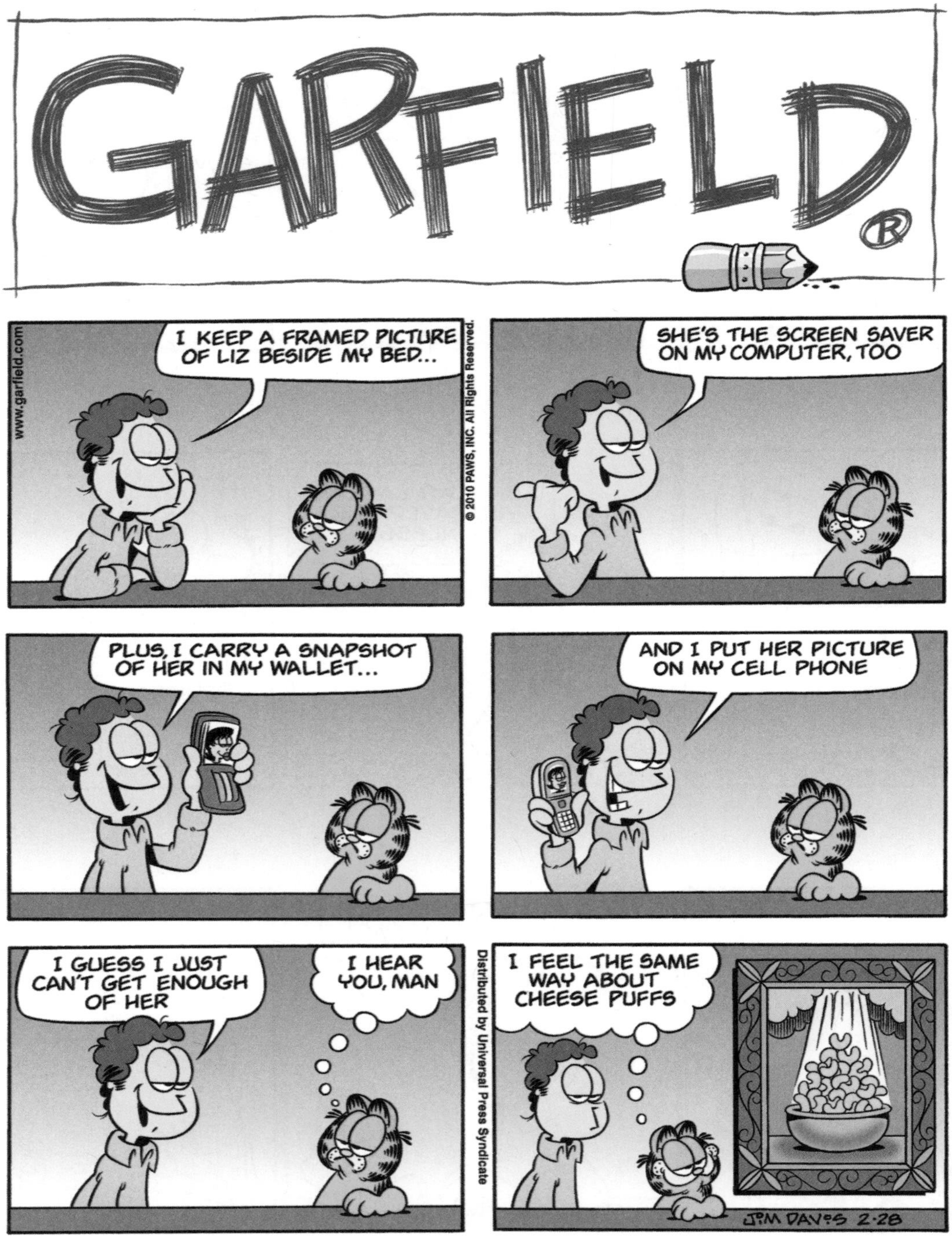
GARFIELD
www.garfield.com
I KEEP A FRAMED PICTURE OF LIZ BESIDE MY BED...
© 2010 PAWS, INC. All Rights Reserved.
SHE'S THE SCREEN SAVER ON MY COMPUTER, TOO
PLUS, I CARRY A SNAPSHOT OF HER IN MY WALLET...
AND I PUT HER PICTURE ON MY CELL PHONE
I GUESS I JUST CAN'T GET ENOUGH OF HER
I HEAR YOU, MAN
Distributed by Universal Press Syndicate
I FEEL THE SAME WAY ABOUT CHEESE PUFFS
JIM DAVIS 2-28

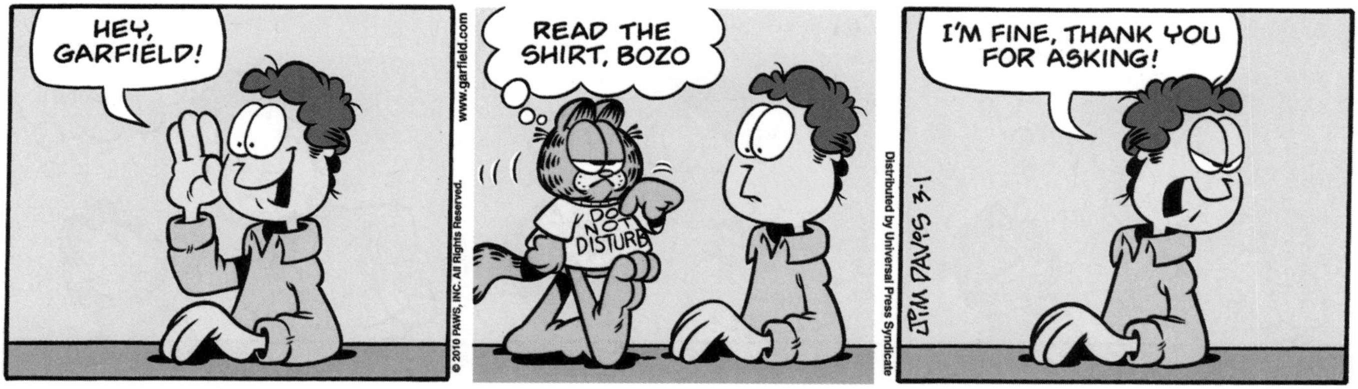
HEY, GARFIELD!
READ THE SHIRT, BOZO
DO NOT DISTURB
I'M FINE, THANK YOU FOR ASKING!
© 2010 PAWS, INC. All Rights Reserved.
www.garfield.com
Distributed by Universal Press Syndicate

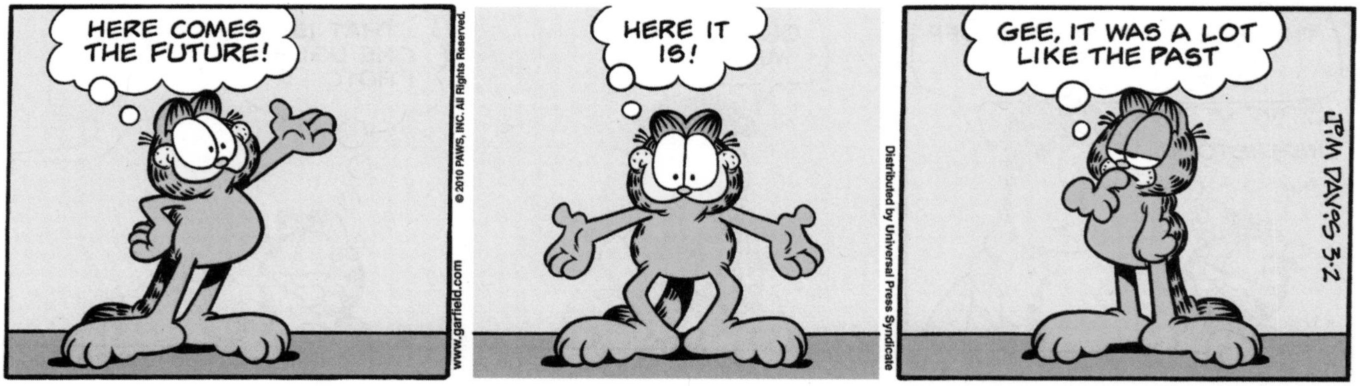
HERE COMES THE FUTURE!
HERE IT IS!
GEE, IT WAS A LOT LIKE THE PAST
© 2010 PAWS, INC. All Rights Reserved.
www.garfield.com
Distributed by Universal Press Syndicate

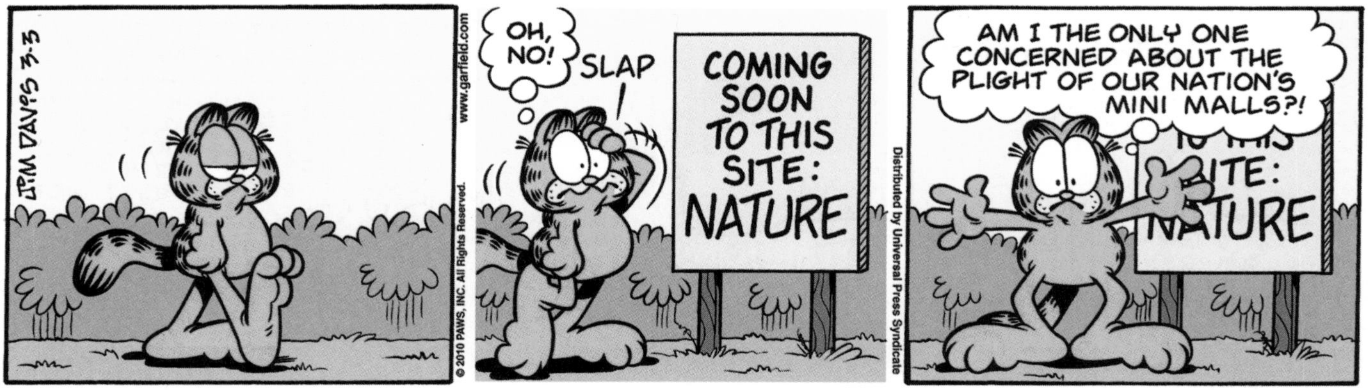
OH, NO!
SLAP
COMING SOON TO THIS SITE: NATURE
AM I THE ONLY ONE CONCERNED ABOUT THE PLIGHT OF OUR NATION'S MINI MALLS?!
© 2010 PAWS, INC. All Rights Reserved.
www.garfield.com
Distributed by Universal Press Syndicate

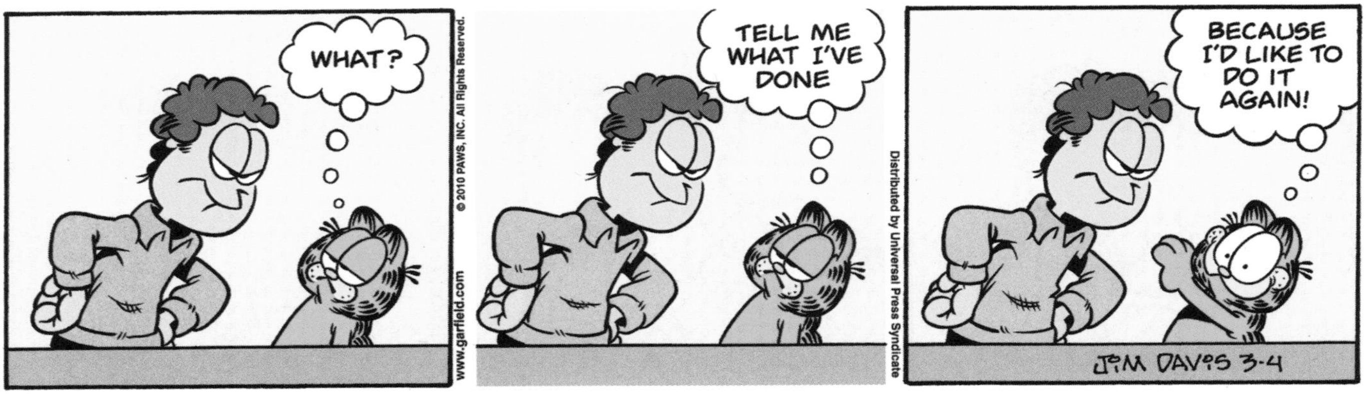
WHAT?
TELL ME WHAT I'VE DONE
BECAUSE I'D LIKE TO DO IT AGAIN!
JIM DAVIS 3-4

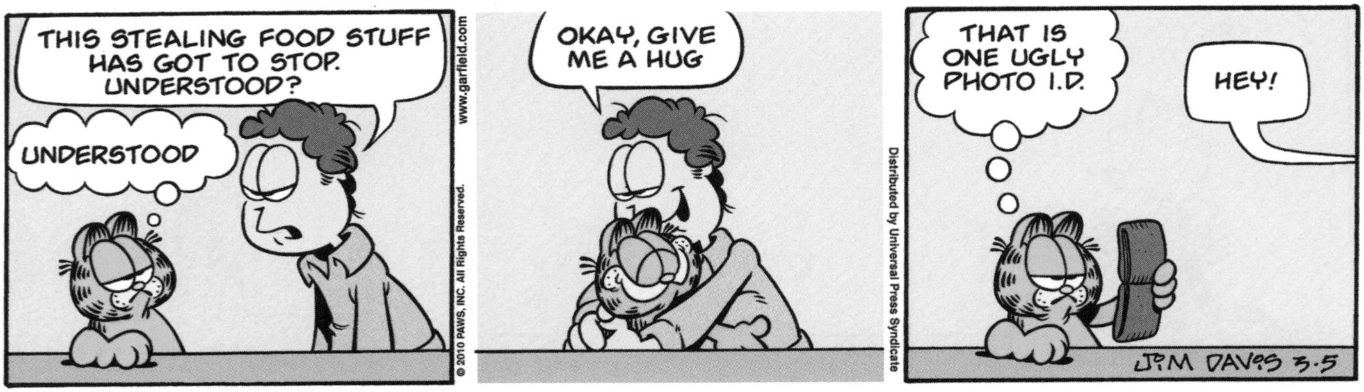
THIS STEALING FOOD STUFF HAS GOT TO STOP. UNDERSTOOD?
UNDERSTOOD
OKAY, GIVE ME A HUG
THAT IS ONE UGLY PHOTO I.D.
HEY!
JIM DAVIS 3-5

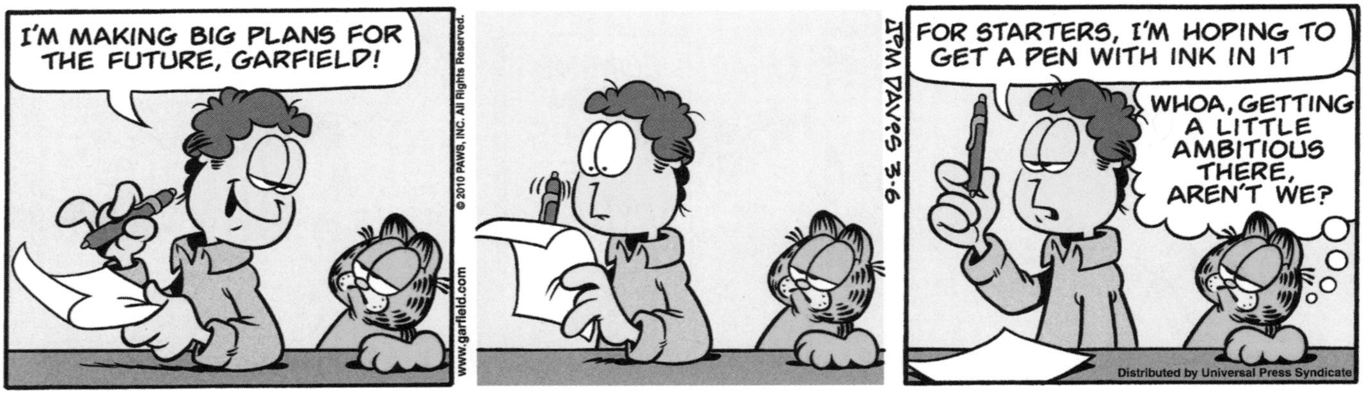
I'M MAKING BIG PLANS FOR THE FUTURE, GARFIELD!
JIM DAVIS 3-6
FOR STARTERS, I'M HOPING TO GET A PEN WITH INK IN IT
WHOA, GETTING A LITTLE AMBITIOUS THERE, AREN'T WE?

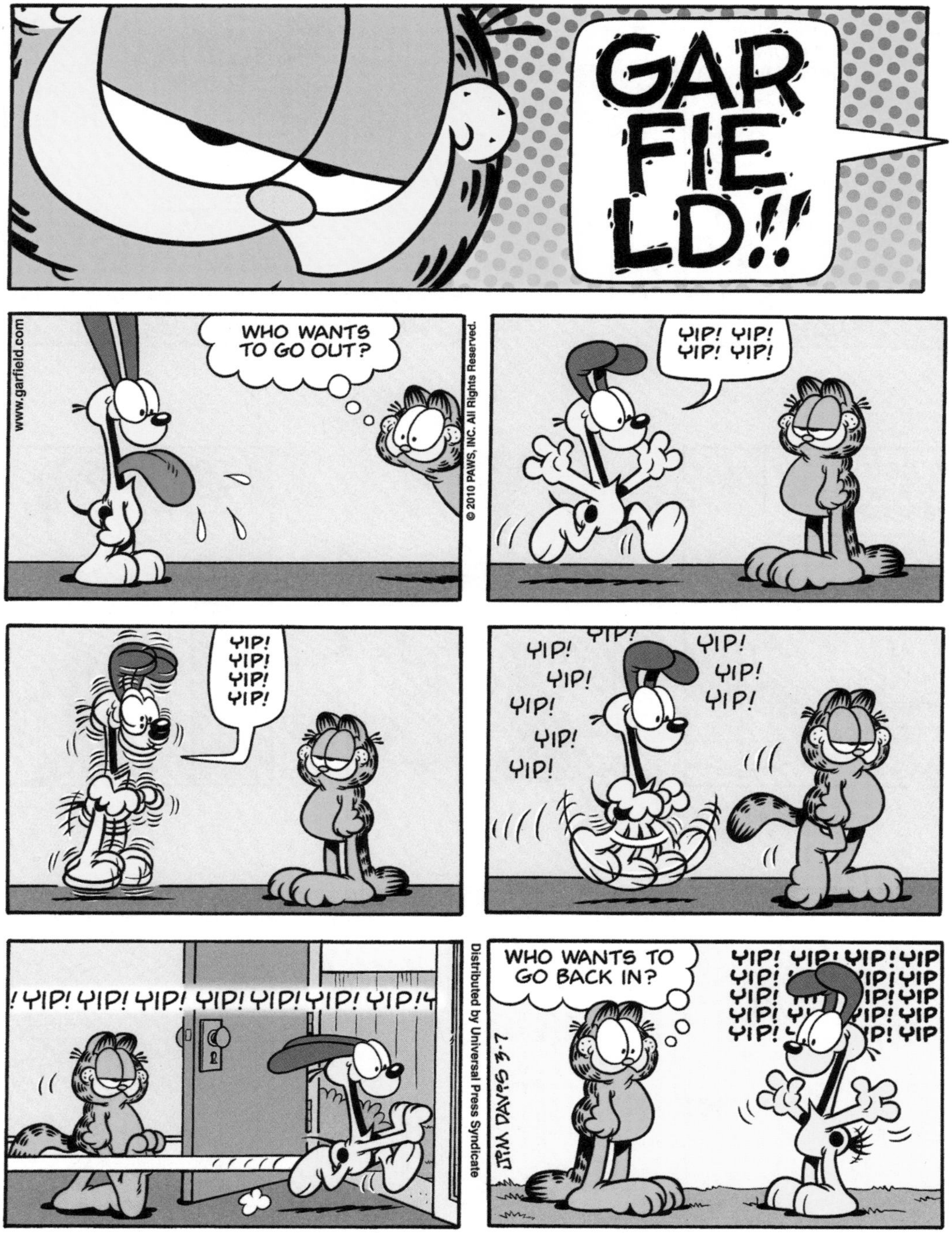
GAR FIE LD!!
www.garfield.com
WHO WANTS TO GO OUT?
© 2010 PAWS, INC. All Rights Reserved.
YIP! YIP! YIP! YIP!
YIP! YIP! YIP! YIP!
YIP! YIP! YIP! YIP! YIP! YIP! YIP! YIP! YIP! YIP!
YIP! YIP! YIP! YIP! YIP! YIP! YIP!
Distributed by Universal Press Syndicate
JIM DAVIS 3-7
WHO WANTS TO GO BACK IN?
YIP! YIP! YIP! YIP

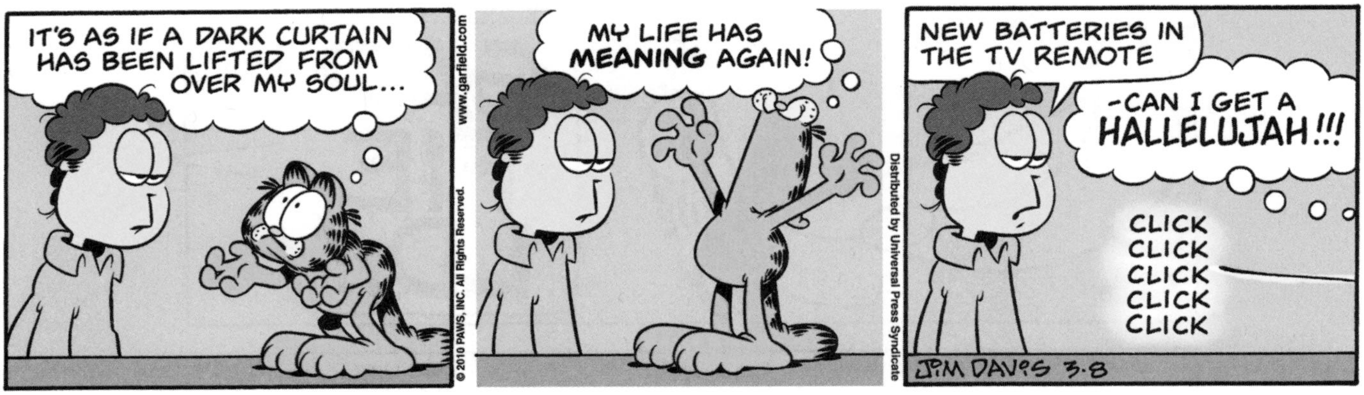
IT'S AS IF A DARK CURTAIN HAS BEEN LIFTED FROM OVER MY SOUL...
© 2010 PAWS, INC. All Rights Reserved. www.garfield.com
MY LIFE HAS **MEANING** AGAIN!
Distributed by Universal Press Syndicate
NEW BATTERIES IN THE TV REMOTE
-CAN I GET A HALLELUJAH!!!
CLICK CLICK CLICK CLICK CLICK
JIM DAVIS 3-8

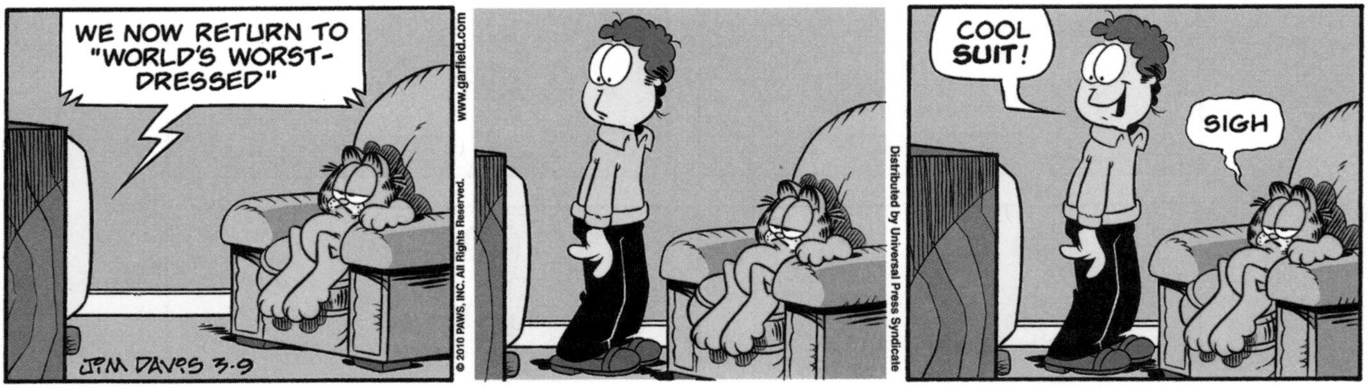
WE NOW RETURN TO "WORLD'S WORST-DRESSED"
JIM DAVIS 3-9
© 2010 PAWS, INC. All Rights Reserved. www.garfield.com
Distributed by Universal Press Syndicate
COOL **SUIT**!
SIGH

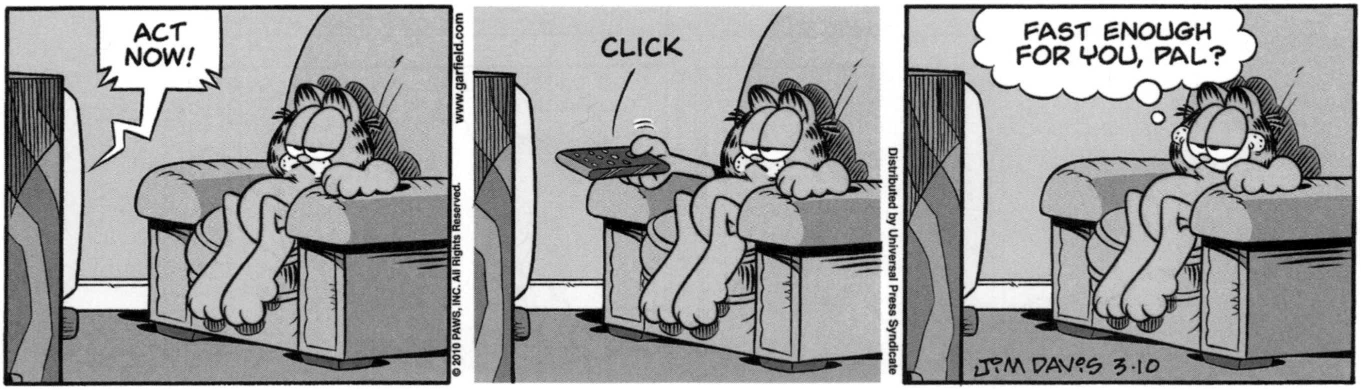
ACT NOW!
© 2010 PAWS, INC. All Rights Reserved. www.garfield.com
CLICK
Distributed by Universal Press Syndicate
FAST ENOUGH FOR YOU, PAL?
JIM DAVIS 3-10

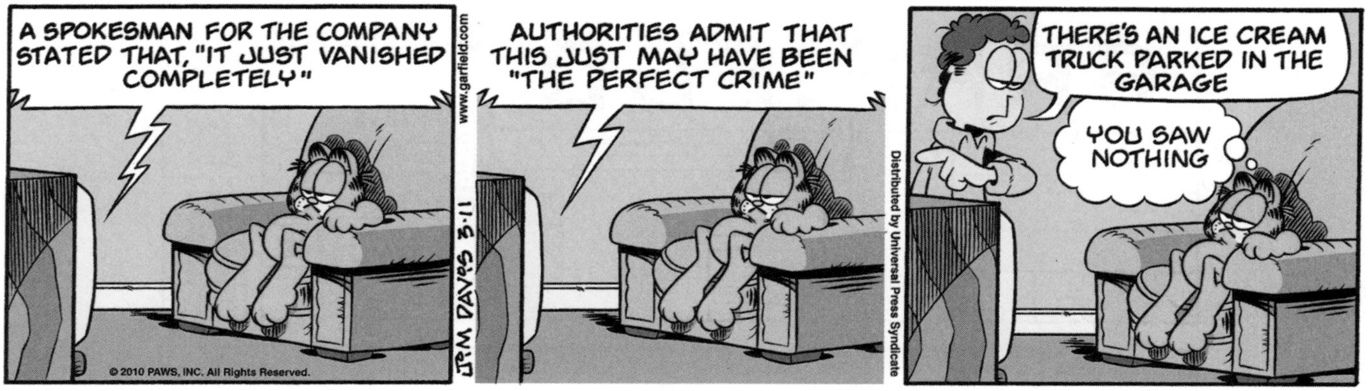

A SPOKESMAN FOR THE COMPANY STATED THAT, "IT JUST VANISHED COMPLETELY"
© 2010 PAWS, INC. All Rights Reserved.
www.garfield.com
JPM DAVPS 3·11
AUTHORITIES ADMIT THAT THIS JUST MAY HAVE BEEN "THE PERFECT CRIME"
Distributed by Universal Press Syndicate
THERE'S AN ICE CREAM TRUCK PARKED IN THE GARAGE
YOU SAW NOTHING

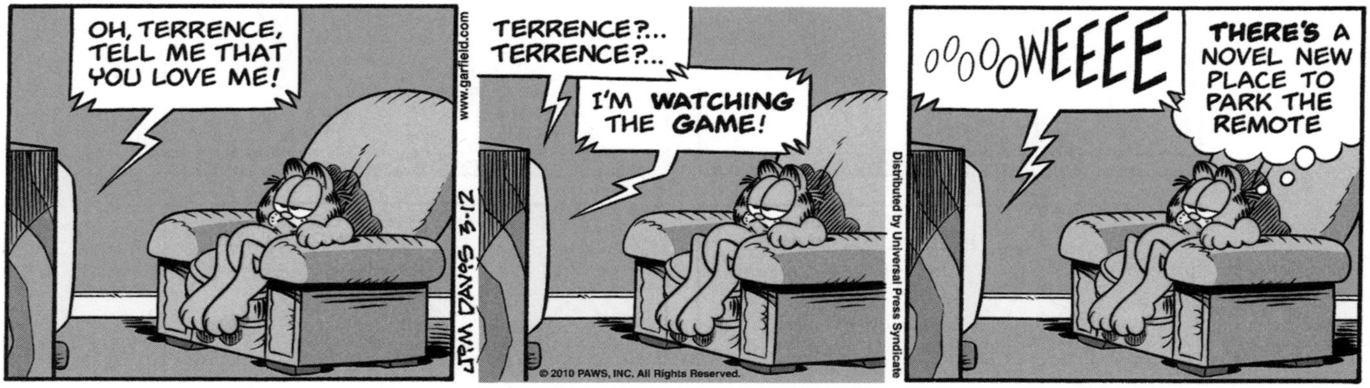

OH, TERRENCE, TELL ME THAT YOU LOVE ME!
www.garfield.com
JPM DAVPS 3·12
TERRENCE?... TERRENCE?...
I'M **WATCHING** THE **GAME**!
© 2010 PAWS, INC. All Rights Reserved.
Distributed by Universal Press Syndicate
OOOOOWEEEE
THERE'S A NOVEL NEW PLACE TO PARK THE REMOTE

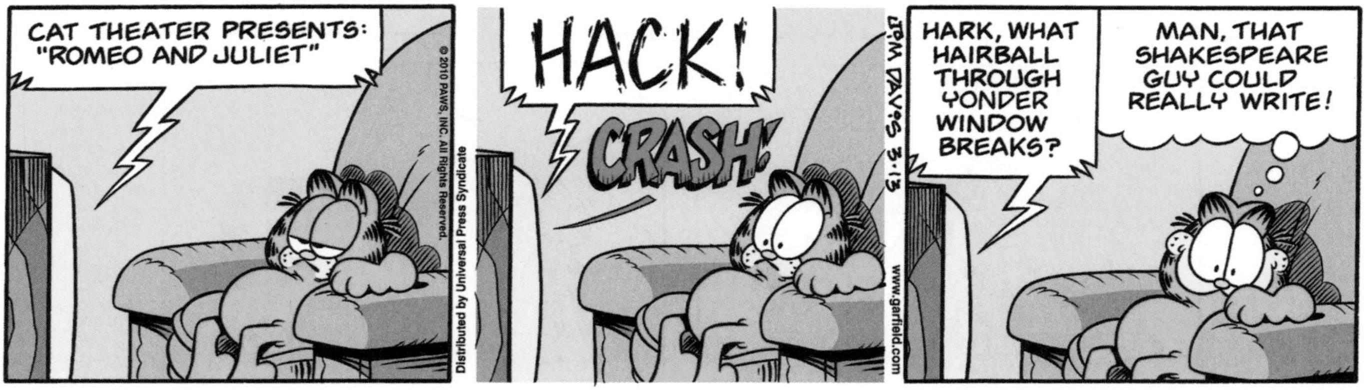

CAT THEATER PRESENTS: "ROMEO AND JULIET"
© 2010 PAWS, INC. All Rights Reserved.
Distributed by Universal Press Syndicate
HACK!
CRASH!
JPM DAVPS 3·13
www.garfield.com
HARK, WHAT HAIRBALL THROUGH YONDER WINDOW BREAKS?
MAN, THAT SHAKESPEARE GUY COULD REALLY WRITE!

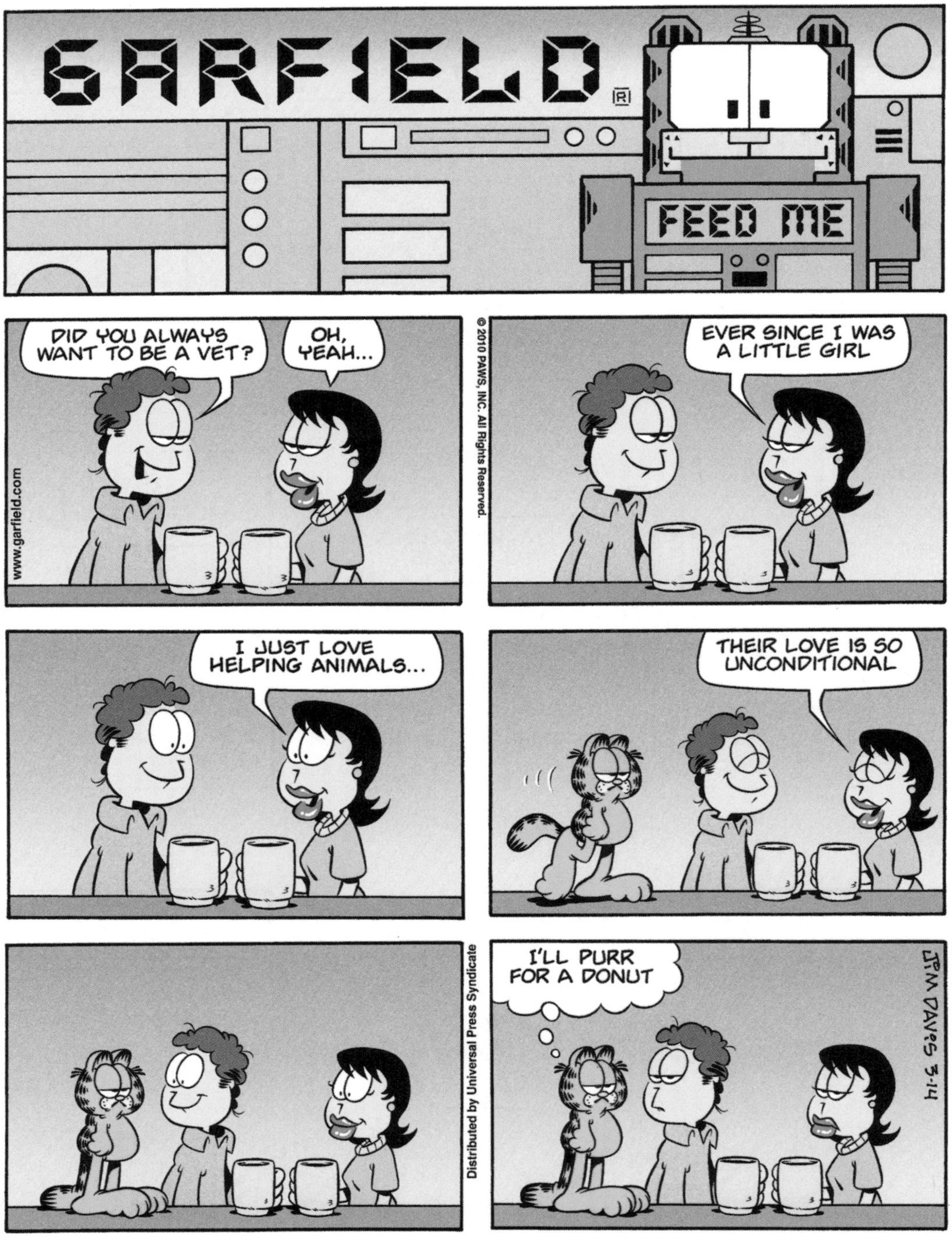
GARFIELD
FEED ME
DID YOU ALWAYS WANT TO BE A VET?
OH, YEAH...
EVER SINCE I WAS A LITTLE GIRL
I JUST LOVE HELPING ANIMALS...
THEIR LOVE IS SO UNCONDITIONAL
I'LL PURR FOR A DONUT
JIM DAVIS 3-14
© 2010 PAWS, INC. All Rights Reserved.
www.garfield.com
Distributed by Universal Press Syndicate

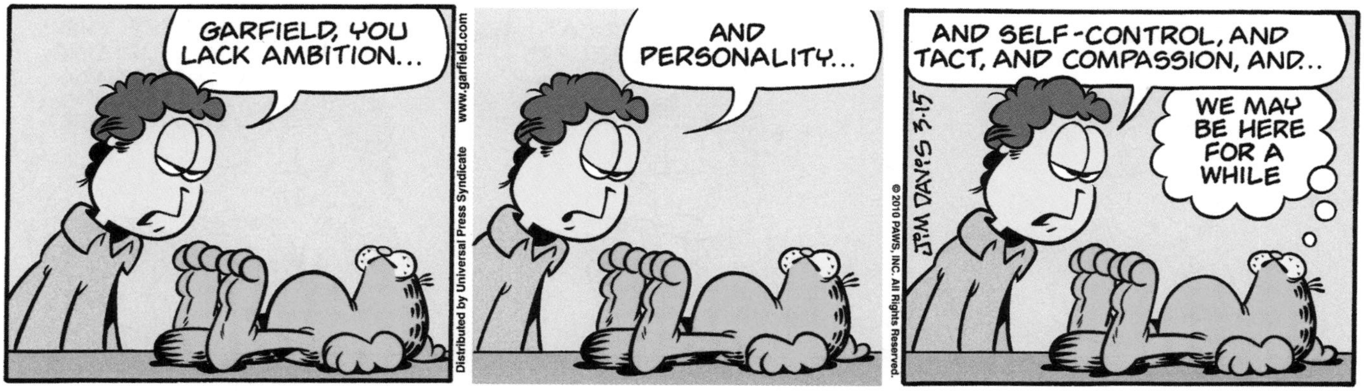
GARFIELD, YOU LACK AMBITION...
AND PERSONALITY...
AND SELF-CONTROL, AND TACT, AND COMPASSION, AND...
WE MAY BE HERE FOR A WHILE
JIM DAVIS 3-15
© 2010 PAWS, INC. All Rights Reserved.
Distributed by Universal Press Syndicate www.garfield.com

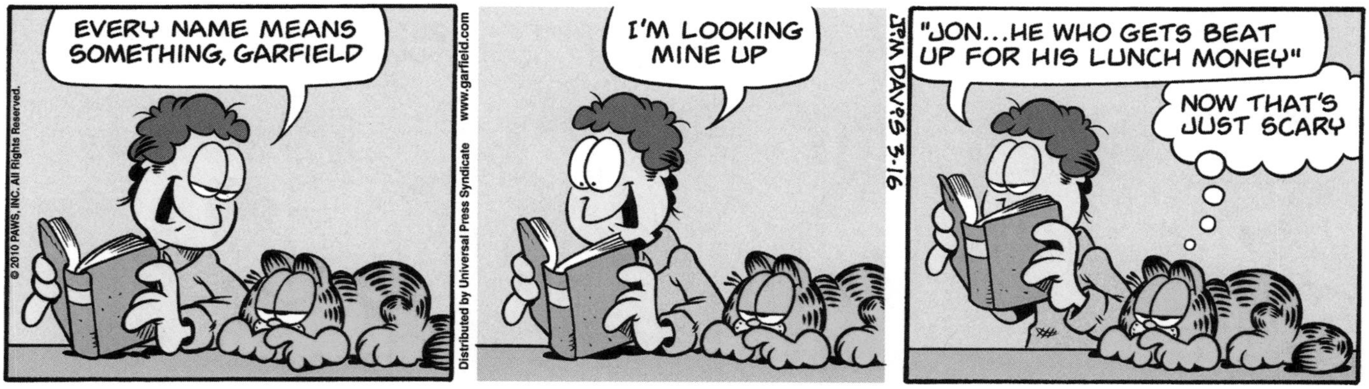
EVERY NAME MEANS SOMETHING, GARFIELD
I'M LOOKING MINE UP
"JON...HE WHO GETS BEAT UP FOR HIS LUNCH MONEY"
NOW THAT'S JUST SCARY
JIM DAVIS 3-16
© 2010 PAWS, INC. All Rights Reserved.
Distributed by Universal Press Syndicate www.garfield.com

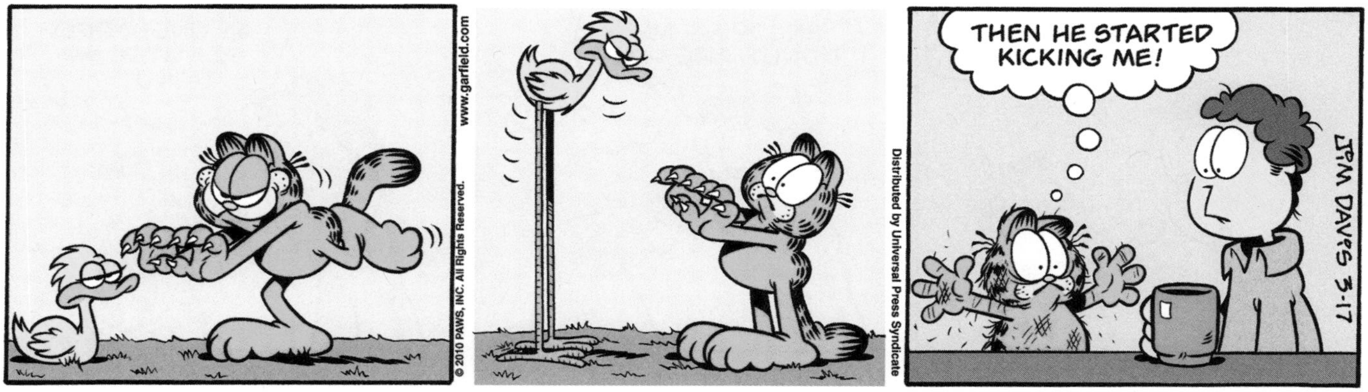
THEN HE STARTED KICKING ME!
JIM DAVIS 3-17
© 2010 PAWS, INC. All Rights Reserved. www.garfield.com
Distributed by Universal Press Syndicate

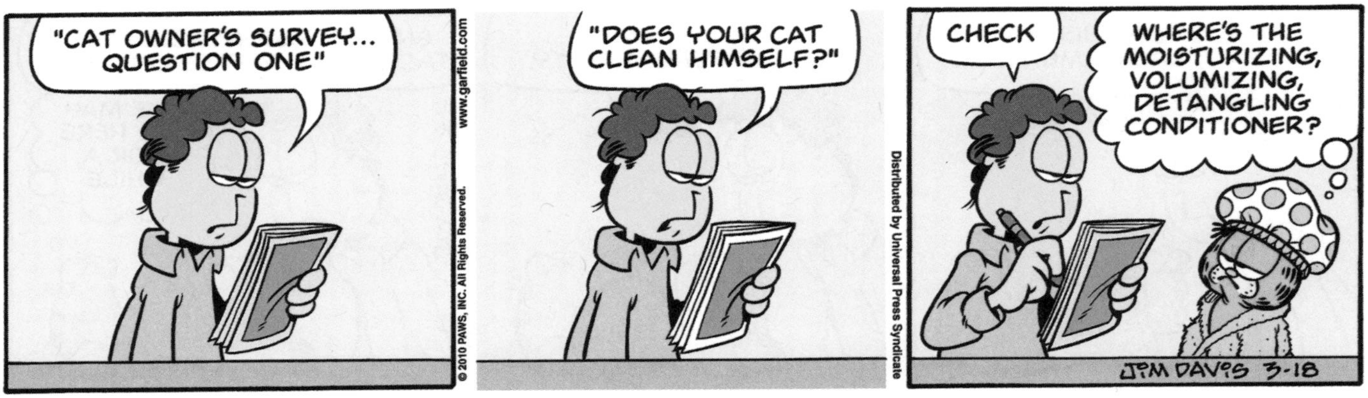
"CAT OWNER'S SURVEY... QUESTION ONE"
© 2010 PAWS, INC. All Rights Reserved. www.garfield.com
"DOES YOUR CAT CLEAN HIMSELF?"
Distributed by Universal Press Syndicate
CHECK
WHERE'S THE MOISTURIZING, VOLUMIZING, DETANGLING CONDITIONER?
JIM DAVIS 3-18

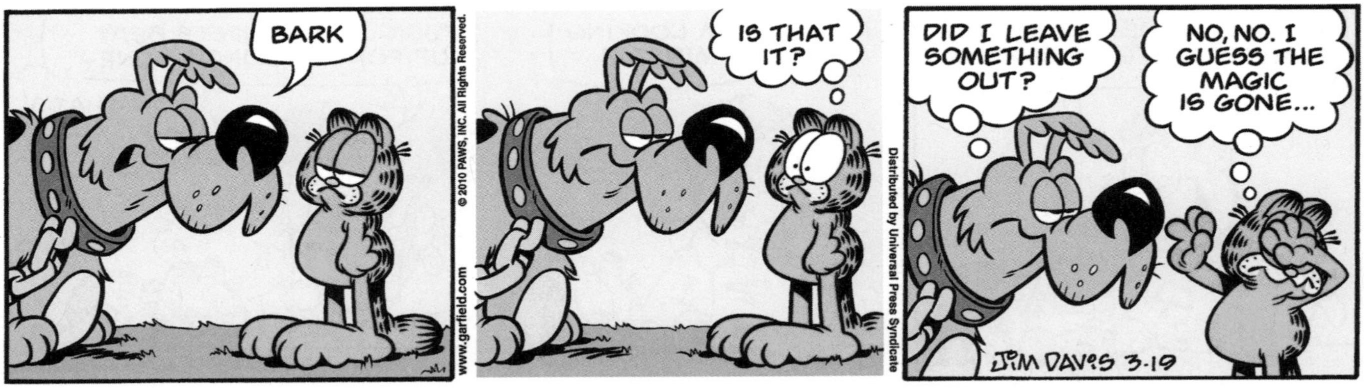
BARK
www.garfield.com © 2010 PAWS, INC. All Rights Reserved.
IS THAT IT?
Distributed by Universal Press Syndicate
DID I LEAVE SOMETHING OUT?
NO, NO. I GUESS THE MAGIC IS GONE...
JIM DAVIS 3-19

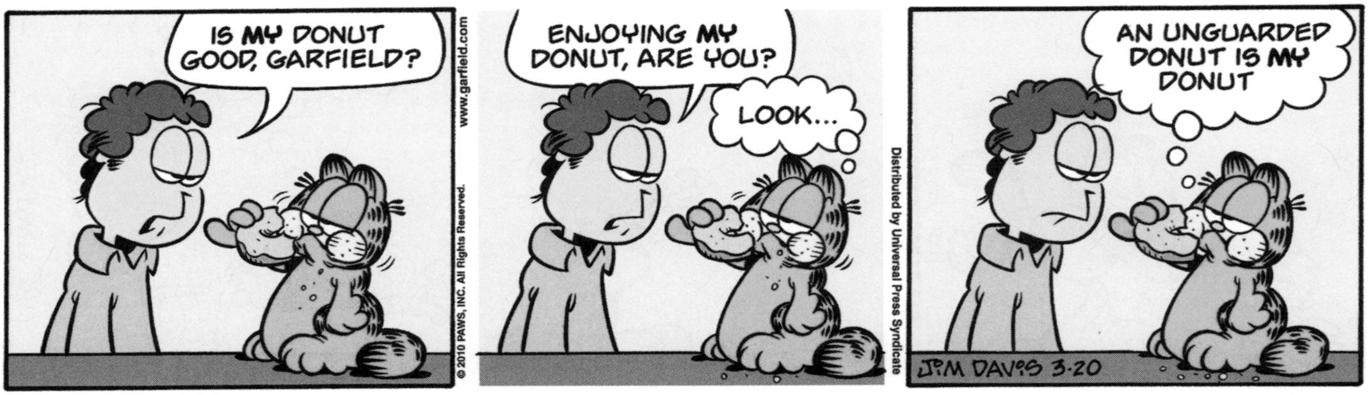
IS **MY** DONUT GOOD, GARFIELD?
© 2010 PAWS, INC. All Rights Reserved. www.garfield.com
ENJOYING **MY** DONUT, ARE YOU?
LOOK...
Distributed by Universal Press Syndicate
AN UNGUARDED DONUT IS **MY** DONUT
JIM DAVIS 3-20

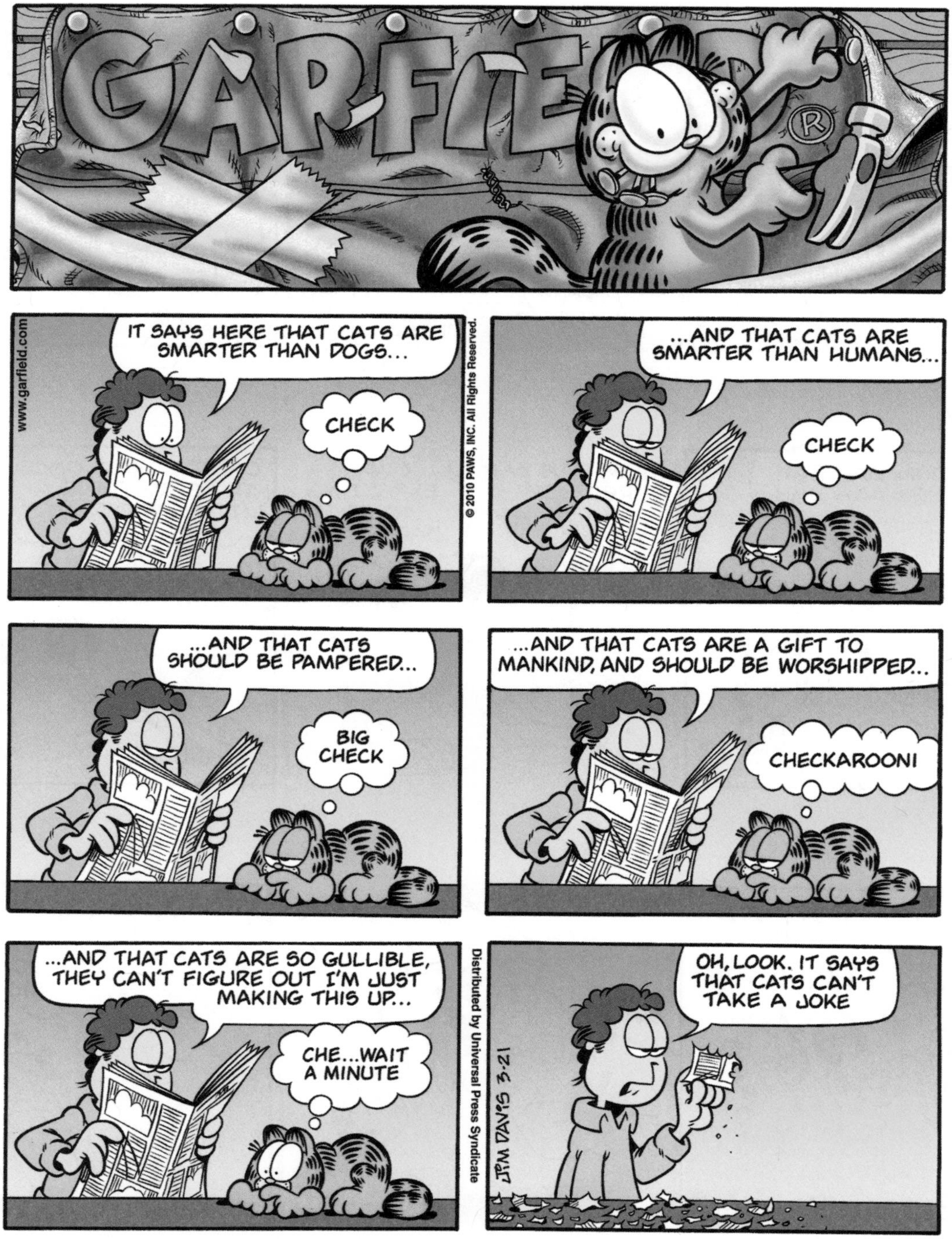
GARFIELD®
www.garfield.com
IT SAYS HERE THAT CATS ARE SMARTER THAN DOGS...
CHECK
© 2010 PAWS, INC. All Rights Reserved.
...AND THAT CATS ARE SMARTER THAN HUMANS...
CHECK
...AND THAT CATS SHOULD BE PAMPERED...
BIG CHECK
...AND THAT CATS ARE A GIFT TO MANKIND, AND SHOULD BE WORSHIPPED...
CHECKAROONI
...AND THAT CATS ARE SO GULLIBLE, THEY CAN'T FIGURE OUT I'M JUST MAKING THIS UP...
CHE...WAIT A MINUTE
Distributed by Universal Press Syndicate
JIM DAVIS 3-21
OH, LOOK. IT SAYS THAT CATS CAN'T TAKE A JOKE

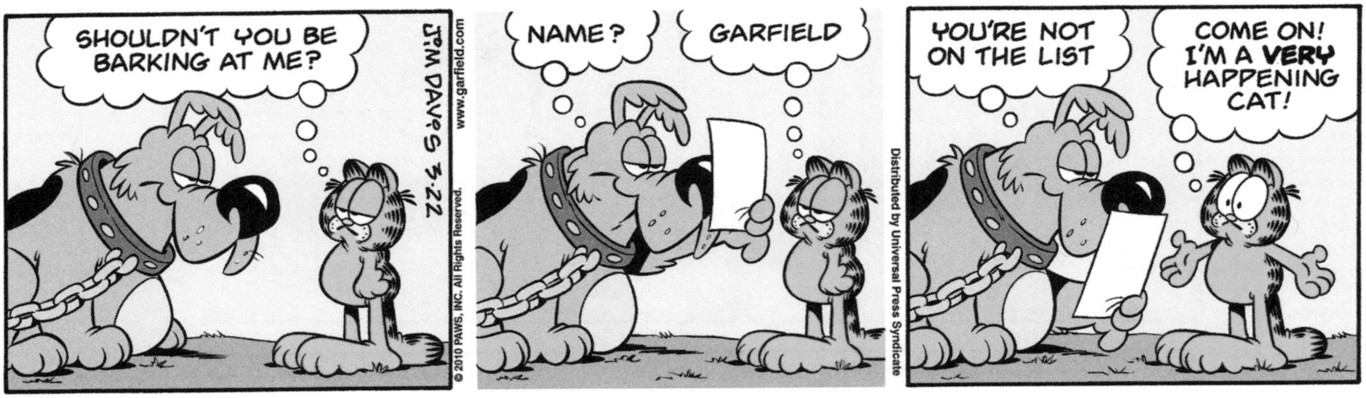
SHOULDN'T YOU BE BARKING AT ME?
JIM DAVIS 3-22
© 2010 PAWS, INC. All Rights Reserved. www.garfield.com
NAME?
GARFIELD
Distributed by Universal Press Syndicate
YOU'RE NOT ON THE LIST
COME ON! I'M A VERY HAPPENING CAT!

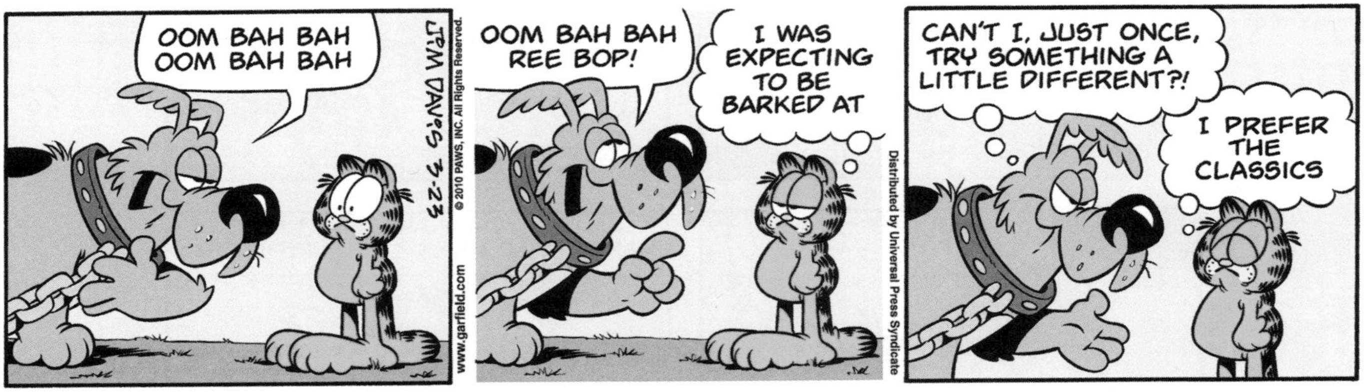
OOM BAH BAH OOM BAH BAH
JIM DAVIS 3-23
© 2010 PAWS, INC. All Rights Reserved. www.garfield.com
OOM BAH BAH REE BOP!
I WAS EXPECTING TO BE BARKED AT
Distributed by Universal Press Syndicate
CAN'T I, JUST ONCE, TRY SOMETHING A LITTLE DIFFERENT?!
I PREFER THE CLASSICS

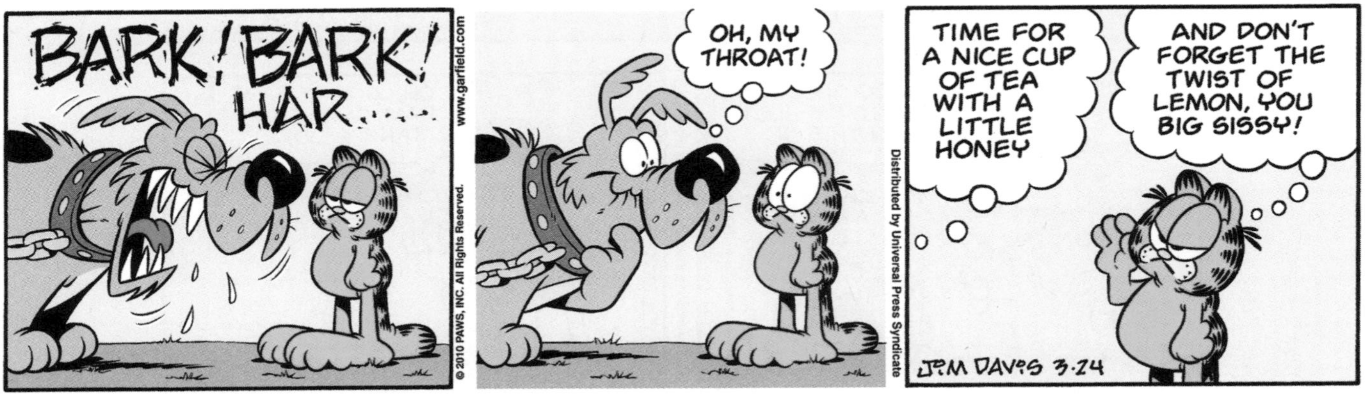
BARK! BARK! HAR.......
© 2010 PAWS, INC. All Rights Reserved. www.garfield.com
OH, MY THROAT!
Distributed by Universal Press Syndicate
TIME FOR A NICE CUP OF TEA WITH A LITTLE HONEY
AND DON'T FORGET THE TWIST OF LEMON, YOU BIG SISSY!
JIM DAVIS 3-24

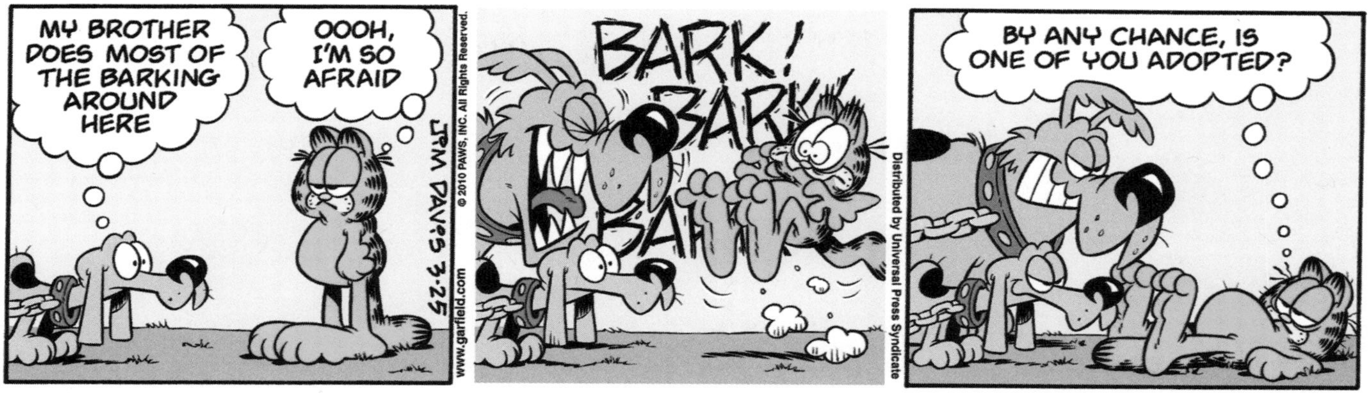
MY BROTHER DOES MOST OF THE BARKING AROUND HERE
OOOH, I'M SO AFRAID
JIM DAVIS 3-25
© 2010 PAWS, INC. All Rights Reserved.
www.garfield.com
BARK! BARK!
BY ANY CHANCE, IS ONE OF YOU ADOPTED?
Distributed by Universal Press Syndicate

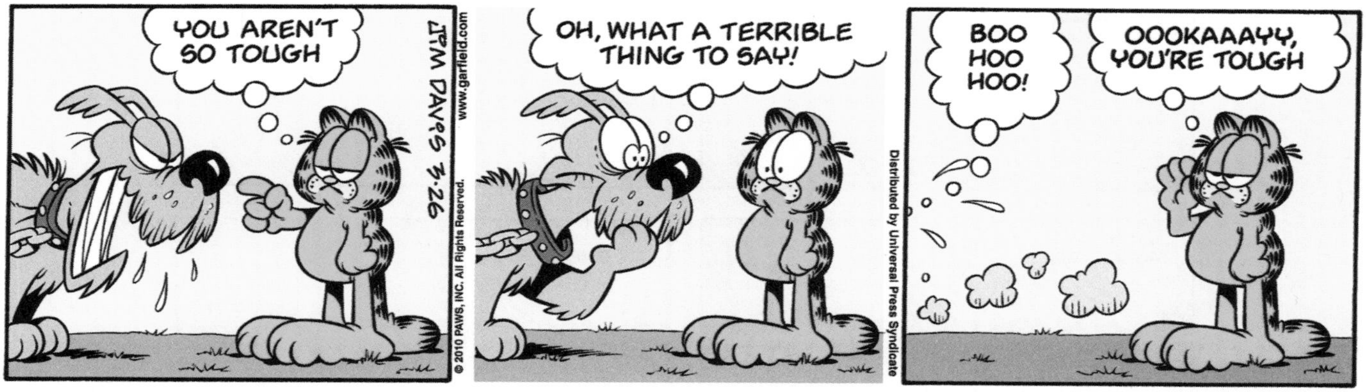
YOU AREN'T SO TOUGH
JIM DAVIS 3-26
www.garfield.com
© 2010 PAWS, INC. All Rights Reserved.
OH, WHAT A TERRIBLE THING TO SAY!
Distributed by Universal Press Syndicate
BOO HOO HOO!
OOOKAAAYY, YOU'RE TOUGH

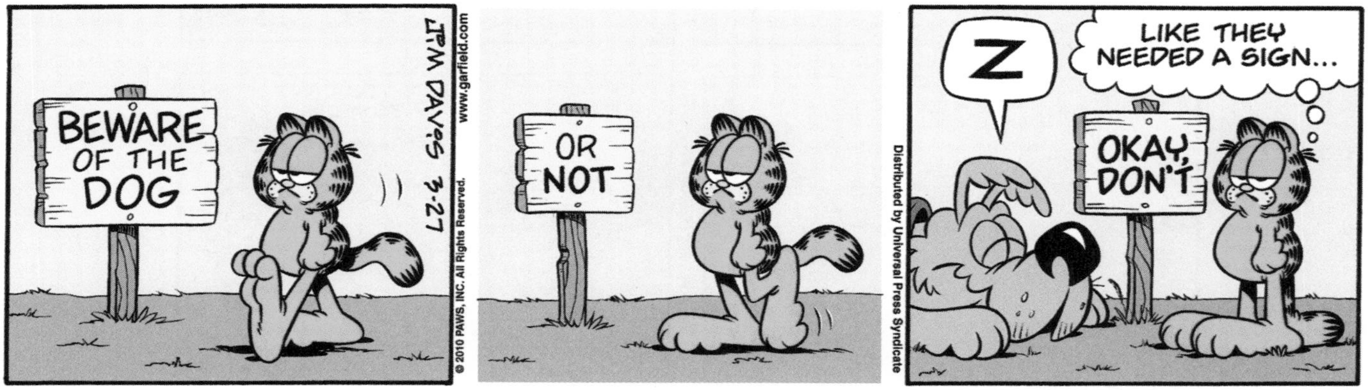
BEWARE OF THE DOG
JIM DAVIS 3-27
www.garfield.com
© 2010 PAWS, INC. All Rights Reserved.
OR NOT
Distributed by Universal Press Syndicate
Z
LIKE THEY NEEDED A SIGN...
OKAY, DON'T

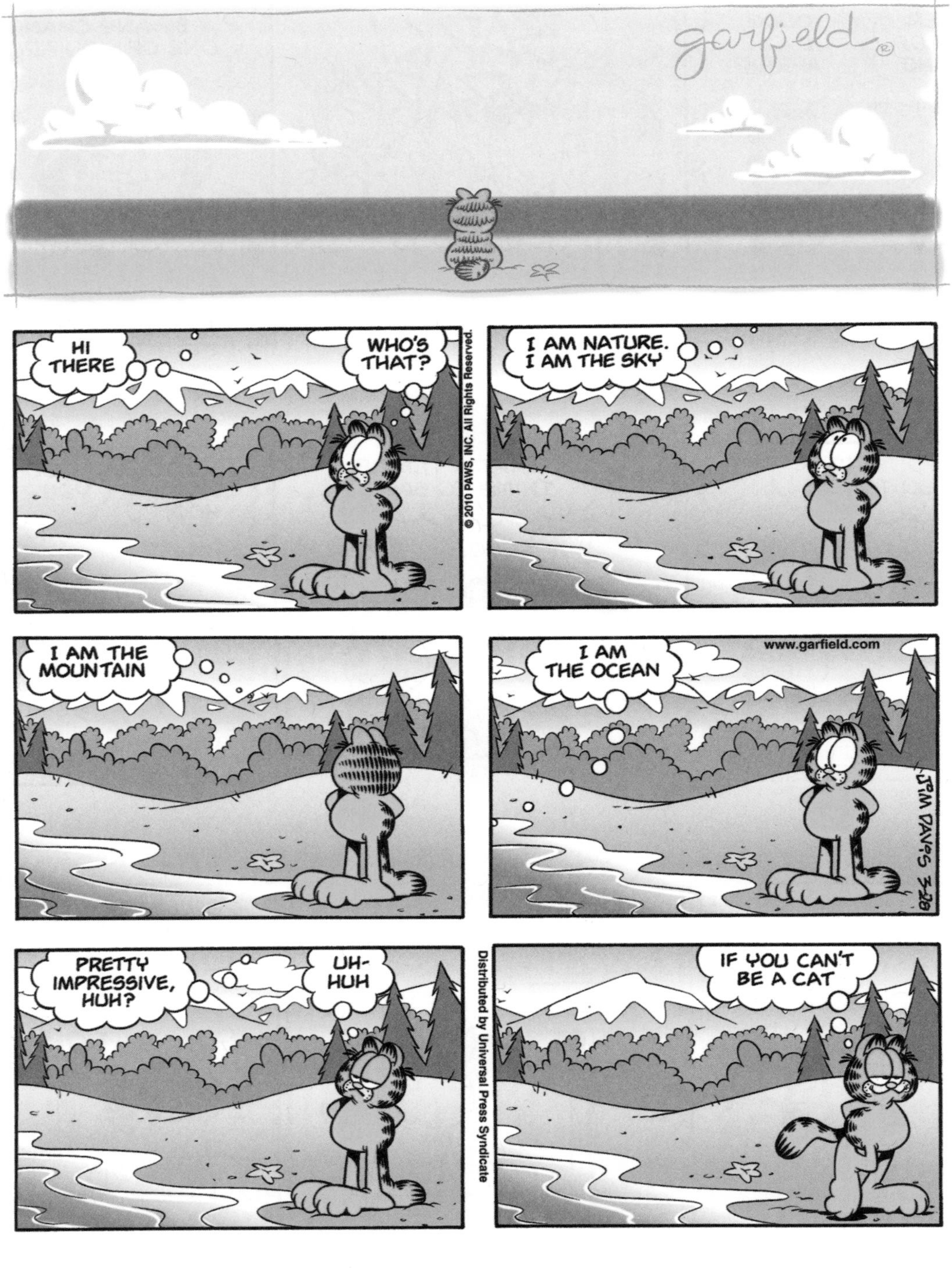
garfield®
HI THERE
WHO'S THAT?
© 2010 PAWS, INC. All Rights Reserved.
I AM NATURE. I AM THE SKY
I AM THE MOUNTAIN
I AM THE OCEAN
www.garfield.com
JIM DAVIS 3-28
PRETTY IMPRESSIVE, HUH?
UH-HUH
Distributed by Universal Press Syndicate
IF YOU CAN'T BE A CAT

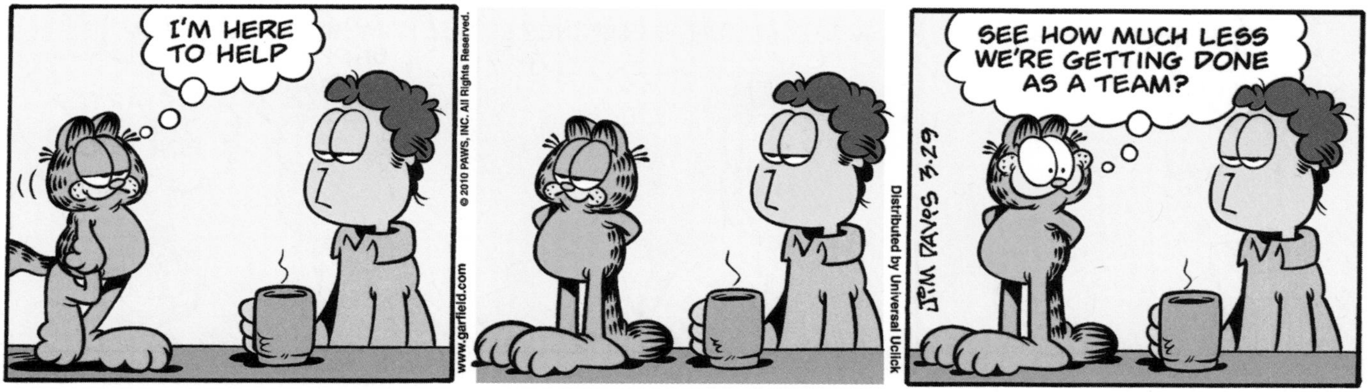
I'M HERE TO HELP
© 2010 PAWS, INC. All Rights Reserved.
www.garfield.com
Distributed by Universal Uclick
SEE HOW MUCH LESS WE'RE GETTING DONE AS A TEAM?
JIM DAVIS 3.29

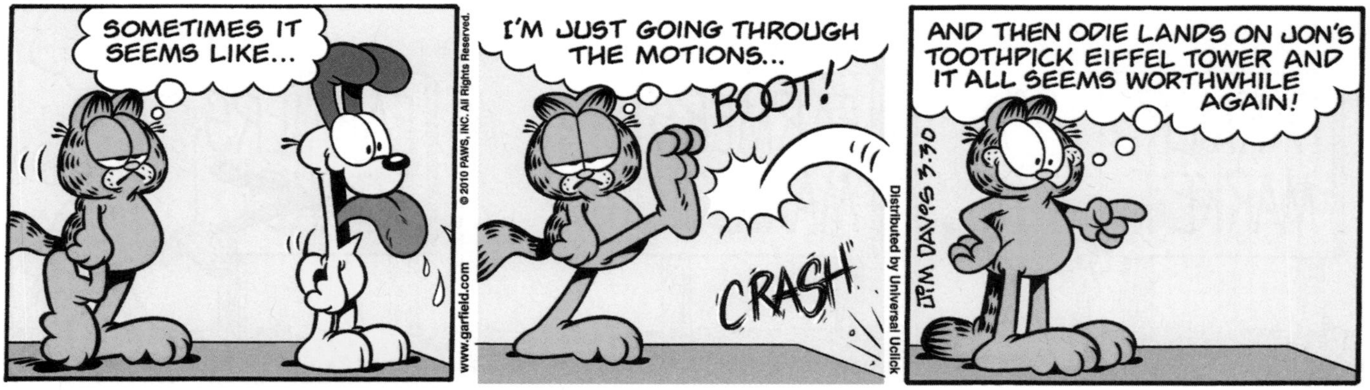
SOMETIMES IT SEEMS LIKE...
© 2010 PAWS, INC. All Rights Reserved.
www.garfield.com
I'M JUST GOING THROUGH THE MOTIONS...
BOOT!
CRASH
Distributed by Universal Uclick
AND THEN ODIE LANDS ON JON'S TOOTHPICK EIFFEL TOWER AND IT ALL SEEMS WORTHWHILE AGAIN!
JIM DAVIS 3.30

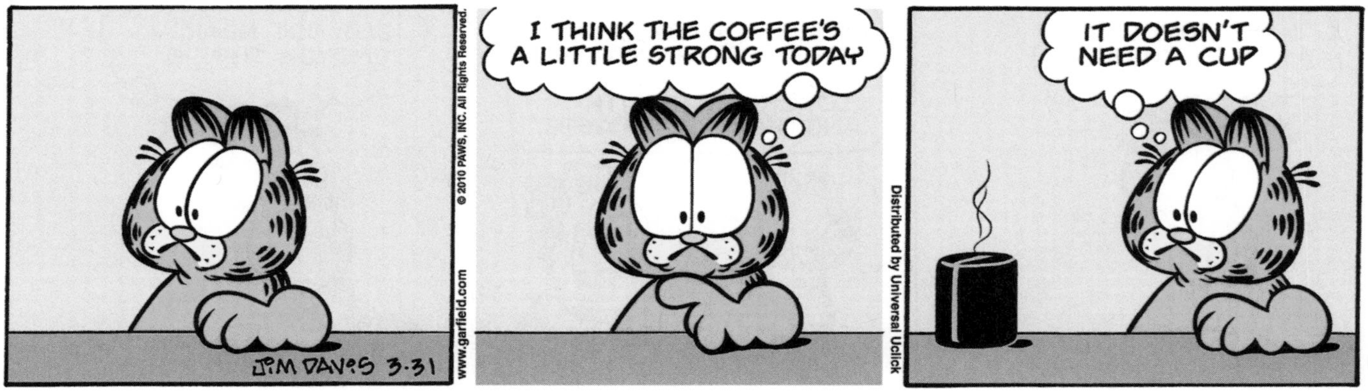
JIM DAVIS 3.31
© 2010 PAWS, INC. All Rights Reserved.
www.garfield.com
I THINK THE COFFEE'S A LITTLE STRONG TODAY
Distributed by Universal Uclick
IT DOESN'T NEED A CUP

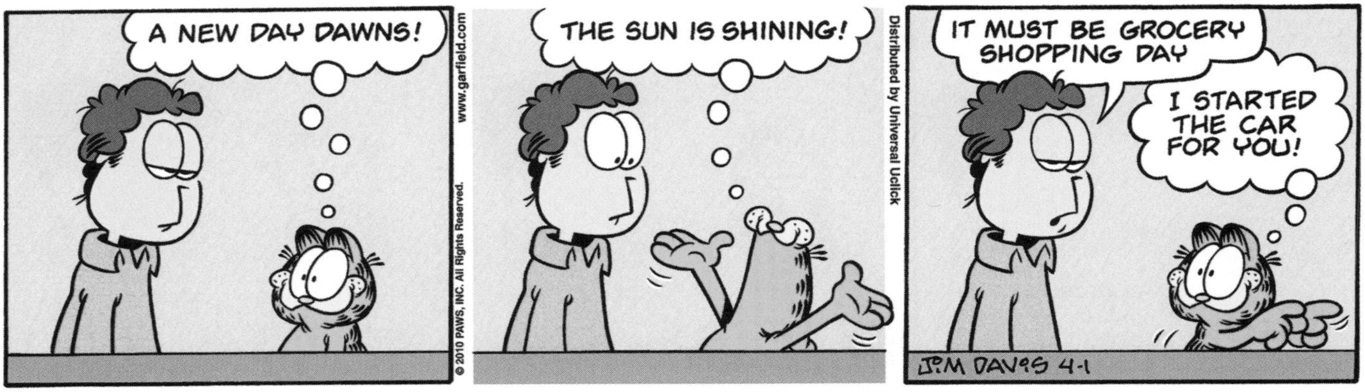
A NEW DAY DAWNS!
THE SUN IS SHINING!
IT MUST BE GROCERY SHOPPING DAY
I STARTED THE CAR FOR YOU!
JIM DAVIS 4-1
© 2010 PAWS, INC. All Rights Reserved.
www.garfield.com
Distributed by Universal Uclick

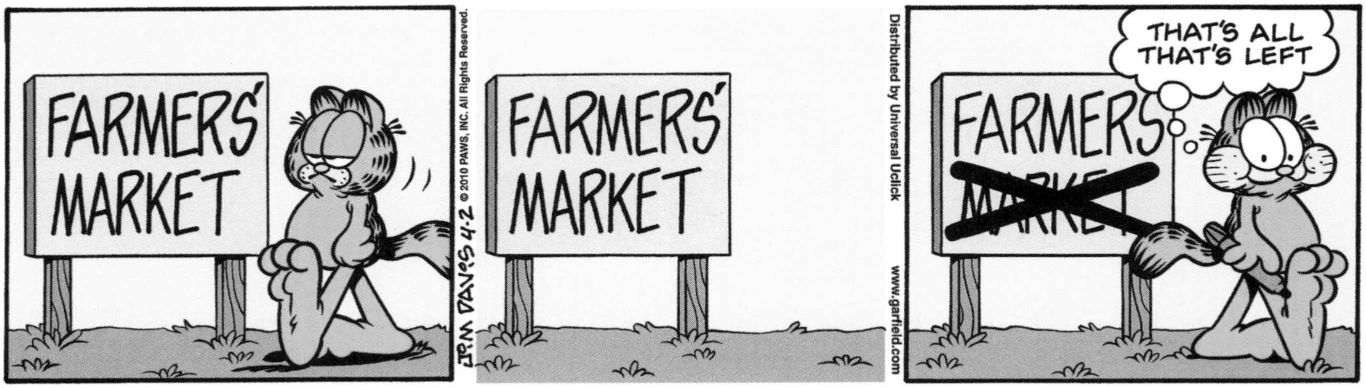
FARMERS' MARKET
FARMERS' MARKET
FARMERS' MARKET
THAT'S ALL THAT'S LEFT
JIM DAVIS 4-2
© 2010 PAWS, INC. All Rights Reserved.
Distributed by Universal Uclick
www.garfield.com

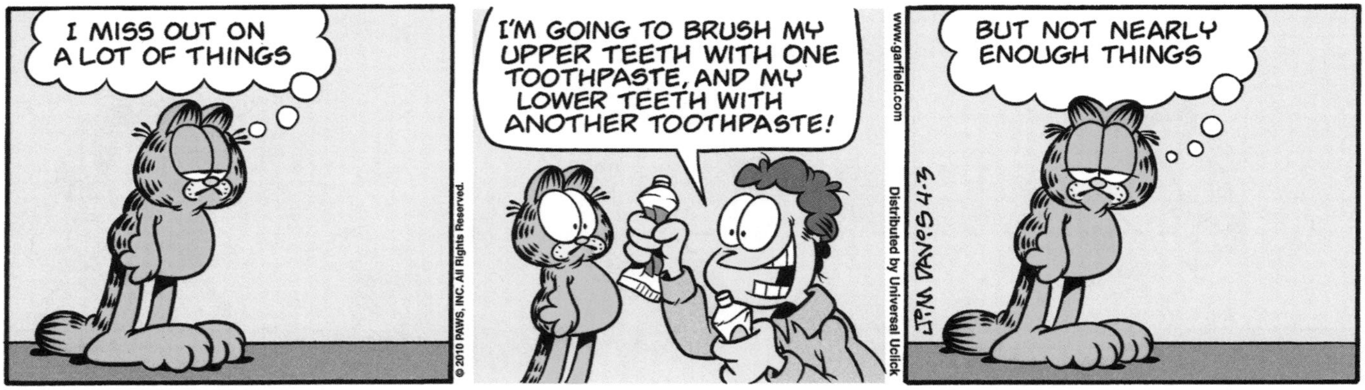
I MISS OUT ON A LOT OF THINGS
I'M GOING TO BRUSH MY UPPER TEETH WITH ONE TOOTHPASTE, AND MY LOWER TEETH WITH ANOTHER TOOTHPASTE!
BUT NOT NEARLY ENOUGH THINGS
JIM DAVIS 4-3
© 2010 PAWS, INC. All Rights Reserved.
www.garfield.com
Distributed by Universal Uclick

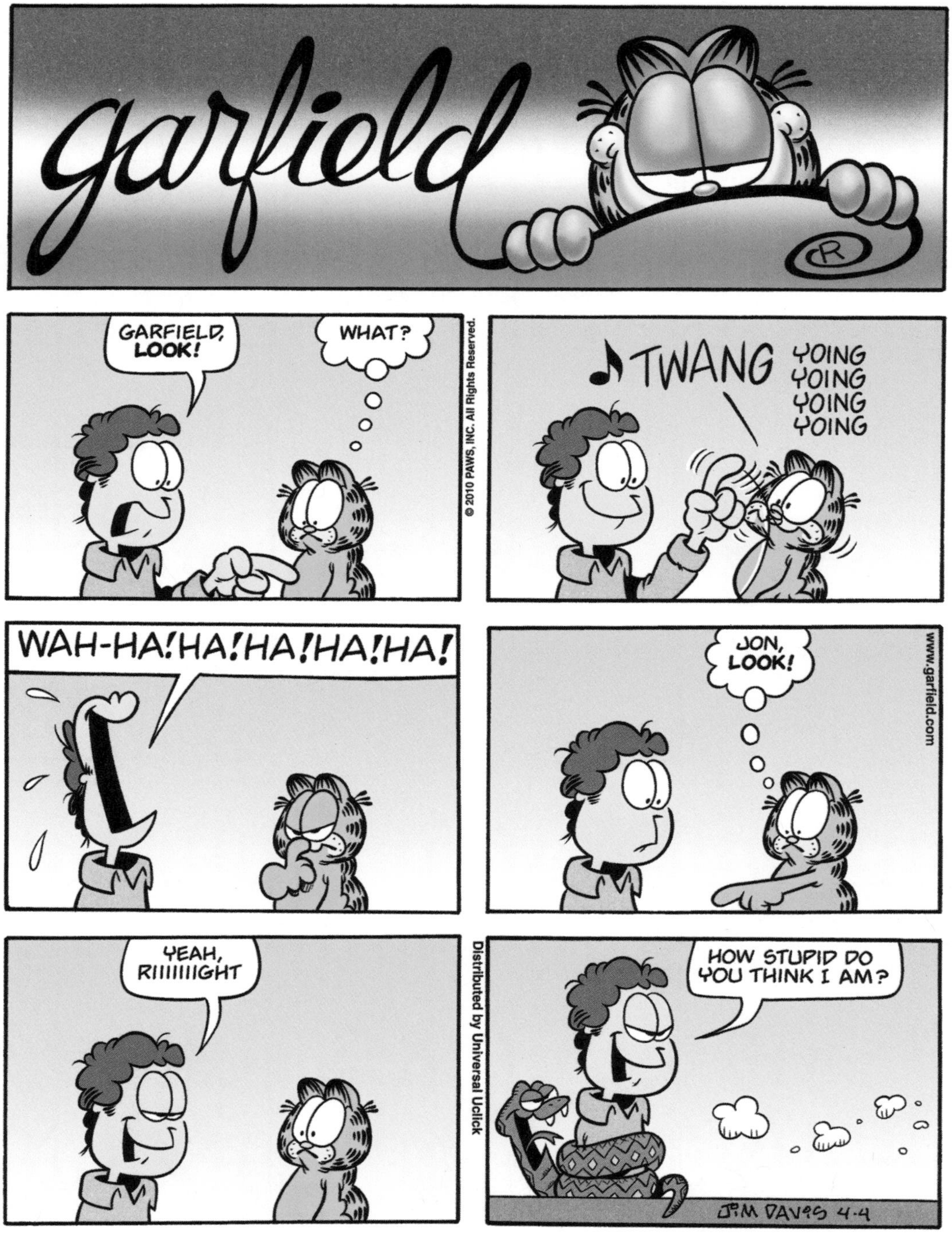
garfield
GARFIELD, LOOK!
WHAT?
© 2010 PAWS, INC. All Rights Reserved.
♪TWANG
YOING YOING YOING YOING
WAH-HA!HA!HA!HA!HA!
JON, LOOK!
www.garfield.com
YEAH, RIIIIIIIGHT
Distributed by Universal Uclick
HOW STUPID DO YOU THINK I AM?
JIM DAVIS 4-4

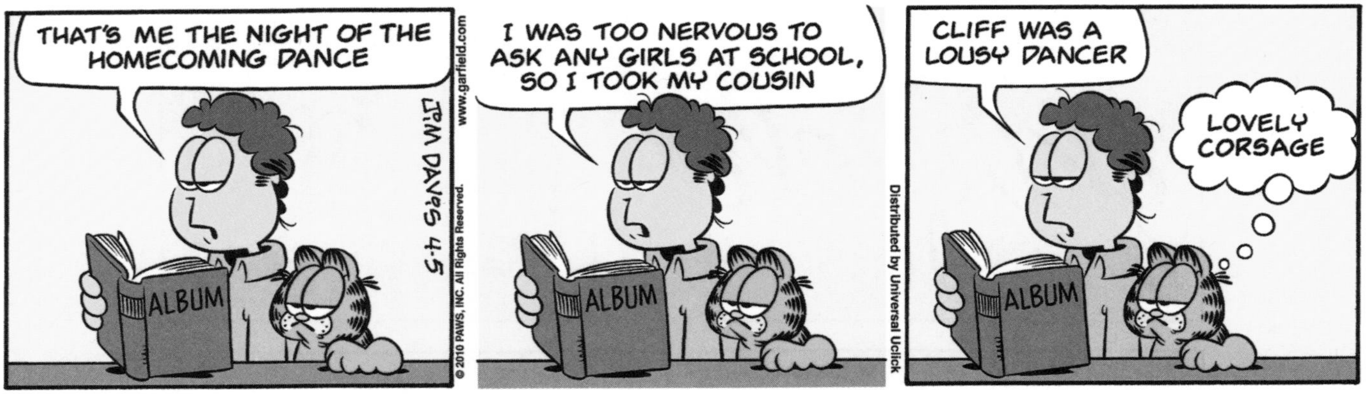
THAT'S ME THE NIGHT OF THE HOMECOMING DANCE
ALBUM
JIM DAVIS 4-5
© 2010 PAWS, INC. All Rights Reserved. www.garfield.com
I WAS TOO NERVOUS TO ASK ANY GIRLS AT SCHOOL, SO I TOOK MY COUSIN
ALBUM
Distributed by Universal Uclick
CLIFF WAS A LOUSY DANCER
LOVELY CORSAGE
ALBUM

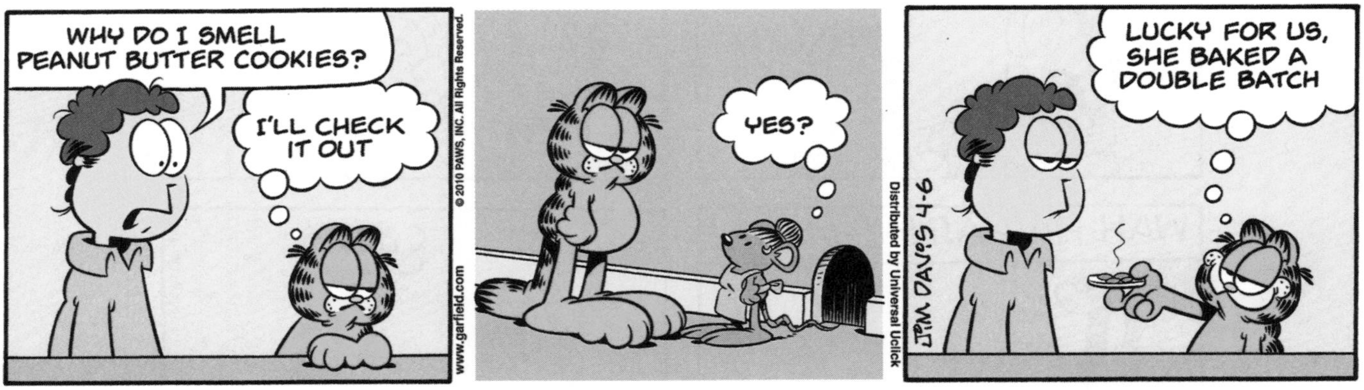
WHY DO I SMELL PEANUT BUTTER COOKIES?
I'LL CHECK IT OUT
© 2010 PAWS, INC. All Rights Reserved. www.garfield.com
YES?
Distributed by Universal Uclick
JIM DAVIS 4-6
LUCKY FOR US, SHE BAKED A DOUBLE BATCH

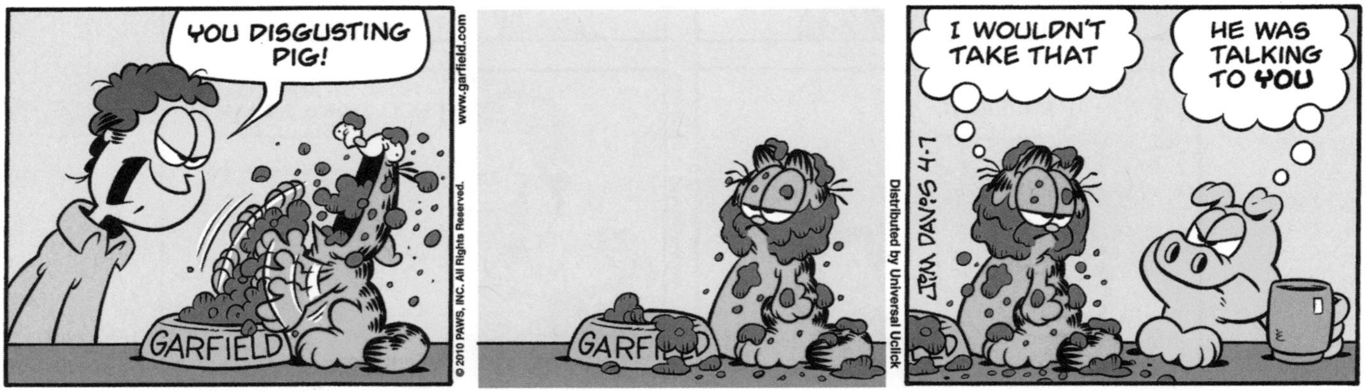
YOU DISGUSTING PIG!
GARFIELD
© 2010 PAWS, INC. All Rights Reserved. www.garfield.com
GARFIELD
Distributed by Universal Uclick
JIM DAVIS 4-7
I WOULDN'T TAKE THAT
HE WAS TALKING TO **YOU**

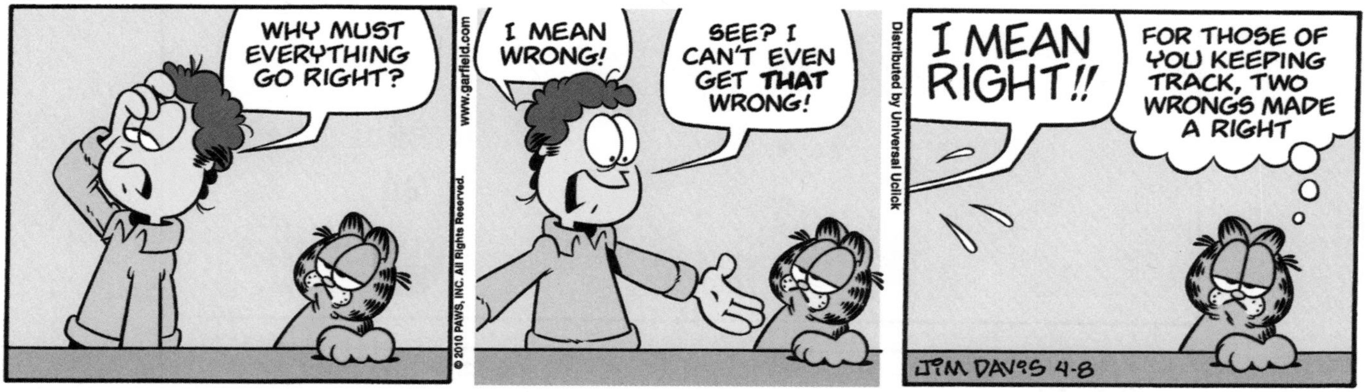
WHY MUST EVERYTHING GO RIGHT?
© 2010 PAWS, INC. All Rights Reserved.
www.garfield.com
I MEAN WRONG!
SEE? I CAN'T EVEN GET **THAT** WRONG!
Distributed by Universal Uclick
I MEAN RIGHT!!
FOR THOSE OF YOU KEEPING TRACK, TWO WRONGS MADE A RIGHT
JIM DAVIS 4-8

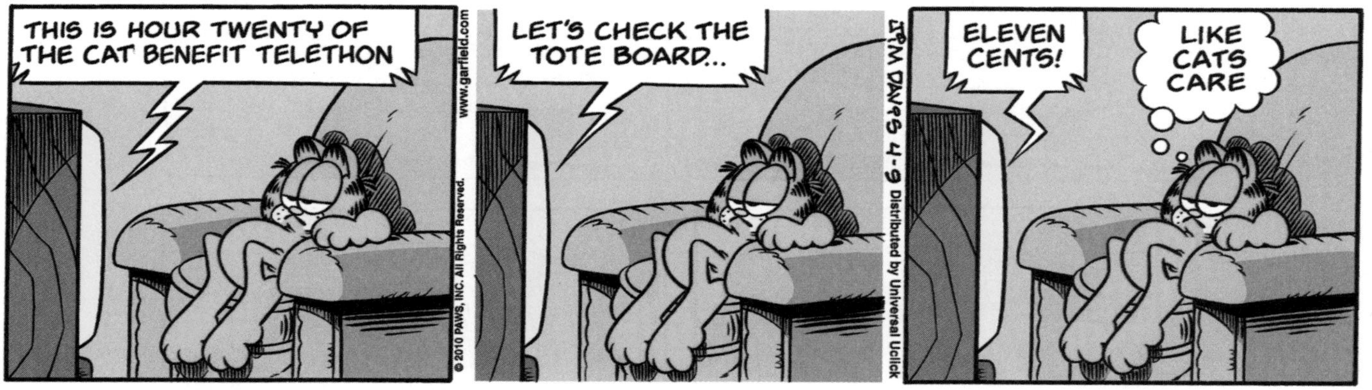
THIS IS HOUR TWENTY OF THE CAT BENEFIT TELETHON
© 2010 PAWS, INC. All Rights Reserved.
www.garfield.com
LET'S CHECK THE TOTE BOARD...
JIM DAVIS 4-9
Distributed by Universal Uclick
ELEVEN CENTS!
LIKE CATS CARE

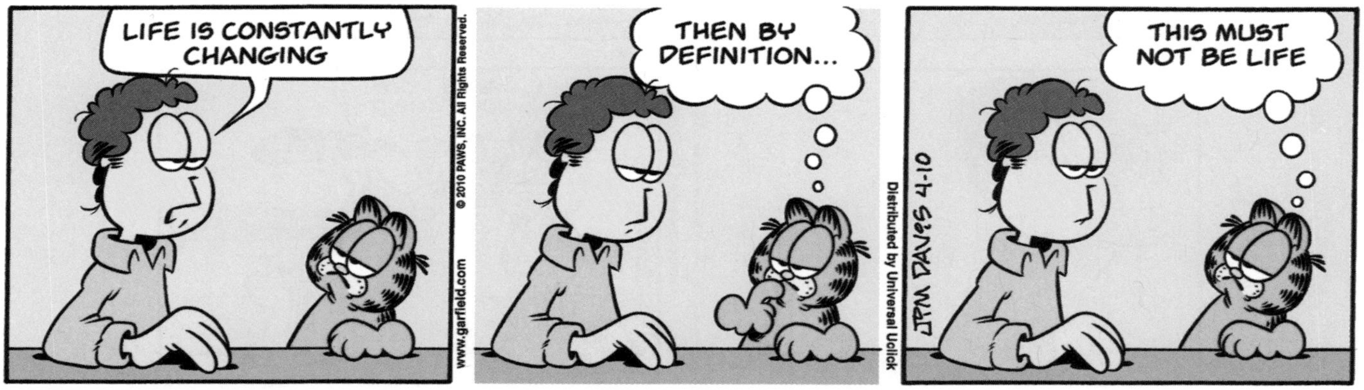
LIFE IS CONSTANTLY CHANGING
© 2010 PAWS, INC. All Rights Reserved.
www.garfield.com
THEN BY DEFINITION...
Distributed by Universal Uclick
JIM DAVIS 4-10
THIS MUST NOT BE LIFE

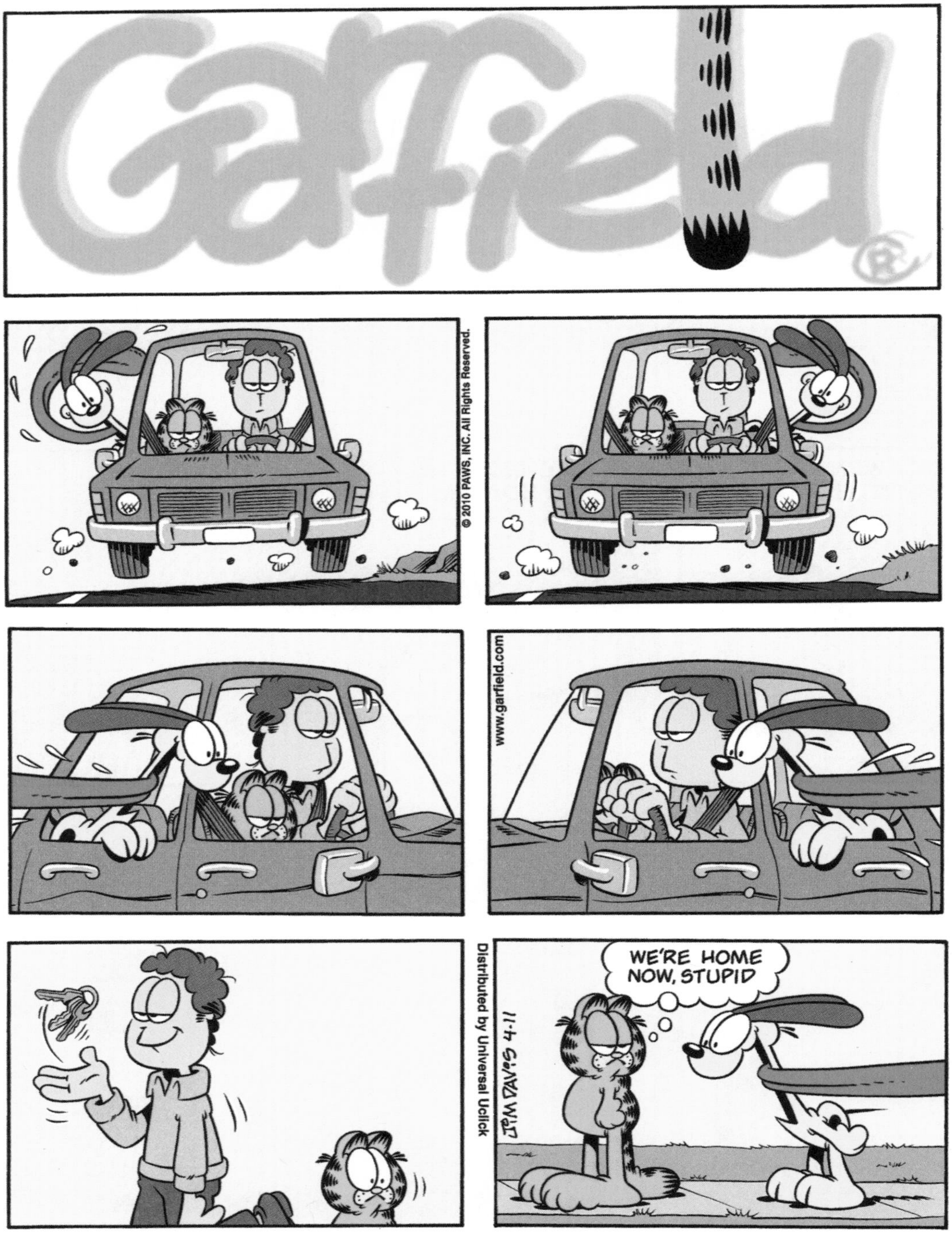
Garfield
© 2010 PAWS, INC. All Rights Reserved.
www.garfield.com
Distributed by Universal Uclick
JPM DAVIS 4-11
WE'RE HOME NOW, STUPID

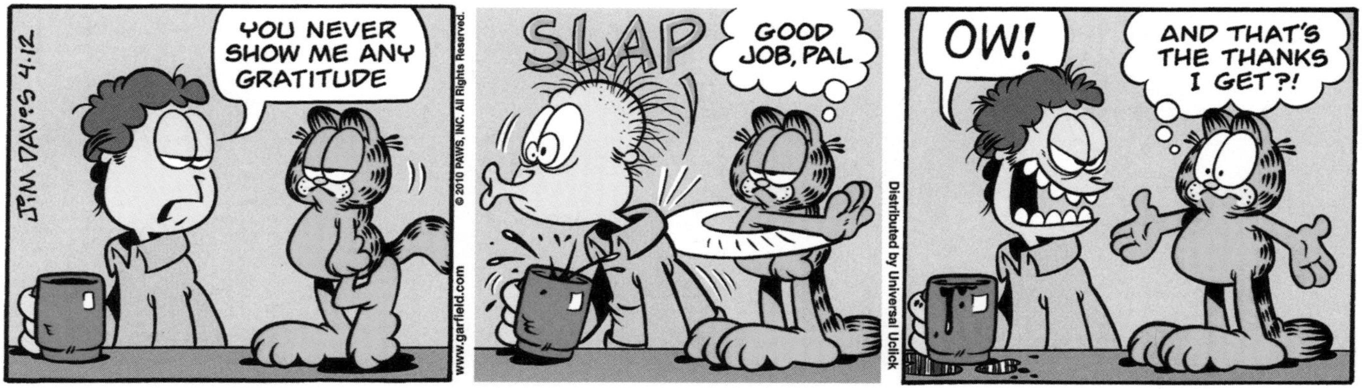
JIM DAVIS 4.12
YOU NEVER SHOW ME ANY GRATITUDE
© 2010 PAWS, INC. All Rights Reserved.
www.garfield.com
SLAP
GOOD JOB, PAL
Distributed by Universal Uclick
OW!
AND THAT'S THE THANKS I GET?!

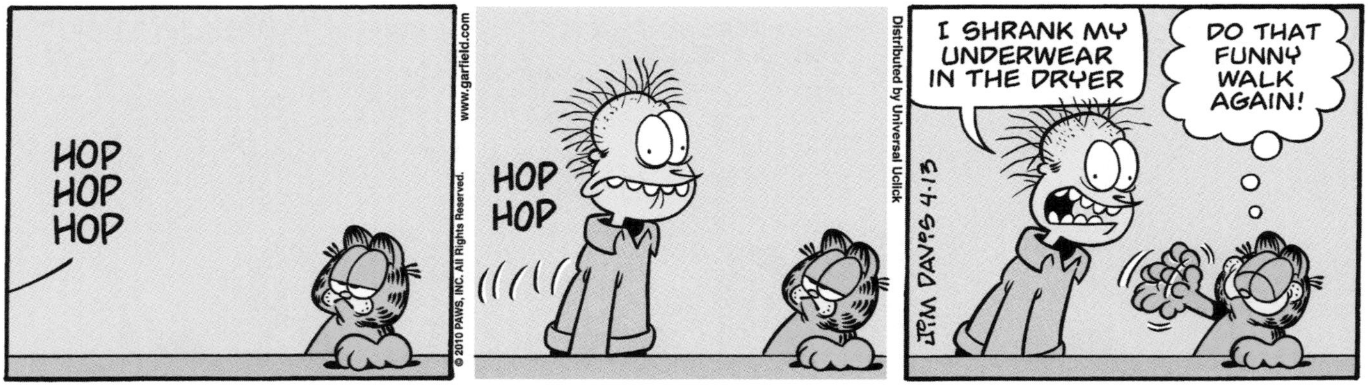
HOP HOP HOP
www.garfield.com
© 2010 PAWS, INC. All Rights Reserved.
HOP HOP
Distributed by Universal Uclick
I SHRANK MY UNDERWEAR IN THE DRYER
DO THAT FUNNY WALK AGAIN!
JIM DAVIS 4.13

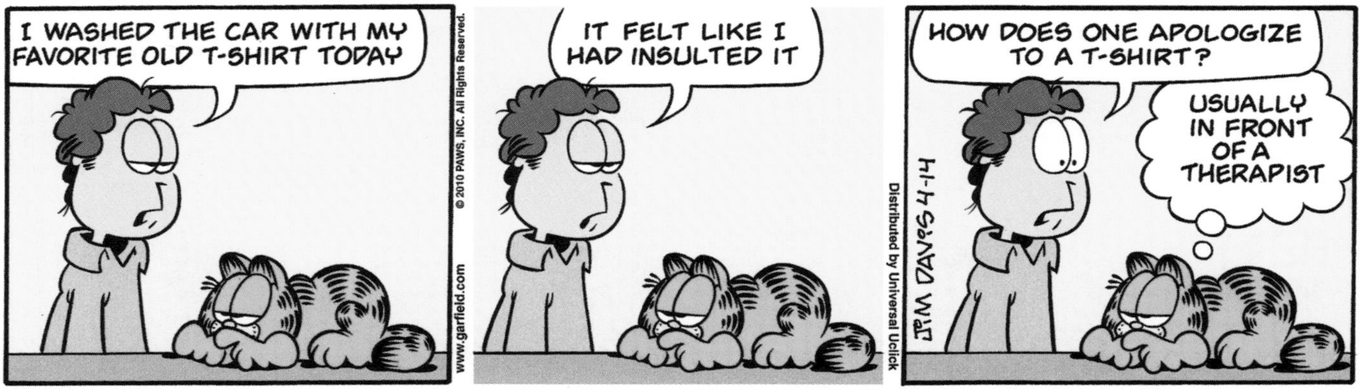
I WASHED THE CAR WITH MY FAVORITE OLD T-SHIRT TODAY
© 2010 PAWS, INC. All Rights Reserved.
www.garfield.com
IT FELT LIKE I HAD INSULTED IT
Distributed by Universal Uclick
HOW DOES ONE APOLOGIZE TO A T-SHIRT?
USUALLY IN FRONT OF A THERAPIST
JIM DAVIS 4.14

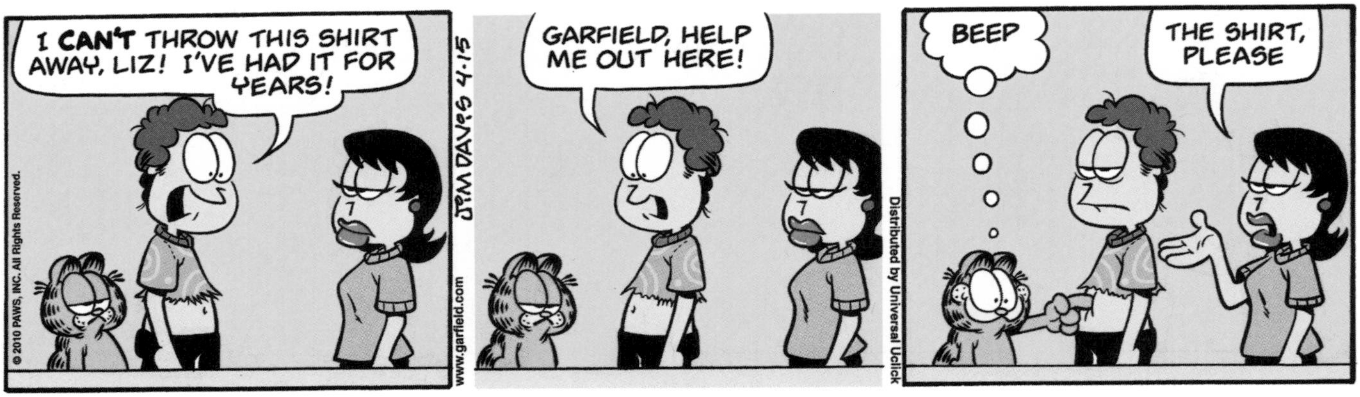
I CAN'T THROW THIS SHIRT AWAY, LIZ! I'VE HAD IT FOR YEARS!
GARFIELD, HELP ME OUT HERE!
BEEP
THE SHIRT, PLEASE
© 2010 PAWS, INC. All Rights Reserved.
JIM DAVIS 4-15
www.garfield.com
Distributed by Universal Uclick

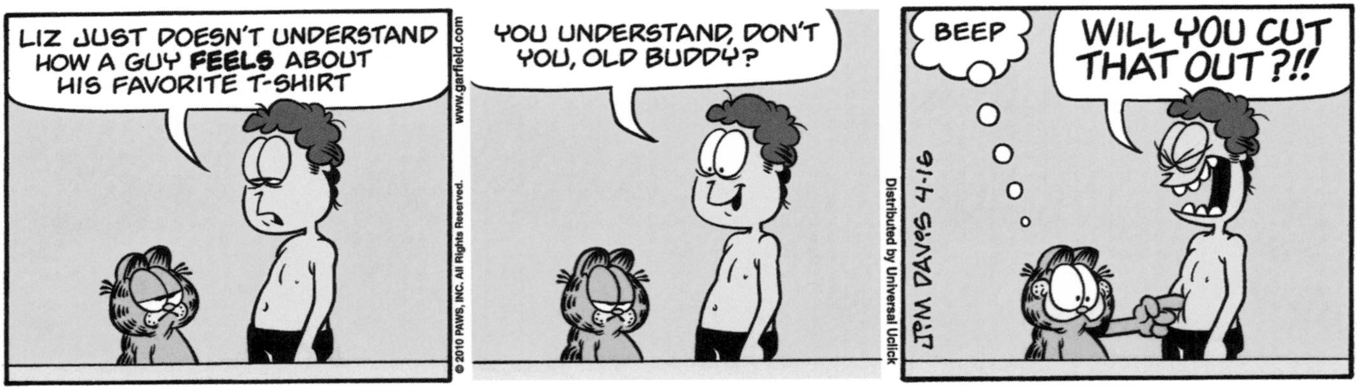
LIZ JUST DOESN'T UNDERSTAND HOW A GUY FEELS ABOUT HIS FAVORITE T-SHIRT
YOU UNDERSTAND, DON'T YOU, OLD BUDDY?
BEEP
WILL YOU CUT THAT OUT?!!
www.garfield.com
© 2010 PAWS, INC. All Rights Reserved.
Distributed by Universal Uclick
JIM DAVIS 4-16

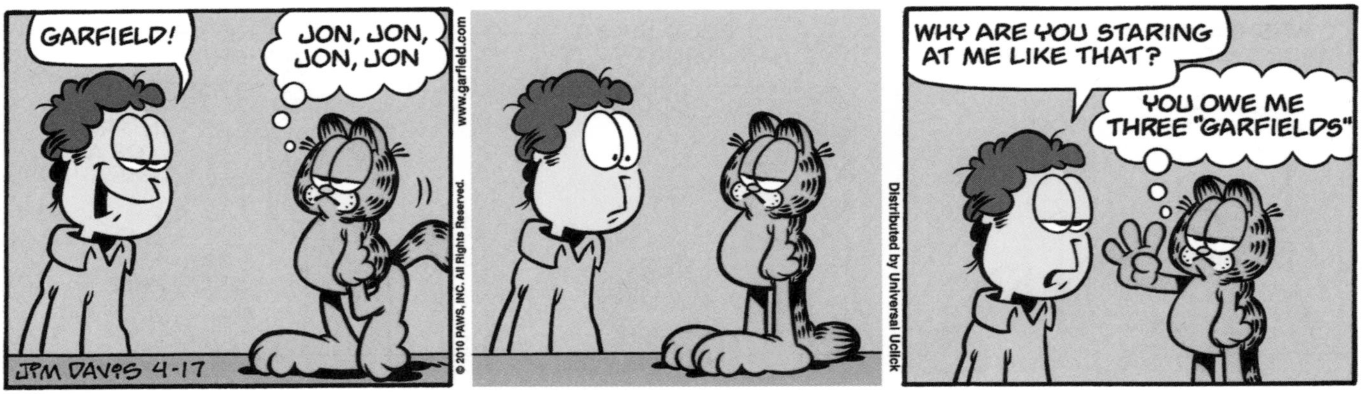
GARFIELD!
JON, JON, JON, JON
WHY ARE YOU STARING AT ME LIKE THAT?
YOU OWE ME THREE "GARFIELDS"
JIM DAVIS 4-17
www.garfield.com
© 2010 PAWS, INC. All Rights Reserved.
Distributed by Universal Uclick

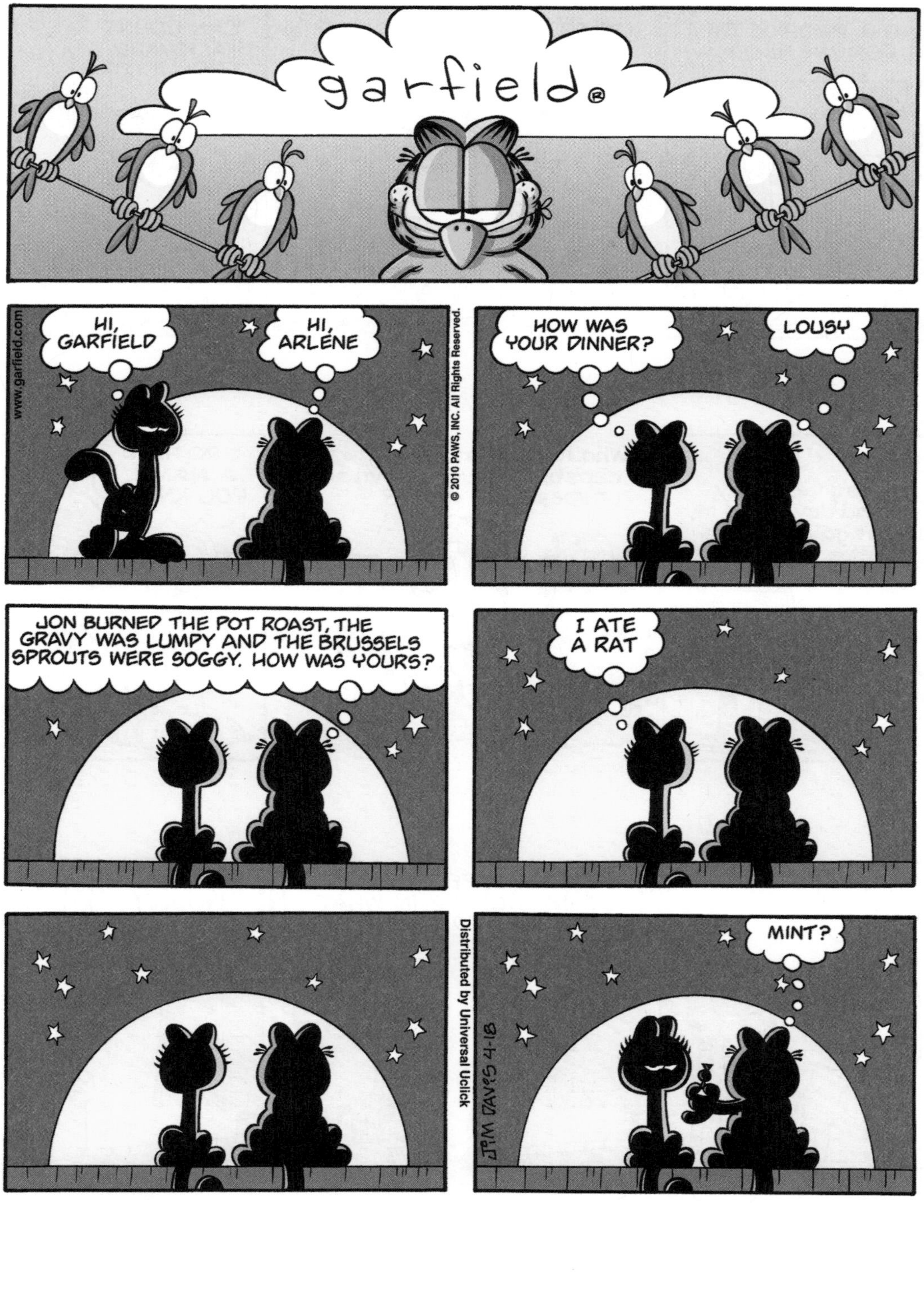
garfield®
www.garfield.com
HI, GARFIELD
HI, ARLENE
© 2010 PAWS, INC. All Rights Reserved.
HOW WAS YOUR DINNER?
LOUSY
JON BURNED THE POT ROAST, THE GRAVY WAS LUMPY AND THE BRUSSELS SPROUTS WERE SOGGY. HOW WAS YOURS?
I ATE A RAT
Distributed by Universal Uclick
JPM DAVIS 4-18
MINT?

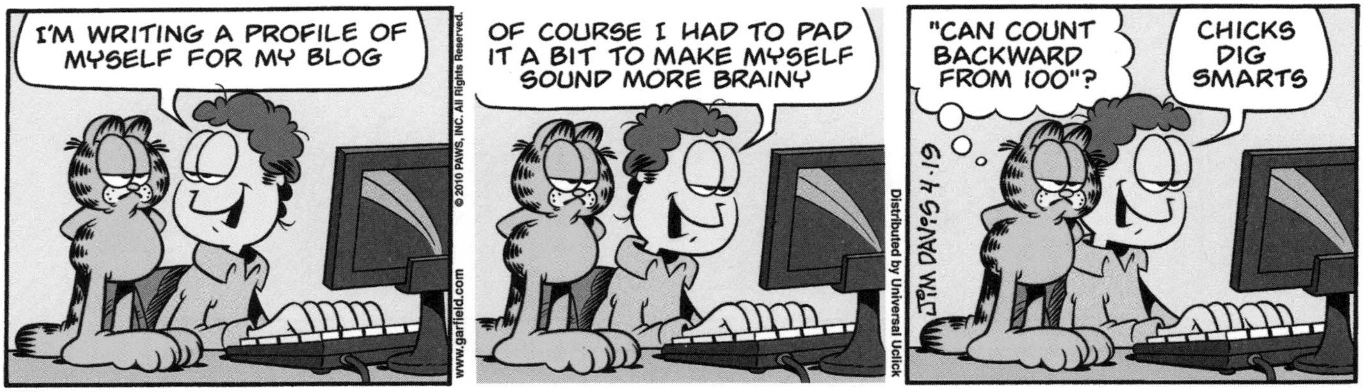
I'M WRITING A PROFILE OF MYSELF FOR MY BLOG
OF COURSE I HAD TO PAD IT A BIT TO MAKE MYSELF SOUND MORE BRAINY
"CAN COUNT BACKWARD FROM 100"?
CHICKS DIG SMARTS
© 2010 PAWS, INC. All Rights Reserved.
www.garfield.com
Distributed by Universal Uclick
JPM DAVPS 4·19

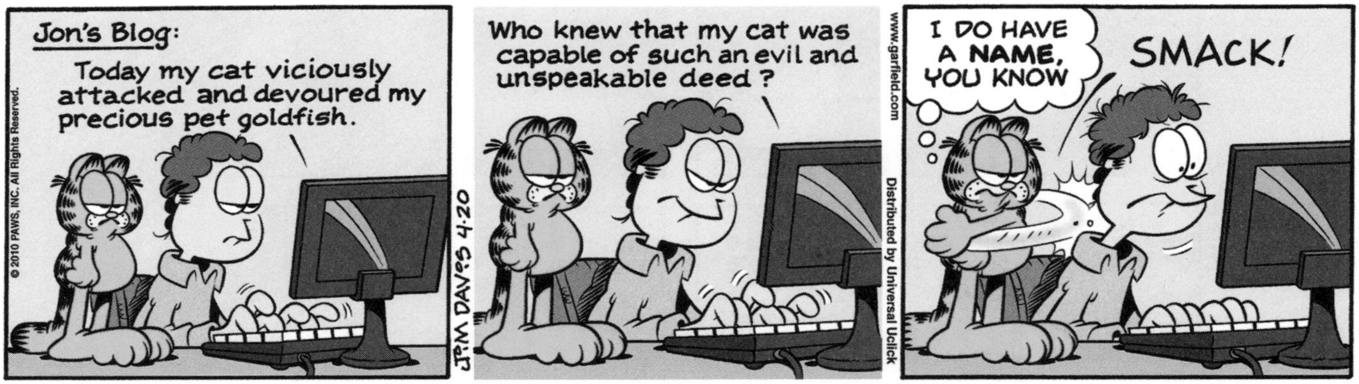
Jon's Blog:
Today my cat viciously attacked and devoured my precious pet goldfish.
Who knew that my cat was capable of such an evil and unspeakable deed?
I DO HAVE A **NAME**, YOU KNOW
SMACK!
© 2010 PAWS, INC. All Rights Reserved.
JPM DAVPS 4·20
www.garfield.com
Distributed by Universal Uclick

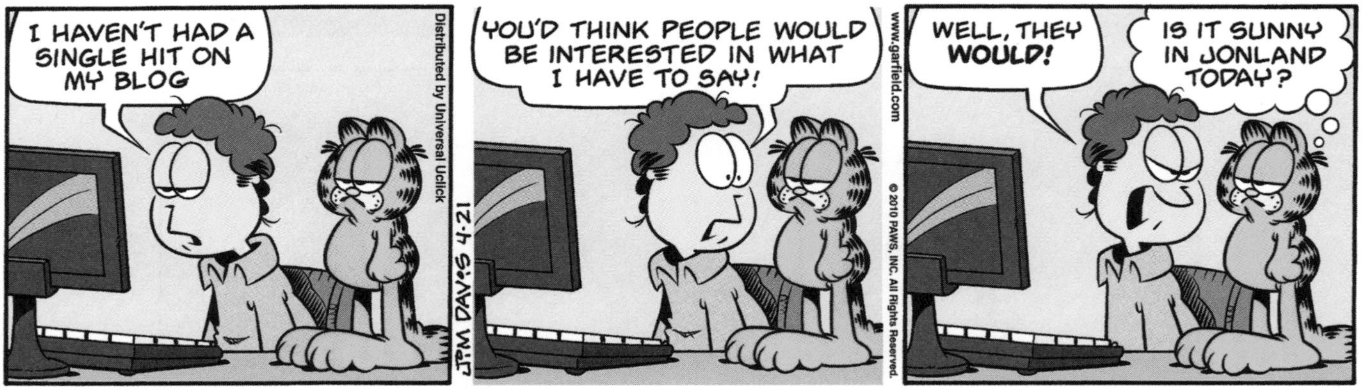
I HAVEN'T HAD A SINGLE HIT ON MY BLOG
YOU'D THINK PEOPLE WOULD BE INTERESTED IN WHAT I HAVE TO SAY!
WELL, THEY **WOULD!**
IS IT SUNNY IN JONLAND TODAY?
Distributed by Universal Uclick
JPM DAVPS 4·21
www.garfield.com
© 2010 PAWS, INC. All Rights Reserved.

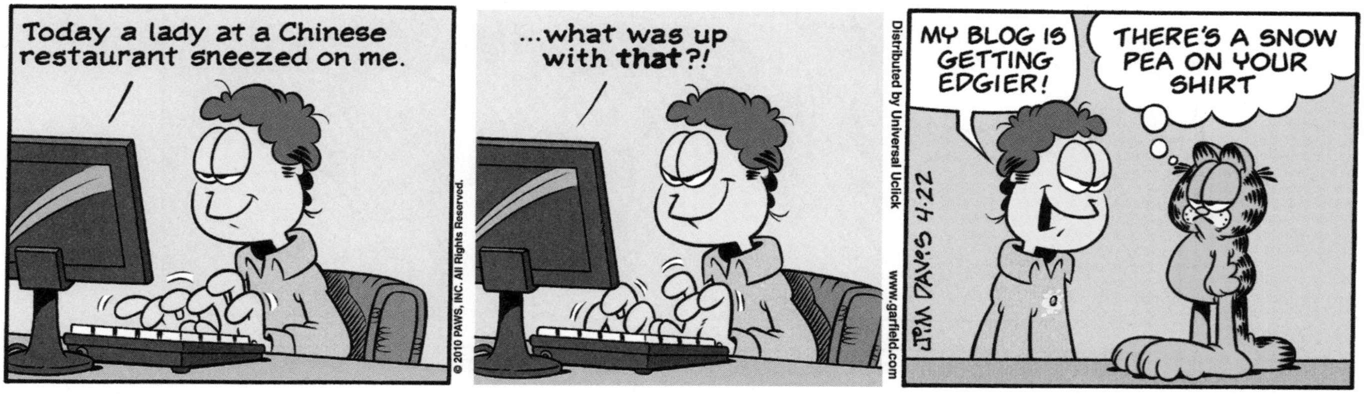
Today a lady at a Chinese restaurant sneezed on me.
...what was up with **that**?!
MY BLOG IS GETTING EDGIER!
THERE'S A SNOW PEA ON YOUR SHIRT
© 2010 PAWS, INC. All Rights Reserved.
Distributed by Universal Uclick
www.garfield.com

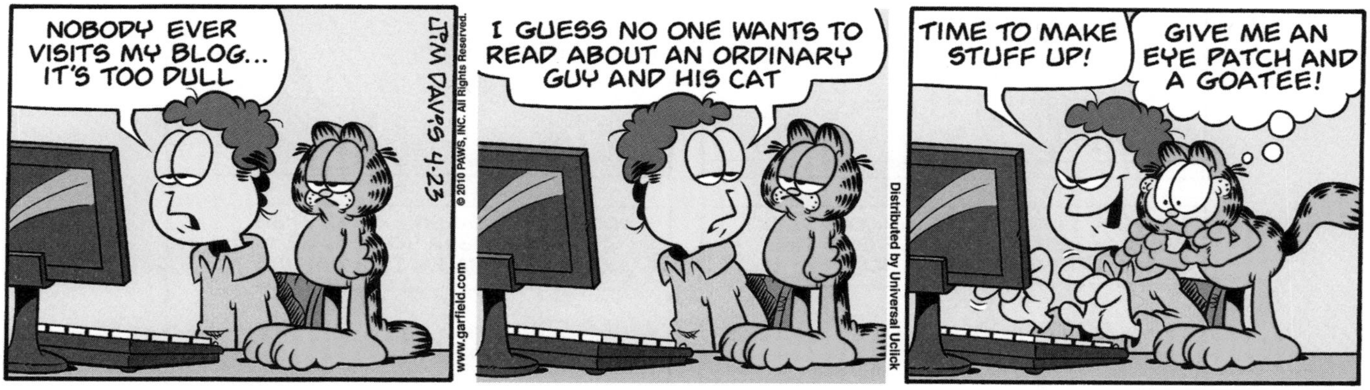
NOBODY EVER VISITS MY BLOG... IT'S TOO DULL
I GUESS NO ONE WANTS TO READ ABOUT AN ORDINARY GUY AND HIS CAT
TIME TO MAKE STUFF UP!
GIVE ME AN EYE PATCH AND A GOATEE!
© 2010 PAWS, INC. All Rights Reserved.
www.garfield.com
Distributed by Universal Uclick

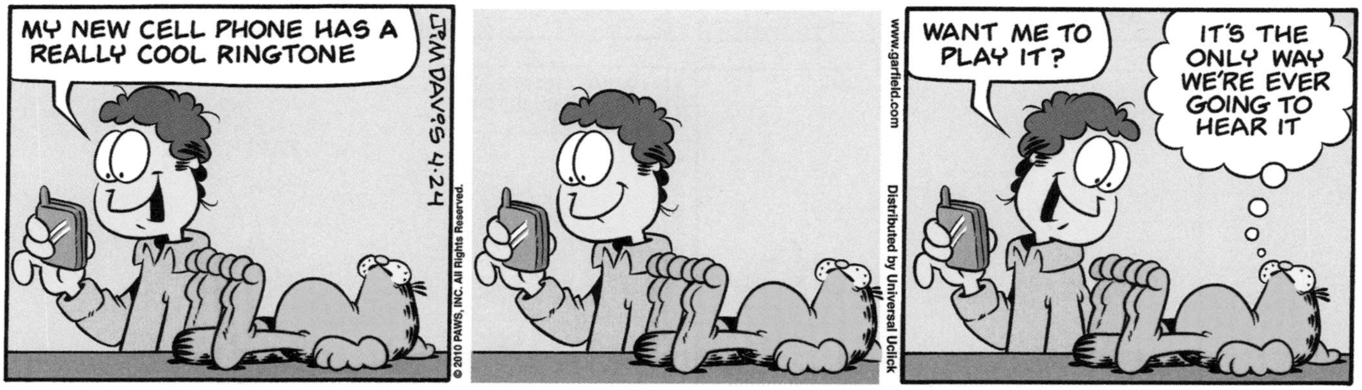
MY NEW CELL PHONE HAS A REALLY COOL RINGTONE
WANT ME TO PLAY IT?
IT'S THE ONLY WAY WE'RE EVER GOING TO HEAR IT
© 2010 PAWS, INC. All Rights Reserved.
www.garfield.com
Distributed by Universal Uclick

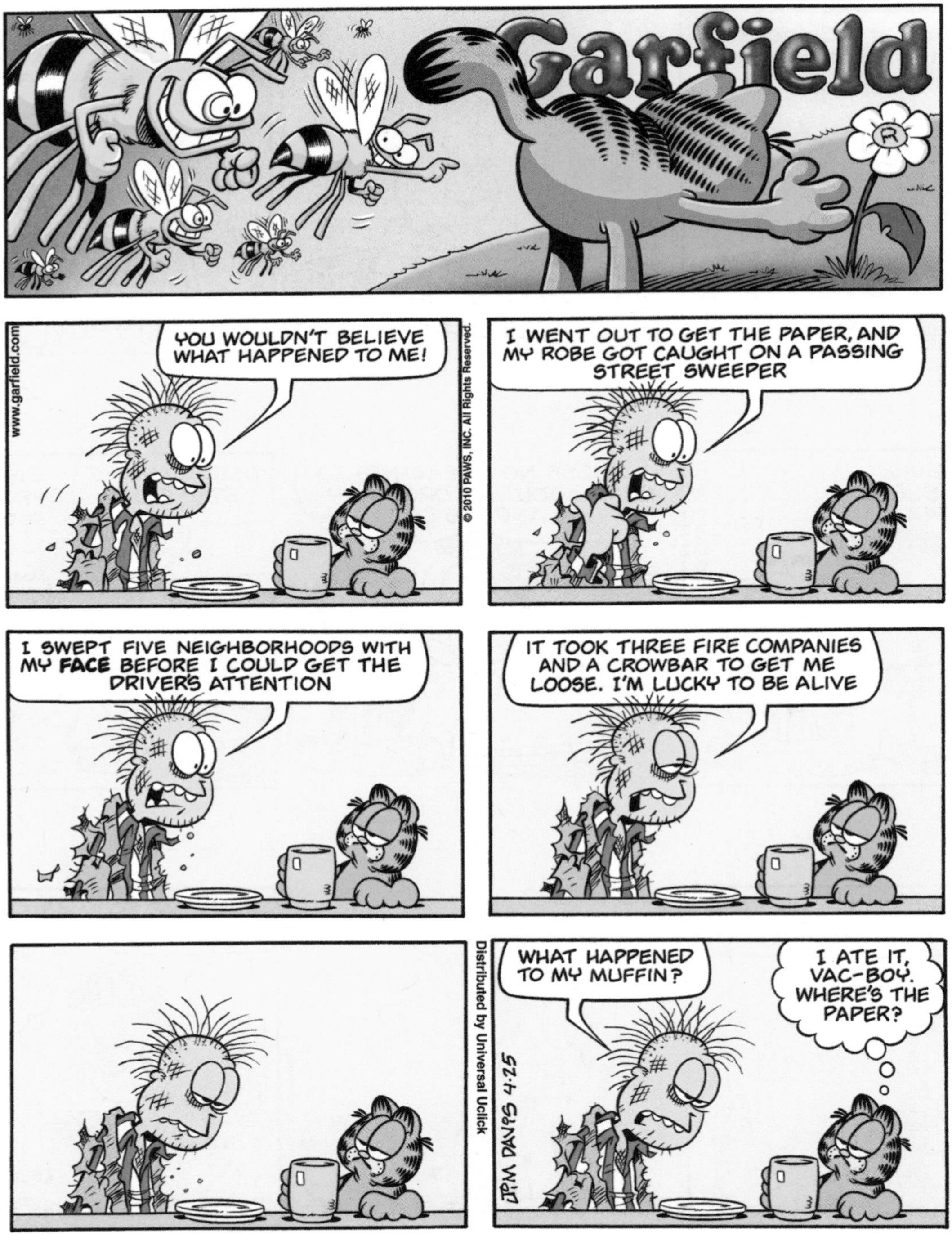
Garfield
www.garfield.com
© 2010 PAWS, INC. All Rights Reserved.
YOU WOULDN'T BELIEVE WHAT HAPPENED TO ME!
I WENT OUT TO GET THE PAPER, AND MY ROBE GOT CAUGHT ON A PASSING STREET SWEEPER
I SWEPT FIVE NEIGHBORHOODS WITH MY FACE BEFORE I COULD GET THE DRIVER'S ATTENTION
IT TOOK THREE FIRE COMPANIES AND A CROWBAR TO GET ME LOOSE. I'M LUCKY TO BE ALIVE
Distributed by Universal Uclick
WHAT HAPPENED TO MY MUFFIN?
I ATE IT, VAC-BOY. WHERE'S THE PAPER?
JPM DAVIS 4·25

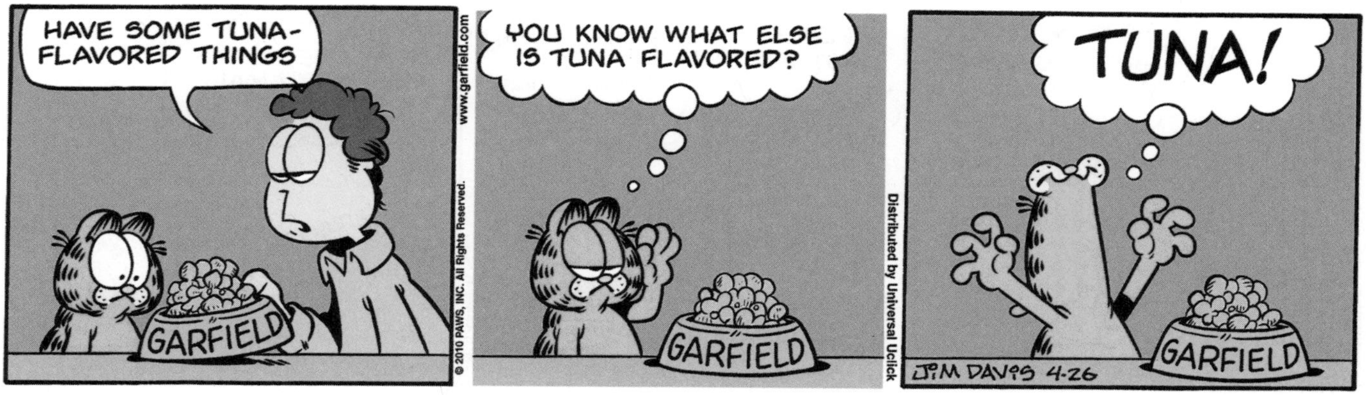
HAVE SOME TUNA-FLAVORED THINGS
YOU KNOW WHAT ELSE IS TUNA FLAVORED?
TUNA!
GARFIELD
© 2010 PAWS, INC. All Rights Reserved.
www.garfield.com
Distributed by Universal Uclick
JIM DAVIS 4-26

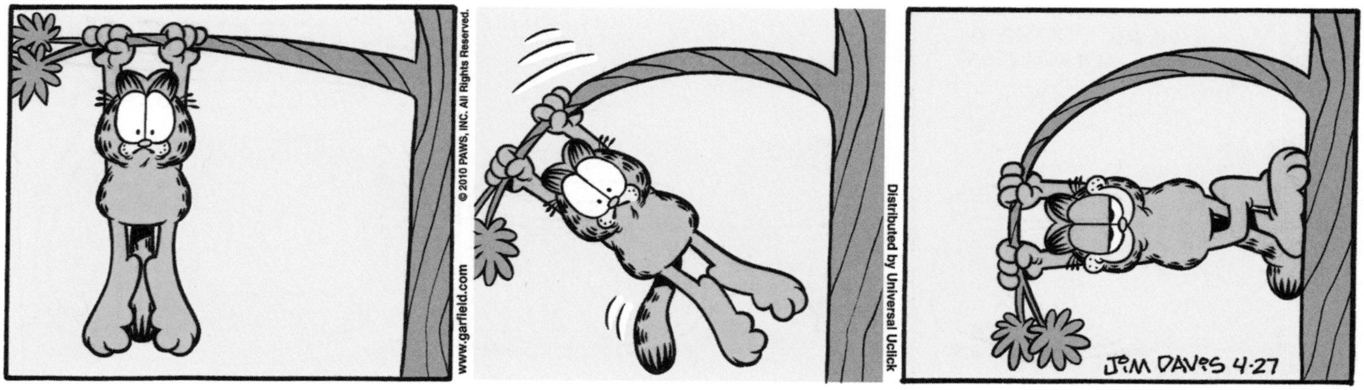
© 2010 PAWS, INC. All Rights Reserved.
www.garfield.com
Distributed by Universal Uclick
JIM DAVIS 4-27

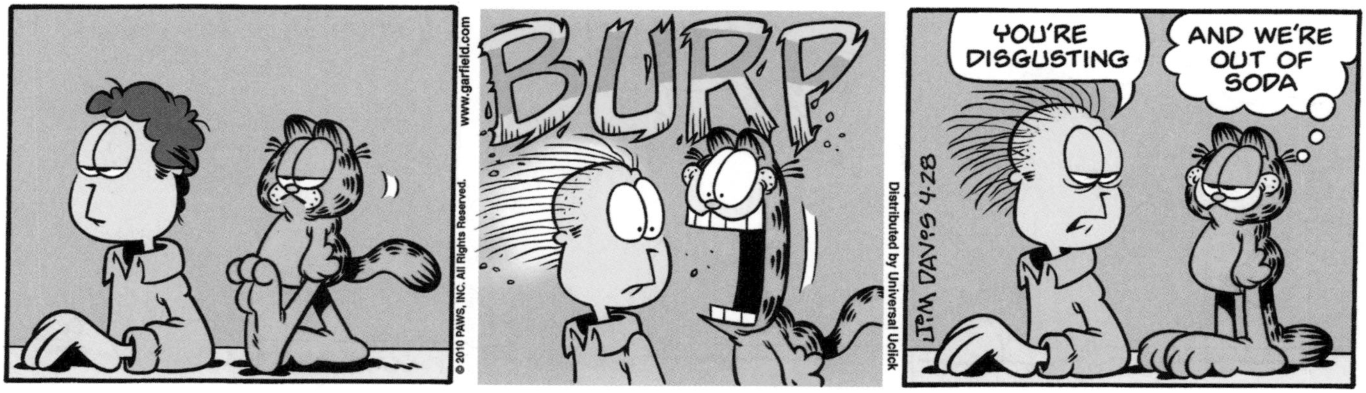
BURP
YOU'RE DISGUSTING
AND WE'RE OUT OF SODA
© 2010 PAWS, INC. All Rights Reserved.
www.garfield.com
Distributed by Universal Uclick
JIM DAVIS 4-28

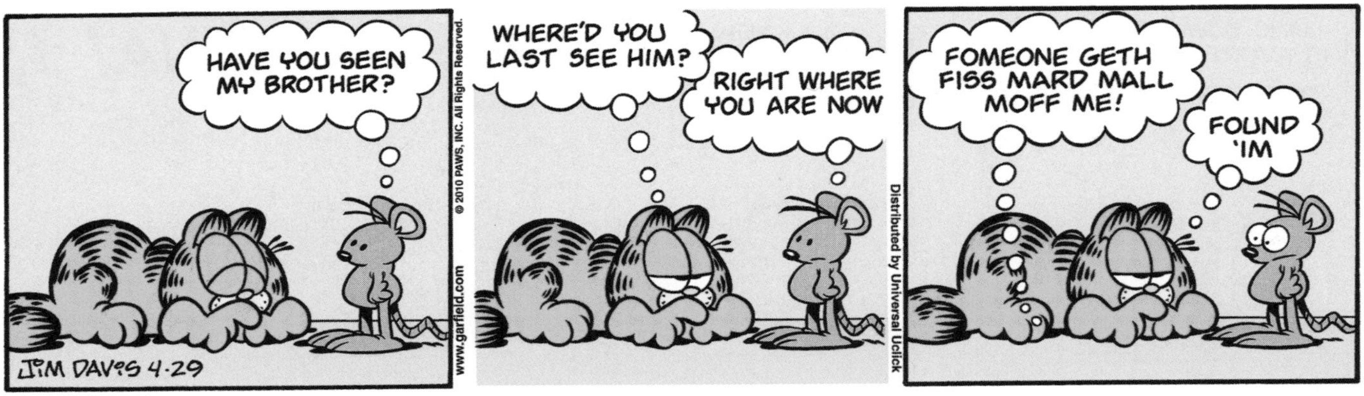
HAVE YOU SEEN MY BROTHER?
JIM DAVIS 4-29
© 2010 PAWS, INC. All Rights Reserved.
www.garfield.com
WHERE'D YOU LAST SEE HIM?
RIGHT WHERE YOU ARE NOW
Distributed by Universal Uclick
FOMEONE GETH FISS MARD MALL MOFF ME!
FOUND 'IM

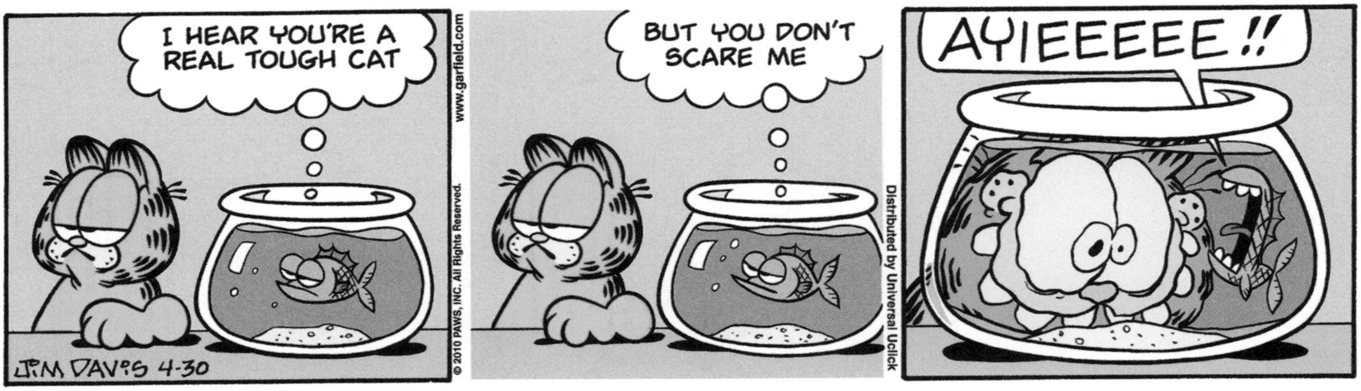
I HEAR YOU'RE A REAL TOUGH CAT
JIM DAVIS 4-30
www.garfield.com
© 2010 PAWS, INC. All Rights Reserved.
BUT YOU DON'T SCARE ME
Distributed by Universal Uclick
AYIEEEEEE!!

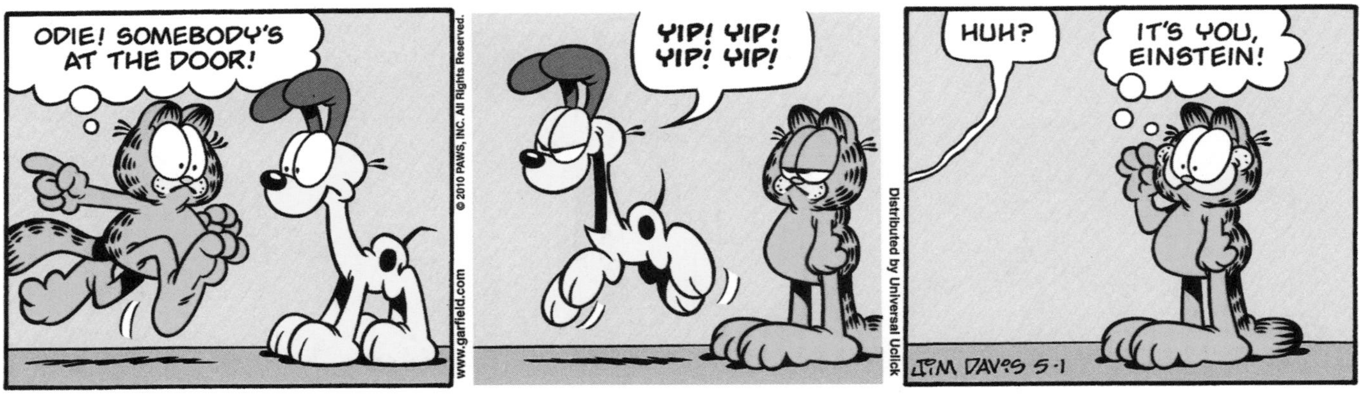
ODIE! SOMEBODY'S AT THE DOOR!
© 2010 PAWS, INC. All Rights Reserved.
www.garfield.com
YIP! YIP! YIP! YIP!
Distributed by Universal Uclick
HUH?
IT'S YOU, EINSTEIN!
JIM DAVIS 5-1

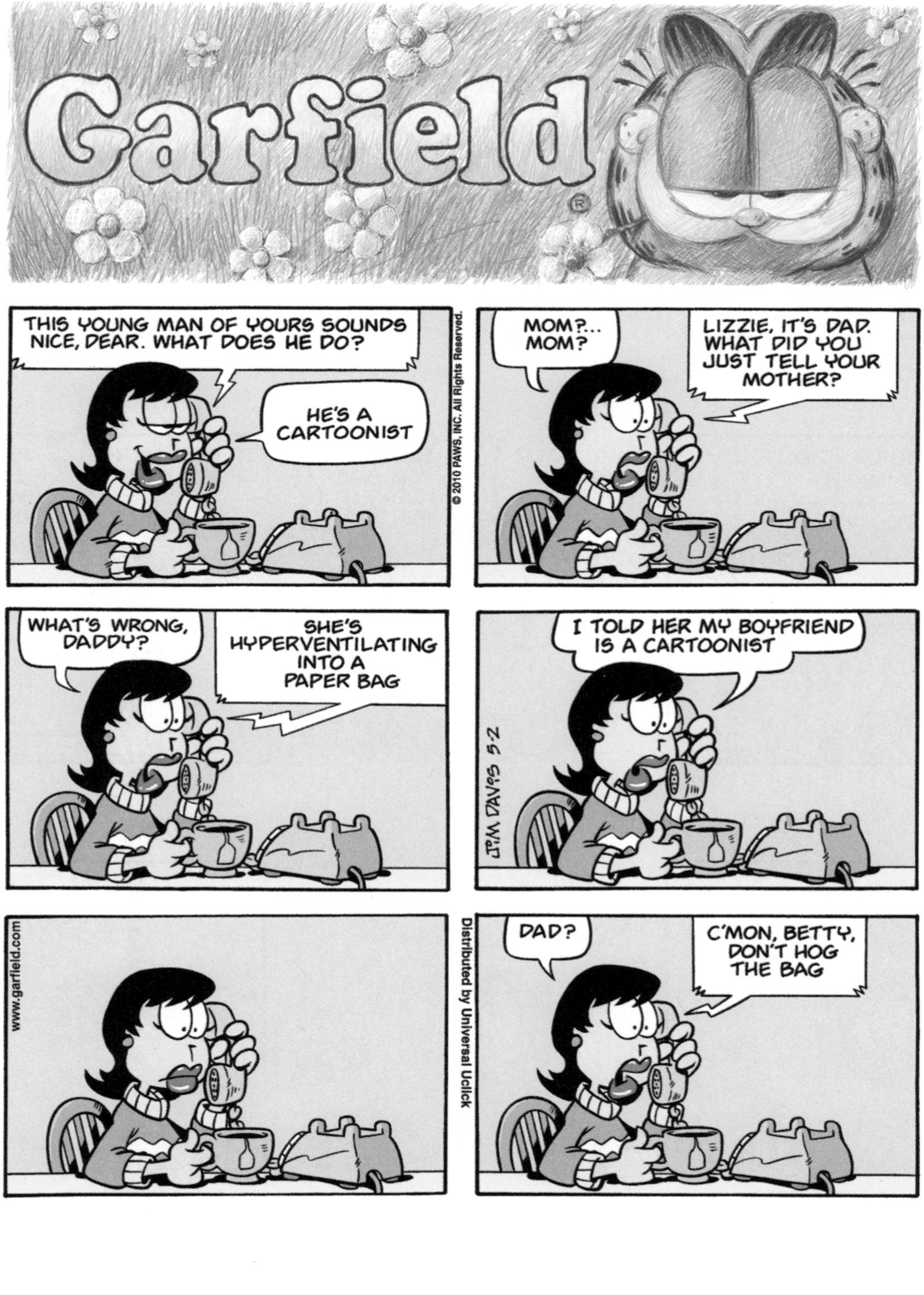
Garfield®
THIS YOUNG MAN OF YOURS SOUNDS NICE, DEAR. WHAT DOES HE DO?
HE'S A CARTOONIST
© 2010 PAWS, INC. All Rights Reserved.
MOM?... MOM?
LIZZIE, IT'S DAD. WHAT DID YOU JUST TELL YOUR MOTHER?
WHAT'S WRONG, DADDY?
SHE'S HYPERVENTILATING INTO A PAPER BAG
I TOLD HER MY BOYFRIEND IS A CARTOONIST
JPM DAVPS 5-2
www.garfield.com
Distributed by Universal Uclick
DAD?
C'MON, BETTY, DON'T HOG THE BAG

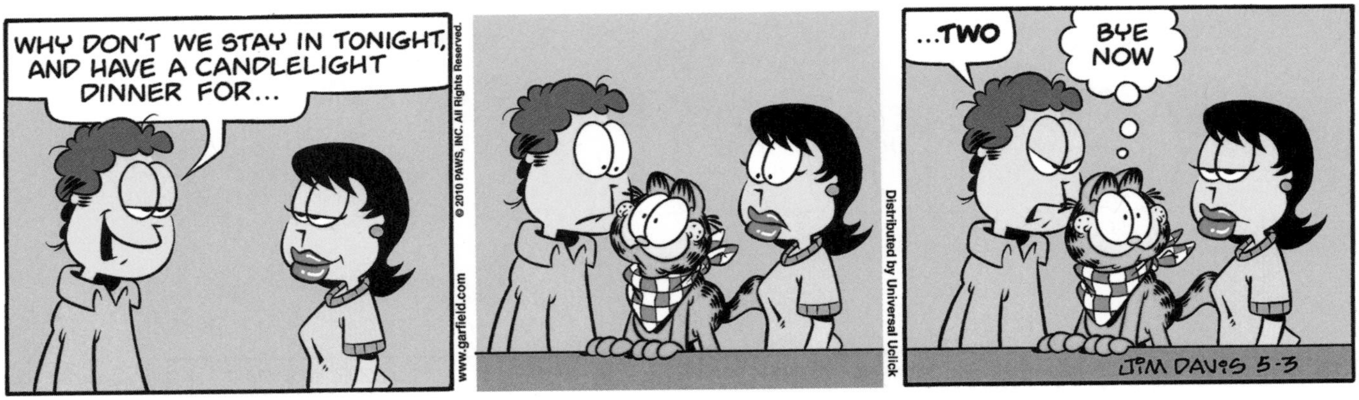
WHY DON'T WE STAY IN TONIGHT, AND HAVE A CANDLELIGHT DINNER FOR...
...TWO
BYE NOW
JIM DAVIS 5-3
© 2010 PAWS, INC. All Rights Reserved.
www.garfield.com
Distributed by Universal Uclick

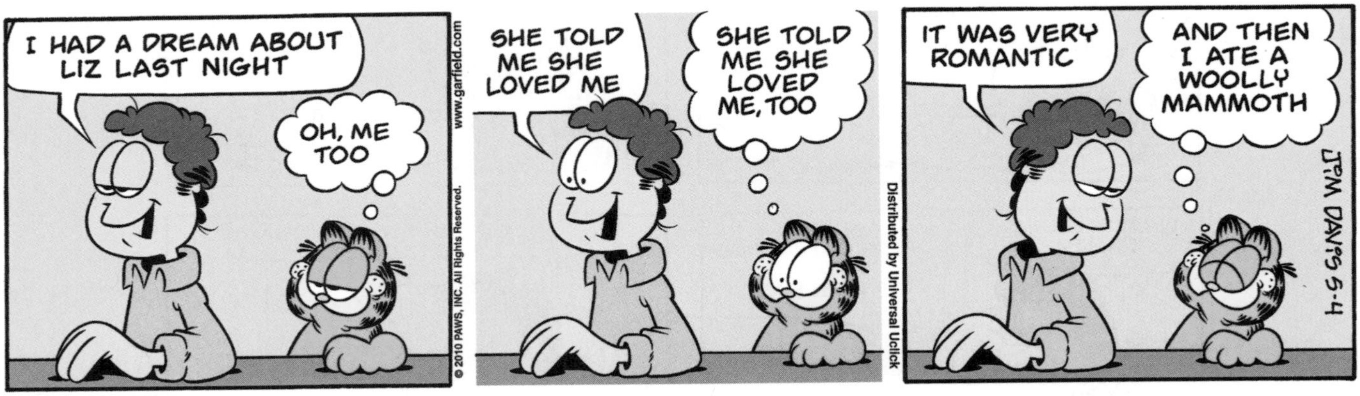
I HAD A DREAM ABOUT LIZ LAST NIGHT
OH, ME TOO
SHE TOLD ME SHE LOVED ME
SHE TOLD ME SHE LOVED ME, TOO
IT WAS VERY ROMANTIC
AND THEN I ATE A WOOLLY MAMMOTH
JIM DAVIS 5-4
© 2010 PAWS, INC. All Rights Reserved.
www.garfield.com
Distributed by Universal Uclick

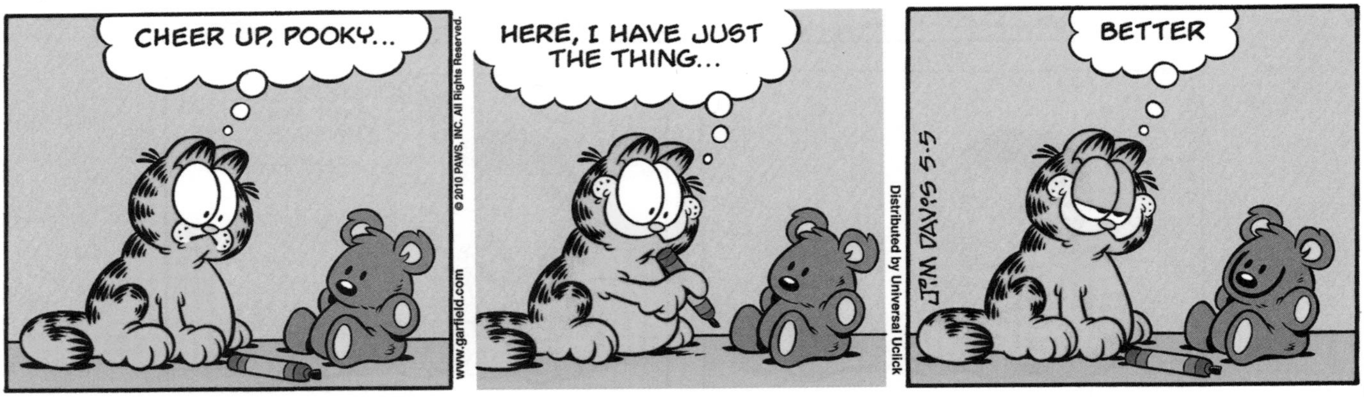
CHEER UP, POOKY...
HERE, I HAVE JUST THE THING...
BETTER
JIM DAVIS 5-5
© 2010 PAWS, INC. All Rights Reserved.
www.garfield.com
Distributed by Universal Uclick

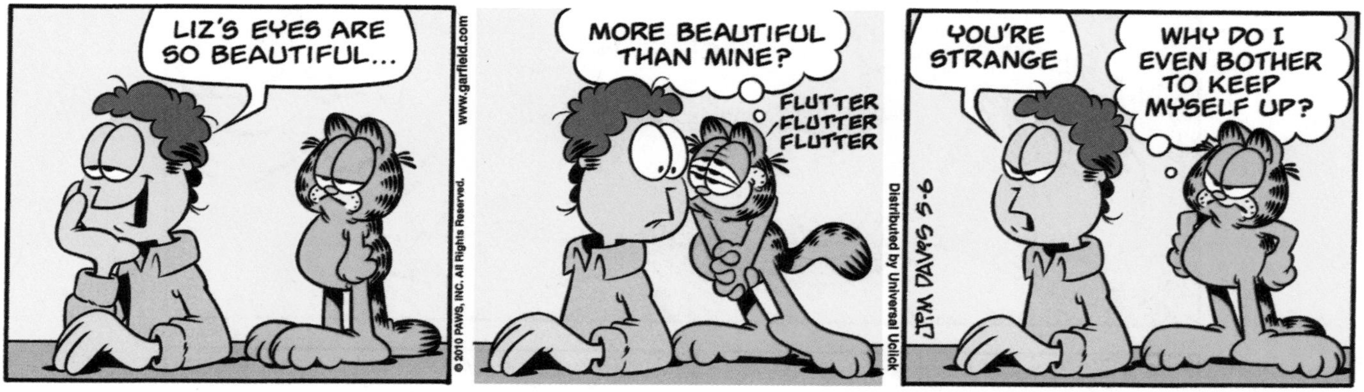
LIZ'S EYES ARE SO BEAUTIFUL...
MORE BEAUTIFUL THAN MINE?
FLUTTER FLUTTER FLUTTER
YOU'RE STRANGE
WHY DO I EVEN BOTHER TO KEEP MYSELF UP?
© 2010 PAWS, INC. All Rights Reserved.
www.garfield.com
Distributed by Universal Uclick
JIM DAVIS 5-6

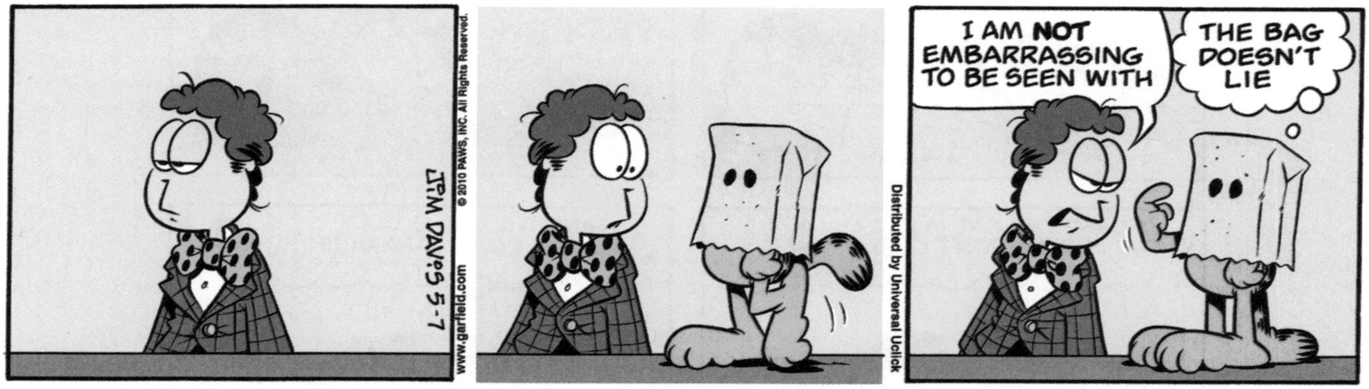
I AM **NOT** EMBARRASSING TO BE SEEN WITH
THE BAG DOESN'T LIE
© 2010 PAWS, INC. All Rights Reserved.
www.garfield.com
Distributed by Universal Uclick
JIM DAVIS 5-7

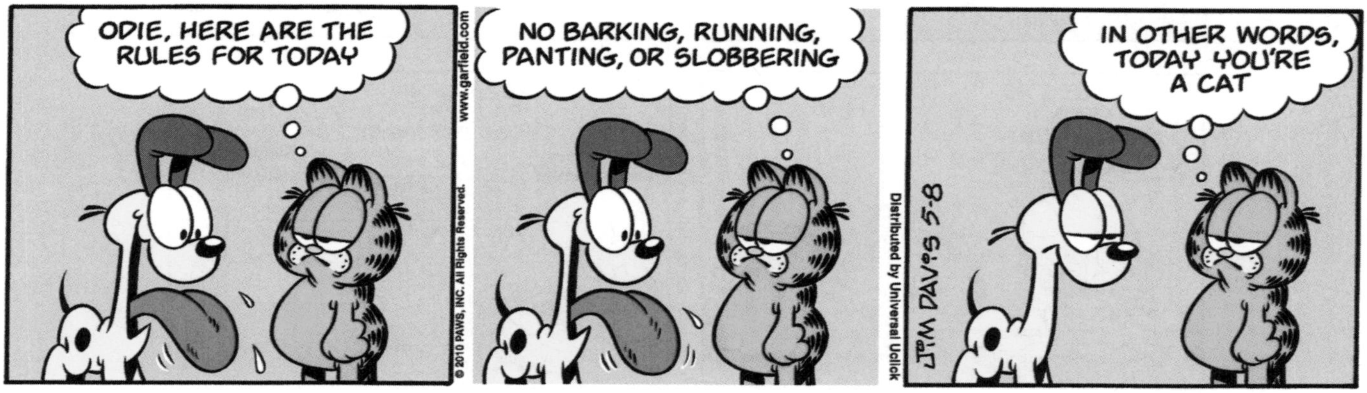
ODIE, HERE ARE THE RULES FOR TODAY
NO BARKING, RUNNING, PANTING, OR SLOBBERING
IN OTHER WORDS, TODAY YOU'RE A CAT
© 2010 PAWS, INC. All Rights Reserved.
www.garfield.com
Distributed by Universal Uclick
JIM DAVIS 5-8

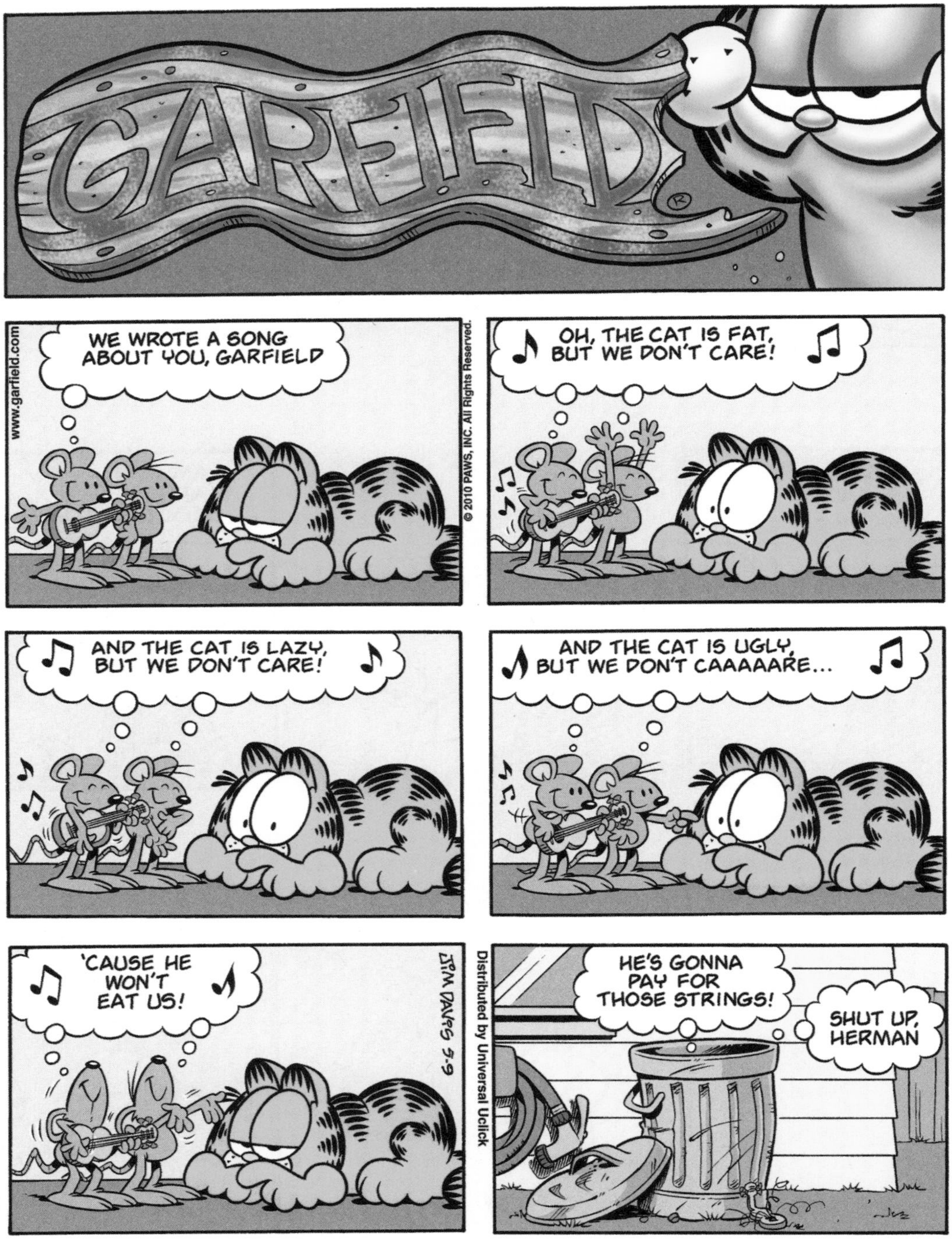
GARFIELD®
www.garfield.com
WE WROTE A SONG ABOUT YOU, GARFIELD
© 2010 PAWS, INC. All Rights Reserved.
OH, THE CAT IS FAT, BUT WE DON'T CARE!
AND THE CAT IS LAZY, BUT WE DON'T CARE!
AND THE CAT IS UGLY, BUT WE DON'T CAAAAARE...
'CAUSE HE WON'T EAT US!
JIM DAVIS 5-9
Distributed by Universal Uclick
HE'S GONNA PAY FOR THOSE STRINGS!
SHUT UP, HERMAN

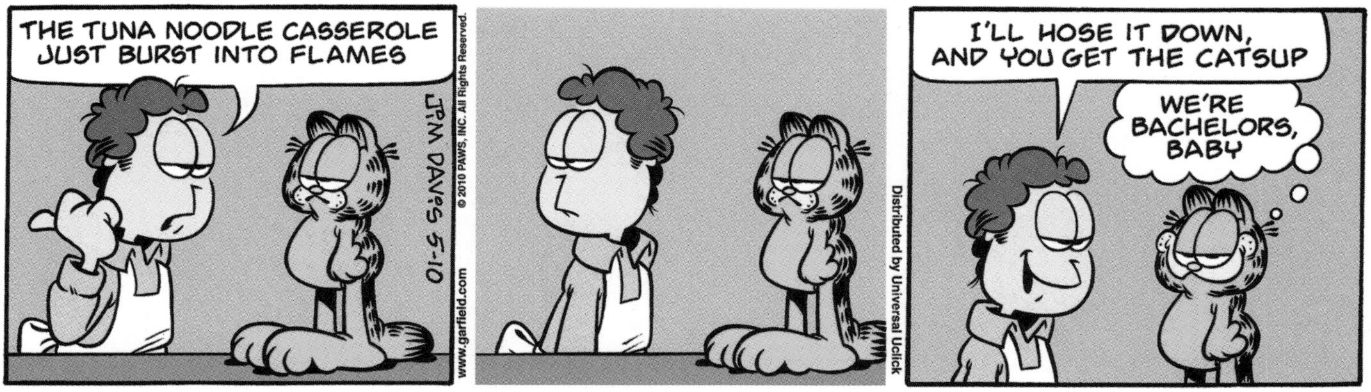
THE TUNA NOODLE CASSEROLE JUST BURST INTO FLAMES
JIM DAVIS 5-10
© 2010 PAWS, INC. All Rights Reserved.
www.garfield.com
Distributed by Universal Uclick
I'LL HOSE IT DOWN, AND YOU GET THE CATSUP
WE'RE BACHELORS, BABY

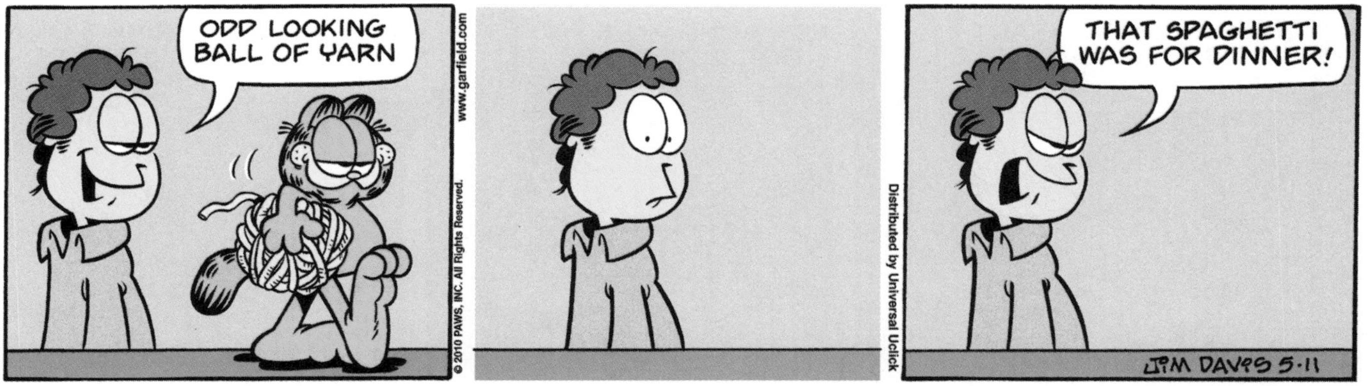
ODD LOOKING BALL OF YARN
© 2010 PAWS, INC. All Rights Reserved.
www.garfield.com
Distributed by Universal Uclick
THAT SPAGHETTI WAS FOR DINNER!
JIM DAVIS 5-11

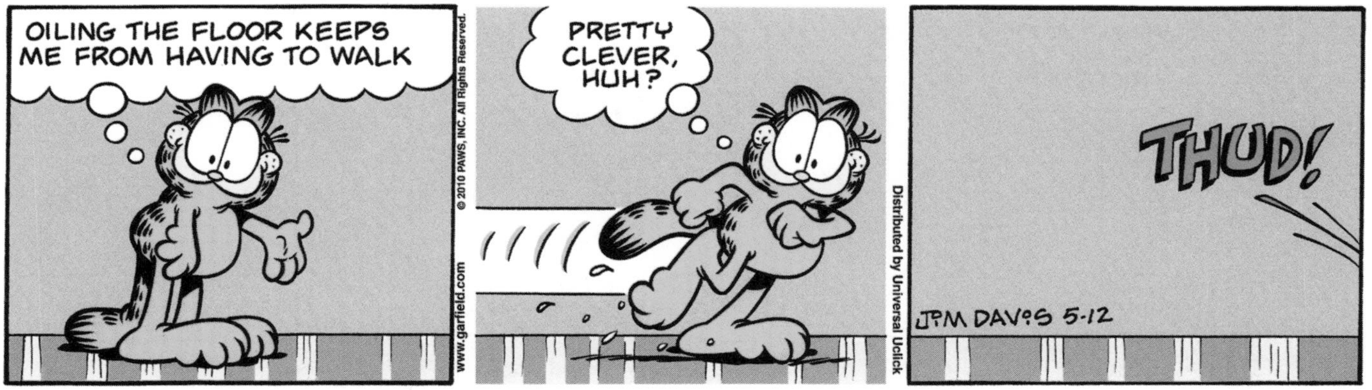
OILING THE FLOOR KEEPS ME FROM HAVING TO WALK
© 2010 PAWS, INC. All Rights Reserved.
www.garfield.com
PRETTY CLEVER, HUH?
Distributed by Universal Uclick
THUD!
JIM DAVIS 5-12

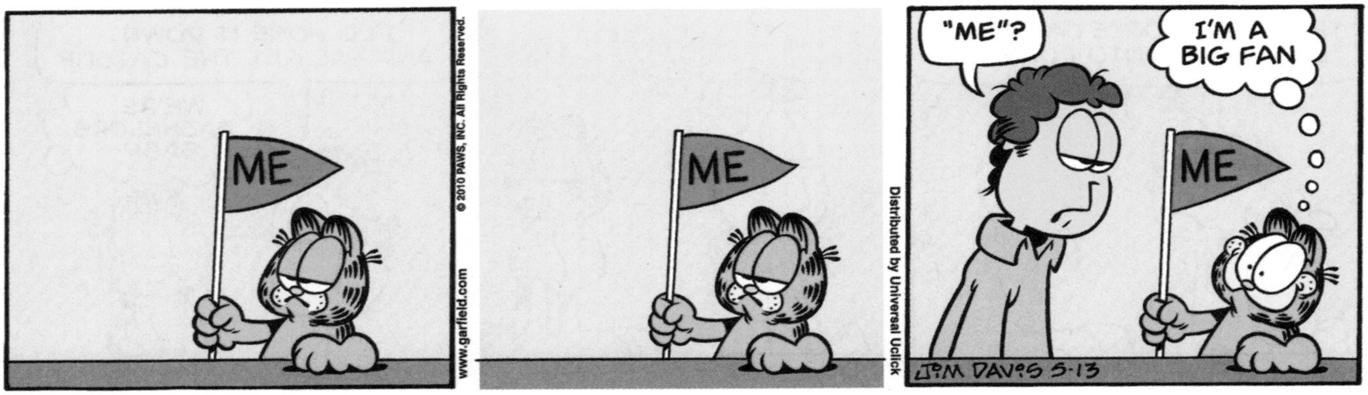
ME
© 2010 PAWS, INC. All Rights Reserved.
www.garfield.com
ME
Distributed by Universal Uclick
"ME"?
I'M A BIG FAN
ME
JIM DAVIS 5-13

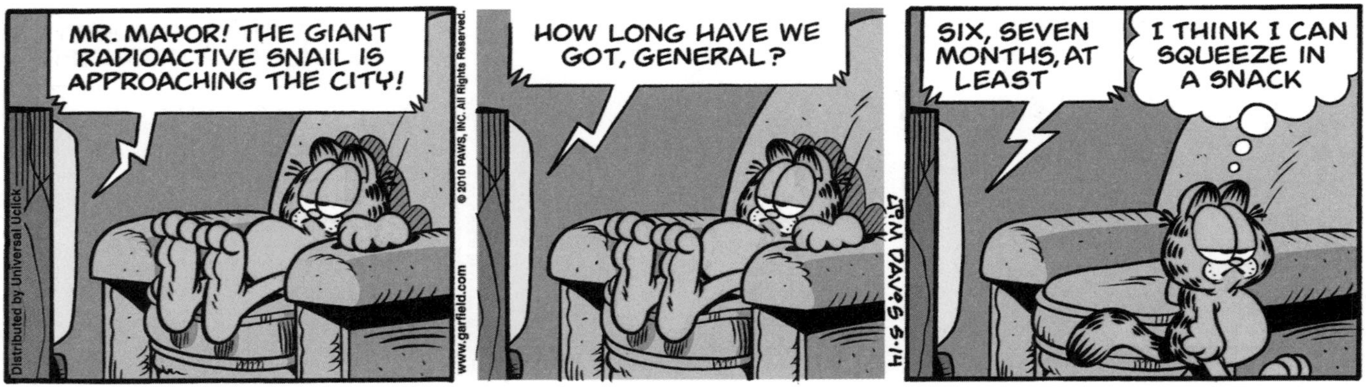
Distributed by Universal Uclick
MR. MAYOR! THE GIANT RADIOACTIVE SNAIL IS APPROACHING THE CITY!
© 2010 PAWS, INC. All Rights Reserved.
www.garfield.com
HOW LONG HAVE WE GOT, GENERAL?
JIM DAVIS 5-14
SIX, SEVEN MONTHS, AT LEAST
I THINK I CAN SQUEEZE IN A SNACK

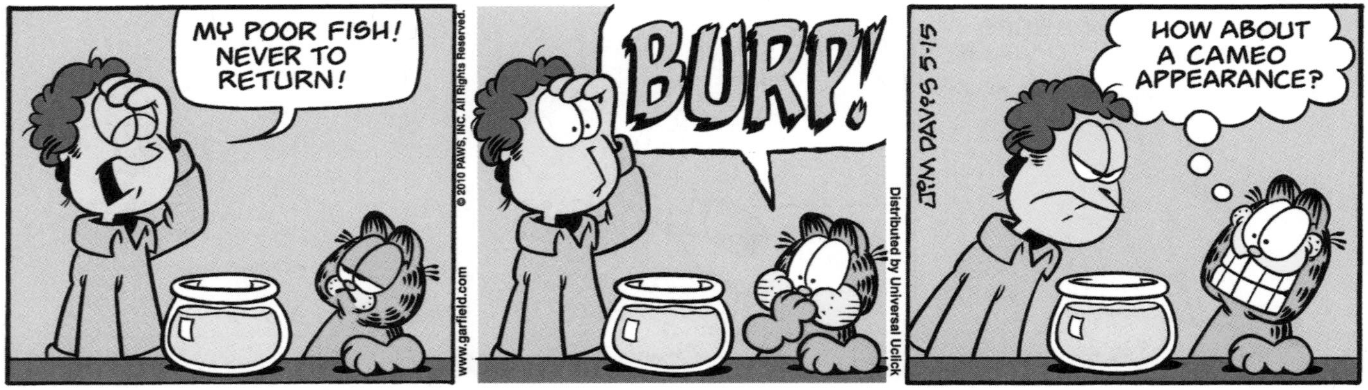
MY POOR FISH! NEVER TO RETURN!
© 2010 PAWS, INC. All Rights Reserved.
www.garfield.com
BURP!
Distributed by Universal Uclick
JIM DAVIS 5-15
HOW ABOUT A CAMEO APPEARANCE?

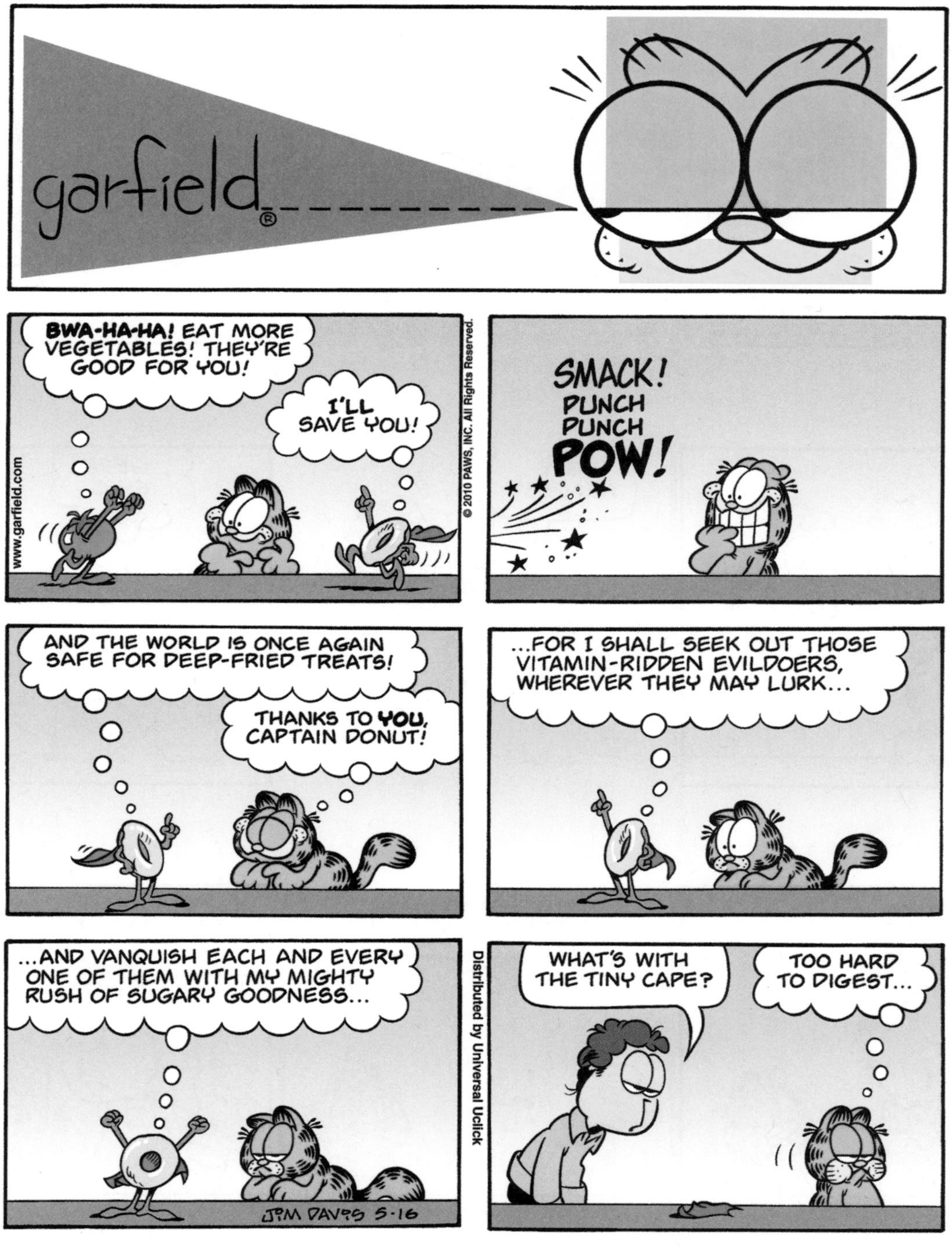

garfield®
www.garfield.com
BWA-HA-HA! EAT MORE VEGETABLES! THEY'RE GOOD FOR YOU!
I'LL SAVE YOU!
© 2010 PAWS, INC. All Rights Reserved.
SMACK! PUNCH PUNCH POW!
AND THE WORLD IS ONCE AGAIN SAFE FOR DEEP-FRIED TREATS!
THANKS TO YOU, CAPTAIN DONUT!
...FOR I SHALL SEEK OUT THOSE VITAMIN-RIDDEN EVILDOERS, WHEREVER THEY MAY LURK...
...AND VANQUISH EACH AND EVERY ONE OF THEM WITH MY MIGHTY RUSH OF SUGARY GOODNESS...
JIM DAVIS 5-16
Distributed by Universal Uclick
WHAT'S WITH THE TINY CAPE?
TOO HARD TO DIGEST...

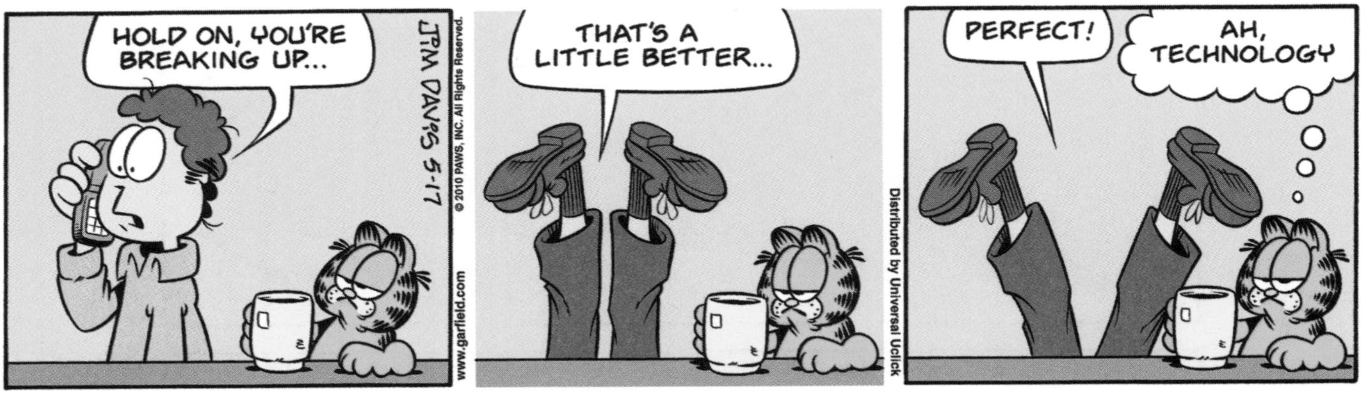
HOLD ON, YOU'RE BREAKING UP...
JIM DAVIS 5-17
THAT'S A LITTLE BETTER...
PERFECT!
AH, TECHNOLOGY

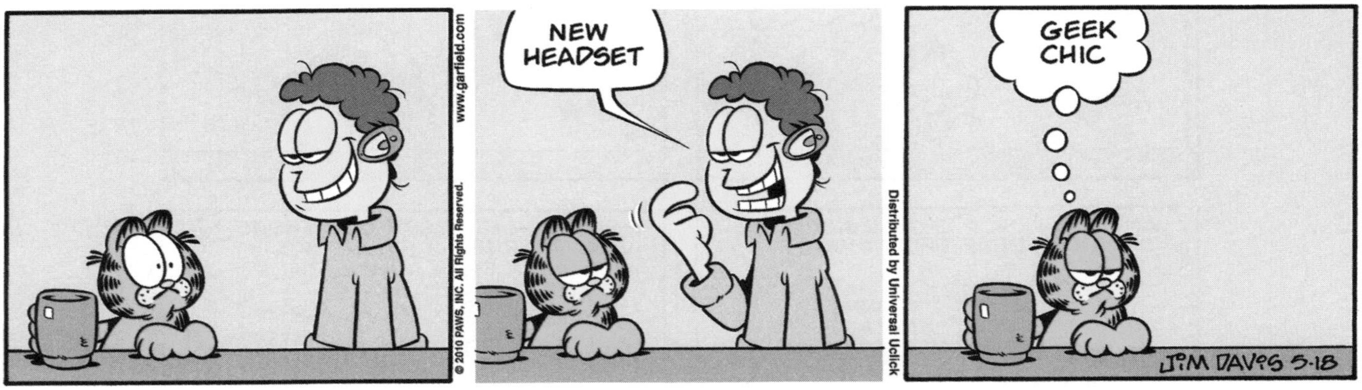
NEW HEADSET
GEEK CHIC
JIM DAVIS 5-18

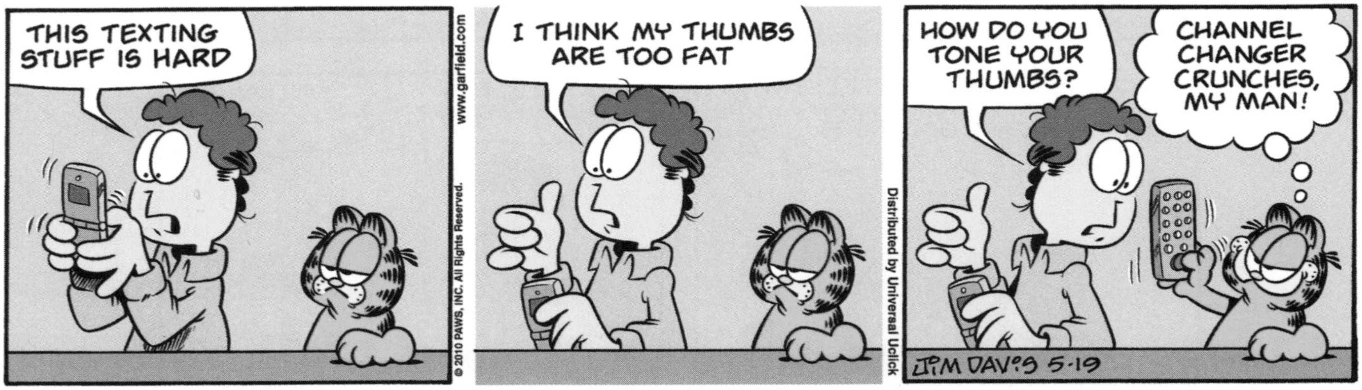
THIS TEXTING STUFF IS HARD
I THINK MY THUMBS ARE TOO FAT
HOW DO YOU TONE YOUR THUMBS?
CHANNEL CHANGER CRUNCHES, MY MAN!
JIM DAVIS 5-19

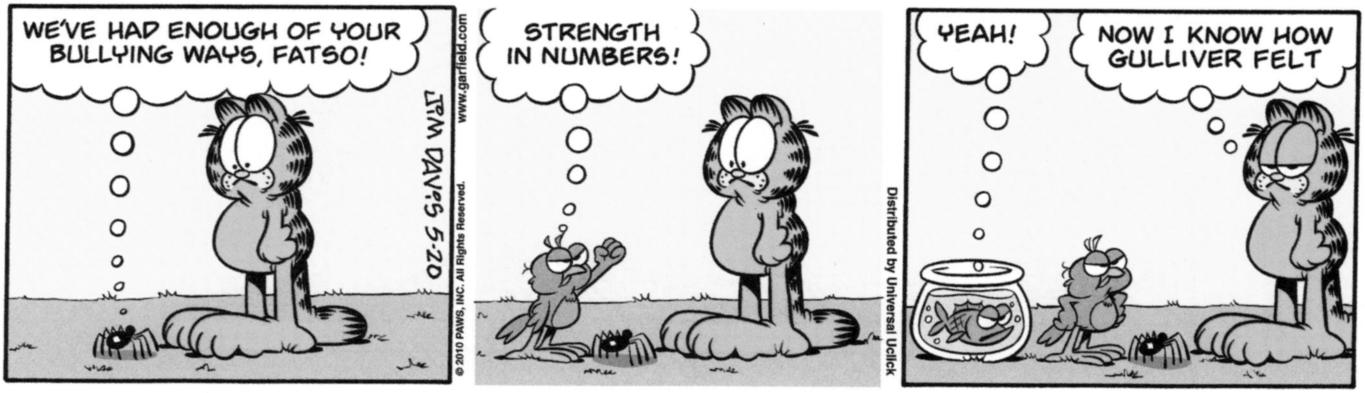
WE'VE HAD ENOUGH OF YOUR BULLYING WAYS, FATSO!
JIM DAVIS 5-20
www.garfield.com
© 2010 PAWS, INC. All Rights Reserved.
STRENGTH IN NUMBERS!
Distributed by Universal Uclick
YEAH!
NOW I KNOW HOW GULLIVER FELT

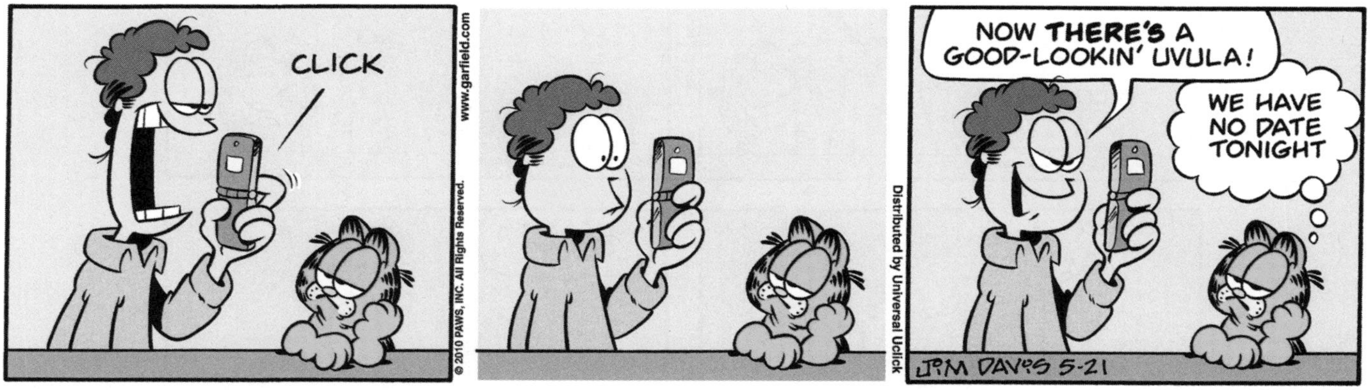
CLICK
www.garfield.com
© 2010 PAWS, INC. All Rights Reserved.
Distributed by Universal Uclick
NOW **THERE'S** A GOOD-LOOKIN' UVULA!
WE HAVE NO DATE TONIGHT
JIM DAVIS 5-21

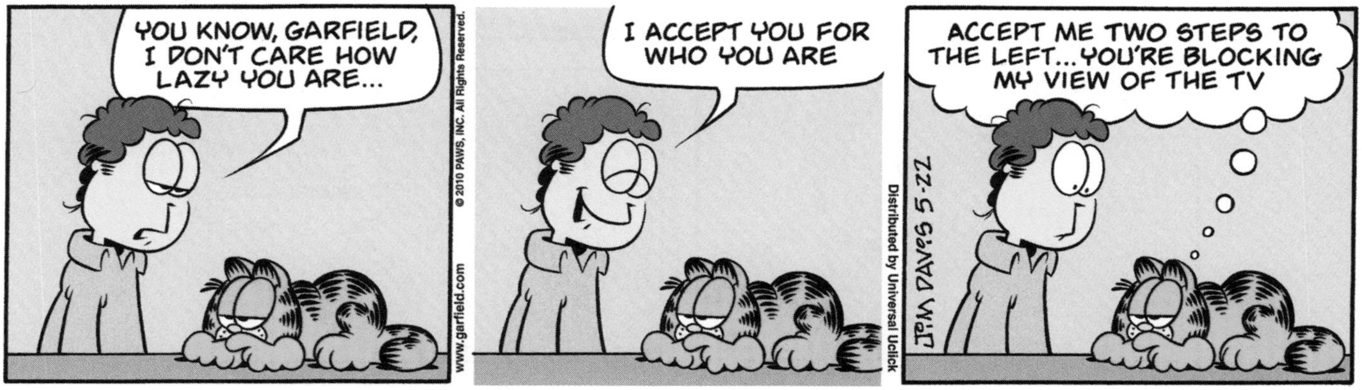
YOU KNOW, GARFIELD, I DON'T CARE HOW LAZY YOU ARE...
www.garfield.com
© 2010 PAWS, INC. All Rights Reserved.
I ACCEPT YOU FOR WHO YOU ARE
Distributed by Universal Uclick
JIM DAVIS 5-22
ACCEPT ME TWO STEPS TO THE LEFT...YOU'RE BLOCKING MY VIEW OF THE TV

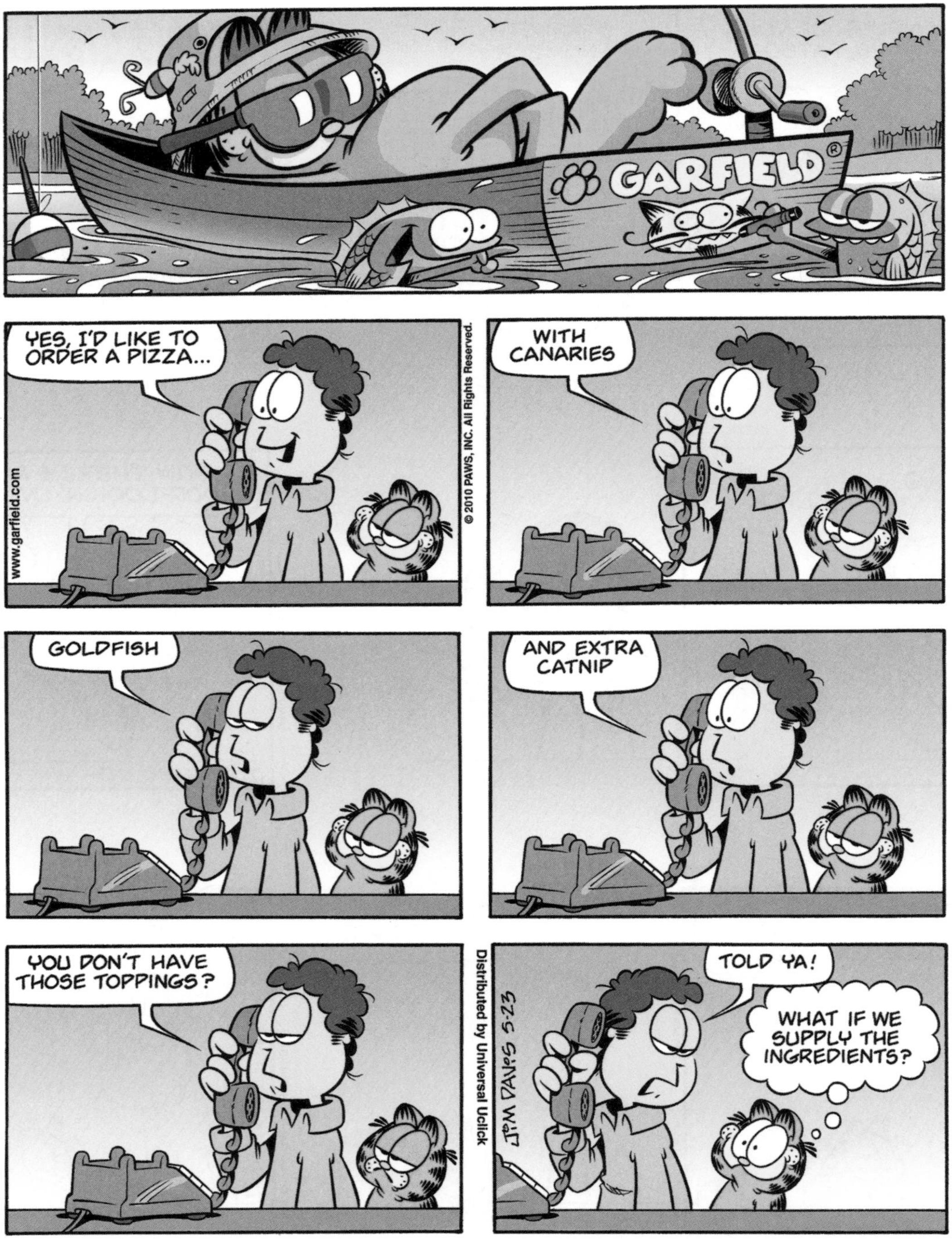
GARFIELD®
YES, I'D LIKE TO ORDER A PIZZA...
WITH CANARIES
GOLDFISH
AND EXTRA CATNIP
YOU DON'T HAVE THOSE TOPPINGS?
TOLD YA!
WHAT IF WE SUPPLY THE INGREDIENTS?
www.garfield.com
© 2010 PAWS, INC. All Rights Reserved.
Distributed by Universal Uclick
JIM DAVIS 5-23

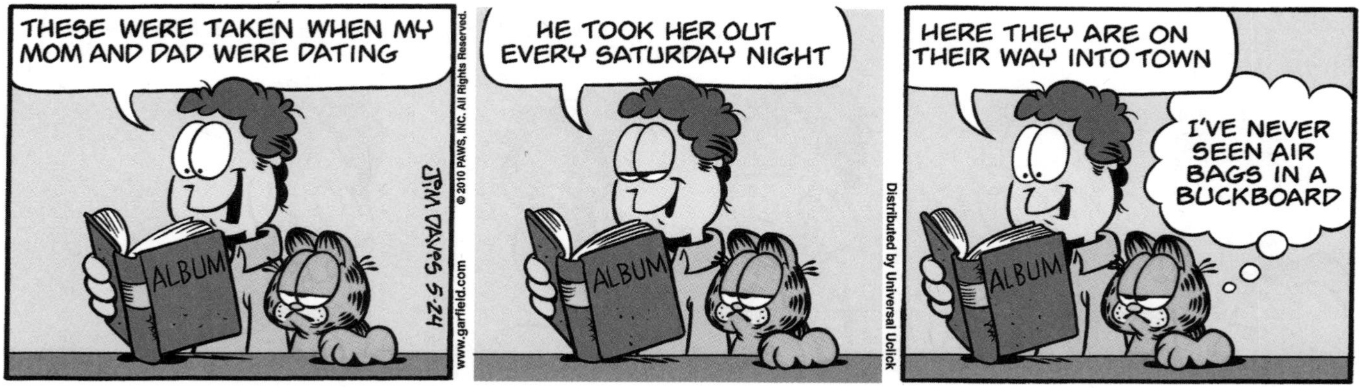
THESE WERE TAKEN WHEN MY MOM AND DAD WERE DATING
ALBUM
HE TOOK HER OUT EVERY SATURDAY NIGHT
HERE THEY ARE ON THEIR WAY INTO TOWN
I'VE NEVER SEEN AIR BAGS IN A BUCKBOARD
JIM DAVIS 5-24
© 2010 PAWS, INC. All Rights Reserved. www.garfield.com
Distributed by Universal Uclick

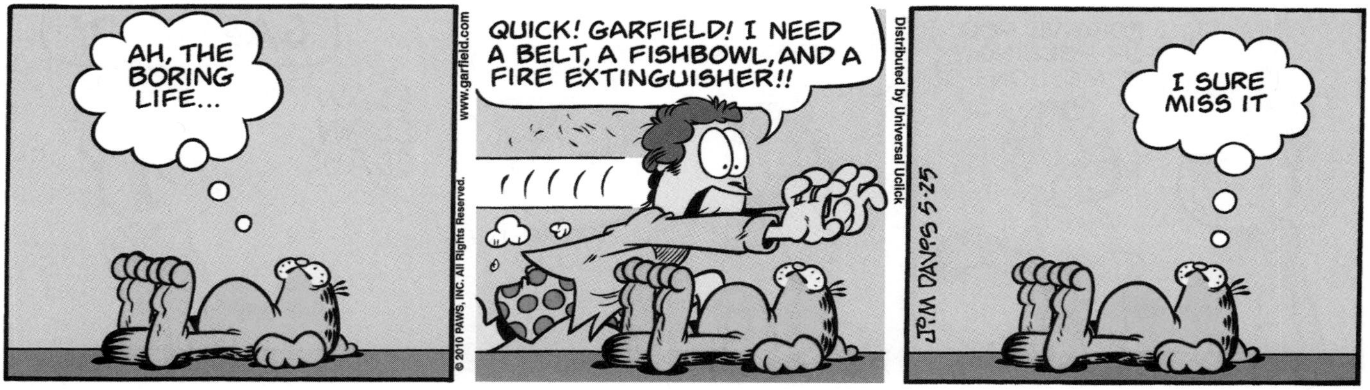
AH, THE BORING LIFE...
QUICK! GARFIELD! I NEED A BELT, A FISHBOWL, AND A FIRE EXTINGUISHER!!
I SURE MISS IT
JIM DAVIS 5-25
© 2010 PAWS, INC. All Rights Reserved. www.garfield.com
Distributed by Universal Uclick

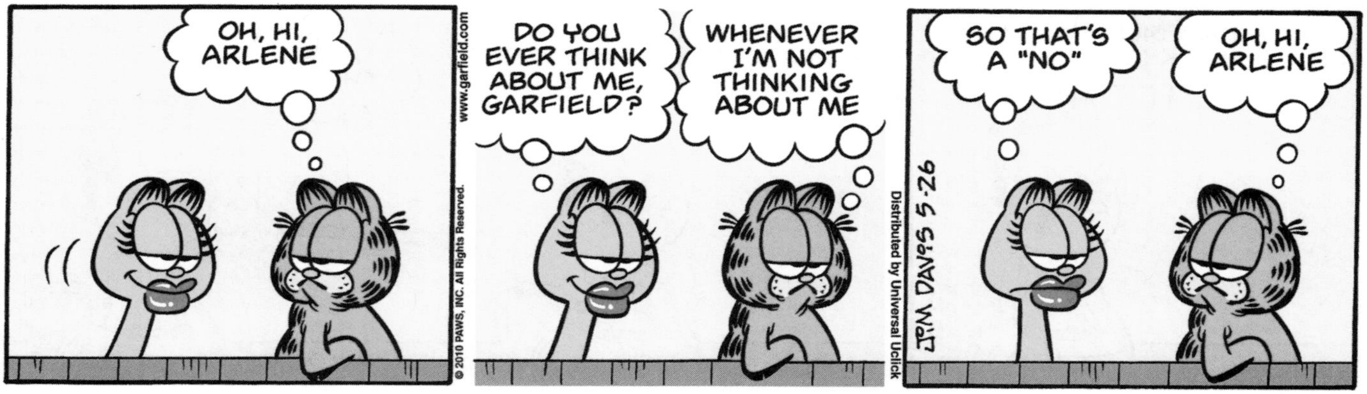
OH, HI, ARLENE
DO YOU EVER THINK ABOUT ME, GARFIELD?
WHENEVER I'M NOT THINKING ABOUT ME
SO THAT'S A "NO"
OH, HI, ARLENE
JIM DAVIS 5-26
© 2010 PAWS, INC. All Rights Reserved. www.garfield.com
Distributed by Universal Uclick

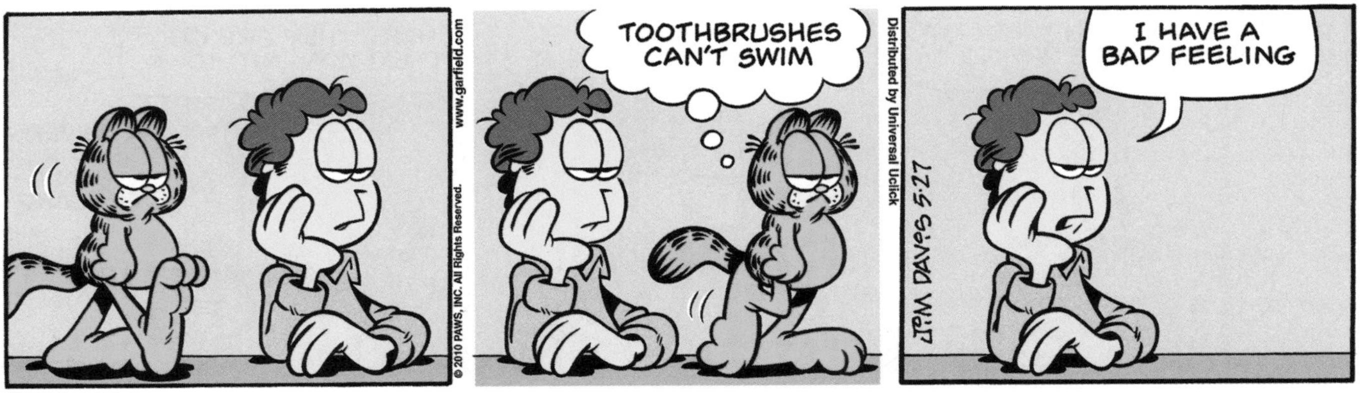

TOOTHBRUSHES CAN'T SWIM
I HAVE A BAD FEELING
JIM DAVIS 5-27

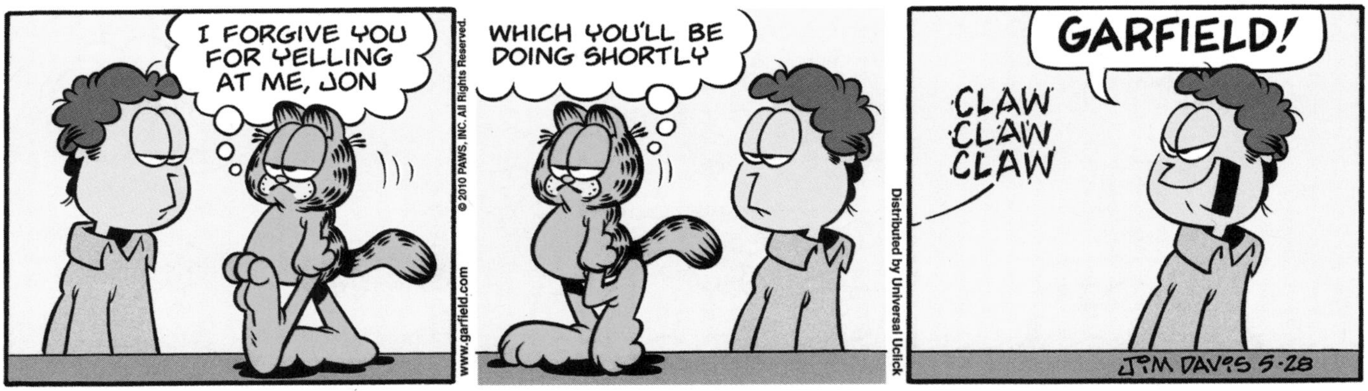

I FORGIVE YOU FOR YELLING AT ME, JON
WHICH YOU'LL BE DOING SHORTLY
CLAW CLAW CLAW
GARFIELD!
JIM DAVIS 5-28

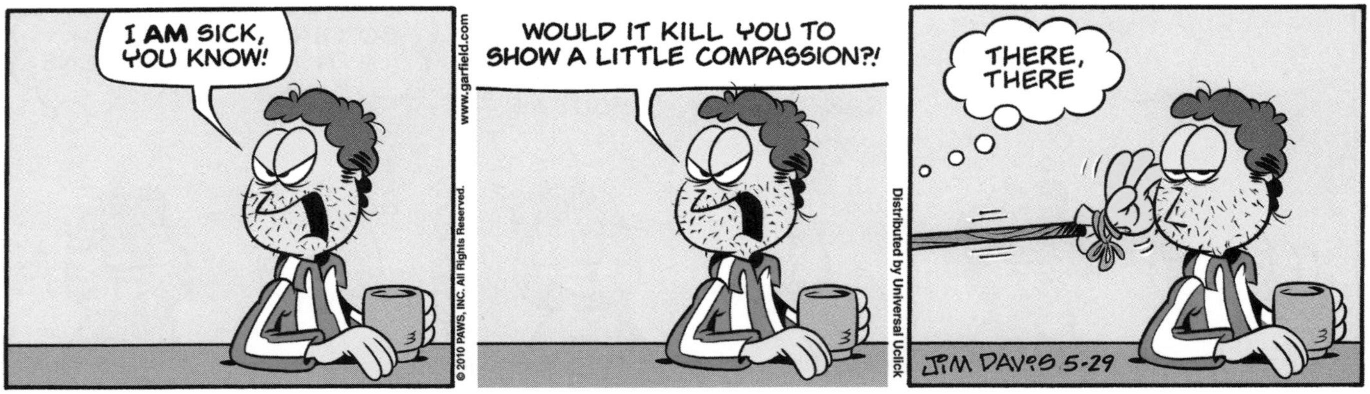

I **AM** SICK, YOU KNOW!
WOULD IT KILL YOU TO SHOW A LITTLE COMPASSION?!
THERE, THERE
JIM DAVIS 5-29

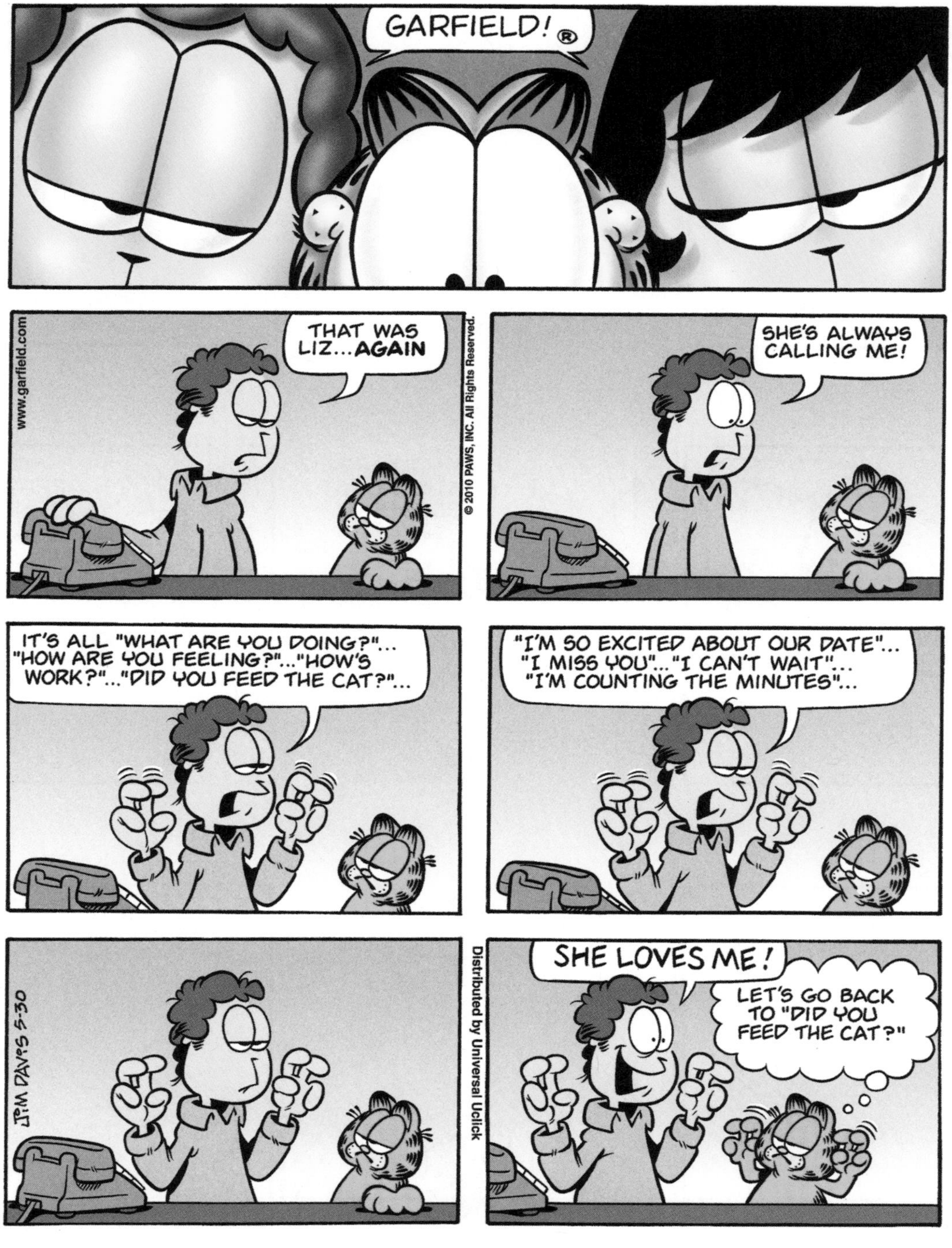
GARFIELD!®
THAT WAS LIZ... AGAIN
SHE'S ALWAYS CALLING ME!
IT'S ALL "WHAT ARE YOU DOING?"... "HOW ARE YOU FEELING?"..."HOW'S WORK?"..."DID YOU FEED THE CAT?"...
"I'M SO EXCITED ABOUT OUR DATE"... "I MISS YOU"..."I CAN'T WAIT"... "I'M COUNTING THE MINUTES"...
SHE LOVES ME!
LET'S GO BACK TO "DID YOU FEED THE CAT?"
www.garfield.com
© 2010 PAWS, INC. All Rights Reserved.
JPM DAVIS 5-30
Distributed by Universal Uclick

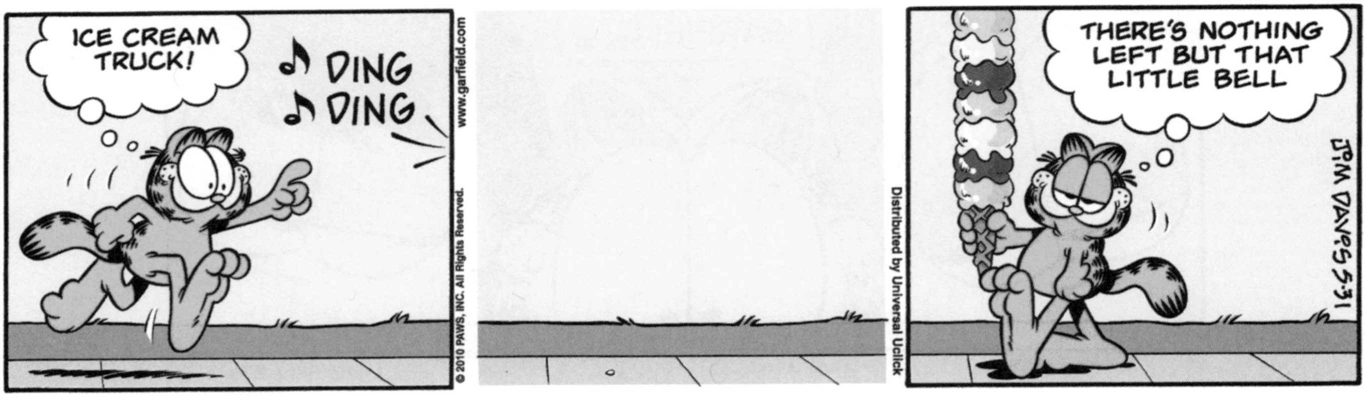
ICE CREAM TRUCK!
♪ DING ♪ DING
THERE'S NOTHING LEFT BUT THAT LITTLE BELL
JIM DAVIS 5-31
© 2010 PAWS, INC. All Rights Reserved. www.garfield.com
Distributed by Universal Uclick

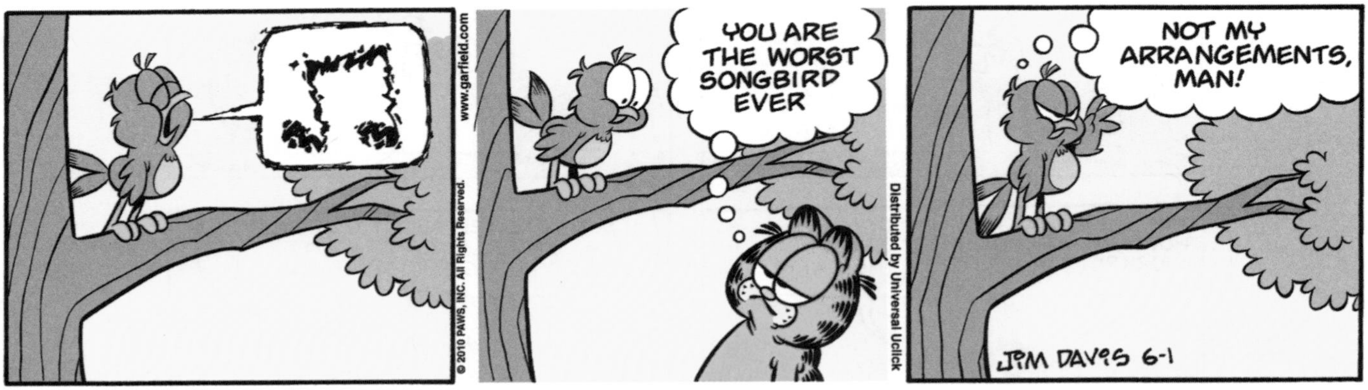
YOU ARE THE WORST SONGBIRD EVER
NOT MY ARRANGEMENTS, MAN!
JIM DAVIS 6-1
© 2010 PAWS, INC. All Rights Reserved. www.garfield.com
Distributed by Universal Uclick

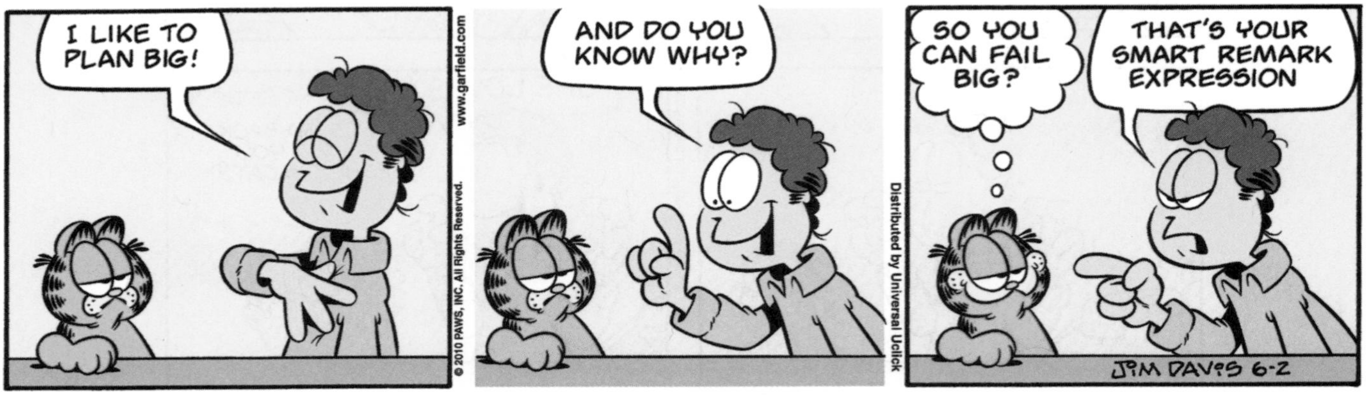
I LIKE TO PLAN BIG!
AND DO YOU KNOW WHY?
SO YOU CAN FAIL BIG?
THAT'S YOUR SMART REMARK EXPRESSION
JIM DAVIS 6-2
© 2010 PAWS, INC. All Rights Reserved. www.garfield.com
Distributed by Universal Uclick

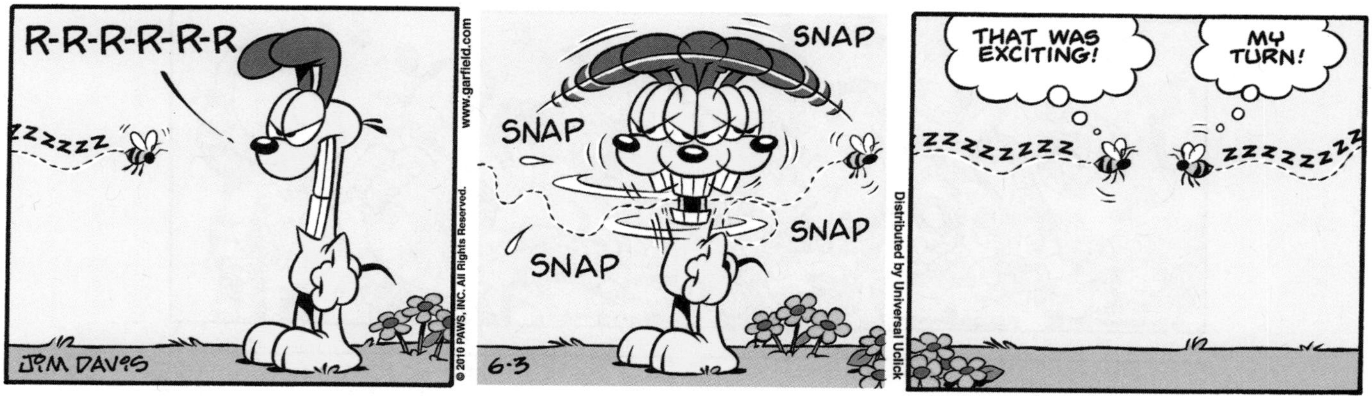
R-R-R-R-R-R
ZZZZZZ
JIM DAVIS
© 2010 PAWS, INC. All Rights Reserved.
www.garfield.com
SNAP
SNAP
SNAP
SNAP
6-3
Distributed by Universal Uclick
THAT WAS EXCITING!
MY TURN!
ZZZZZZZZ
ZZZZZZZZ

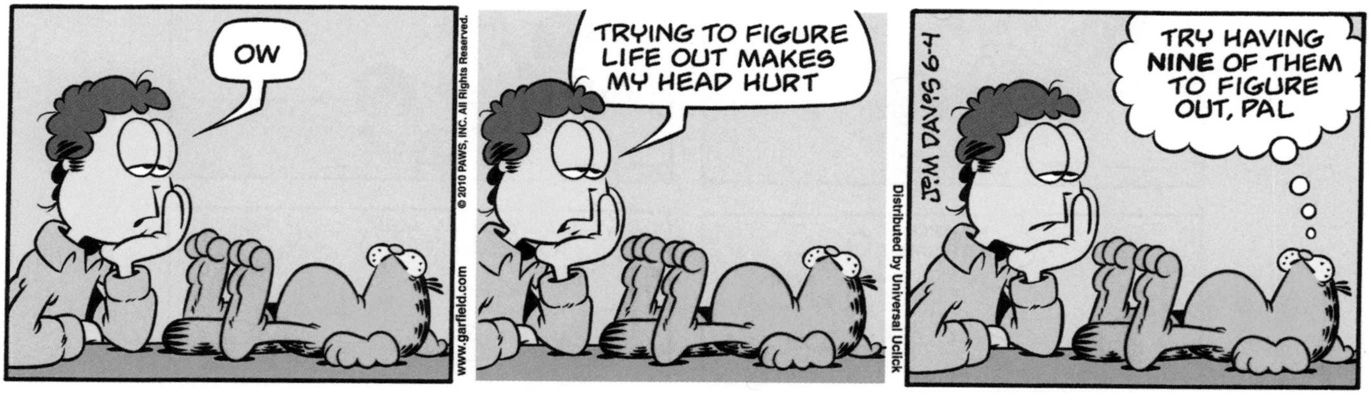
OW
© 2010 PAWS, INC. All Rights Reserved.
www.garfield.com
TRYING TO FIGURE LIFE OUT MAKES MY HEAD HURT
Distributed by Universal Uclick
JIM DAVIS 6-4
TRY HAVING NINE OF THEM TO FIGURE OUT, PAL

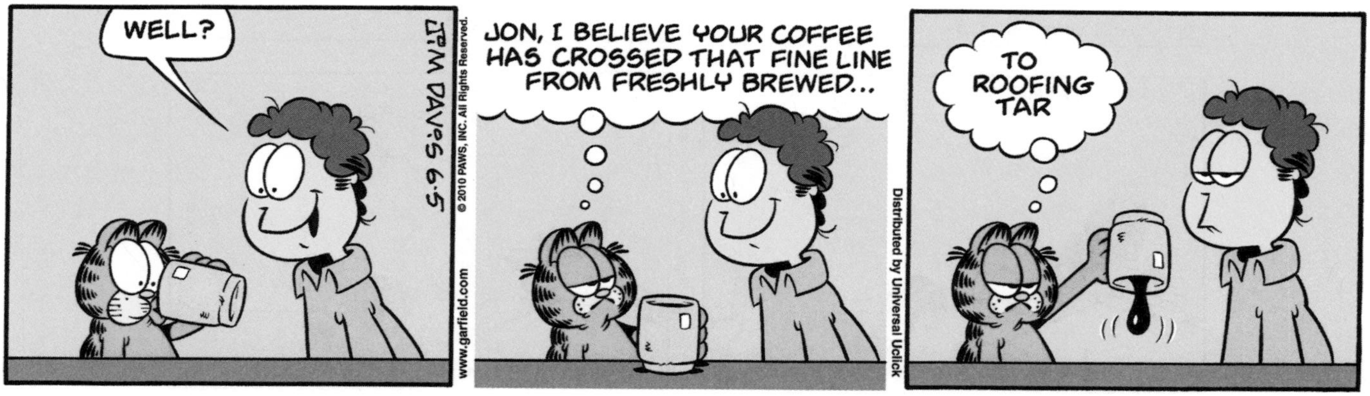
WELL?
JIM DAVIS 6-5
© 2010 PAWS, INC. All Rights Reserved.
www.garfield.com
JON, I BELIEVE YOUR COFFEE HAS CROSSED THAT FINE LINE FROM FRESHLY BREWED...
Distributed by Universal Uclick
TO ROOFING TAR

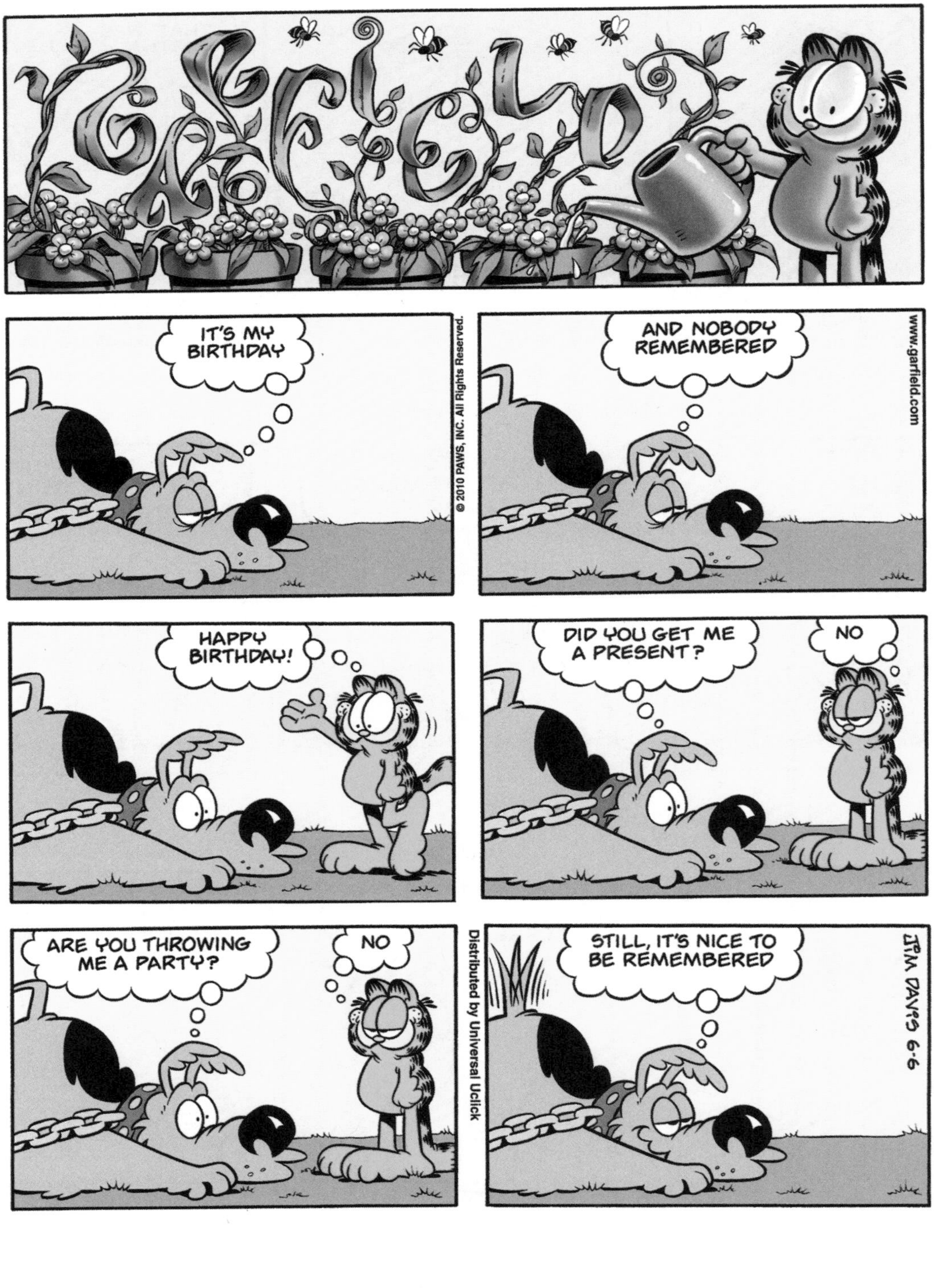
GARFIELD
IT'S MY BIRTHDAY
© 2010 PAWS, INC. All Rights Reserved.
AND NOBODY REMEMBERED
www.garfield.com
HAPPY BIRTHDAY!
DID YOU GET ME A PRESENT?
NO
ARE YOU THROWING ME A PARTY?
NO
Distributed by Universal Uclick
STILL, IT'S NICE TO BE REMEMBERED
JPM DAVIS 6-6

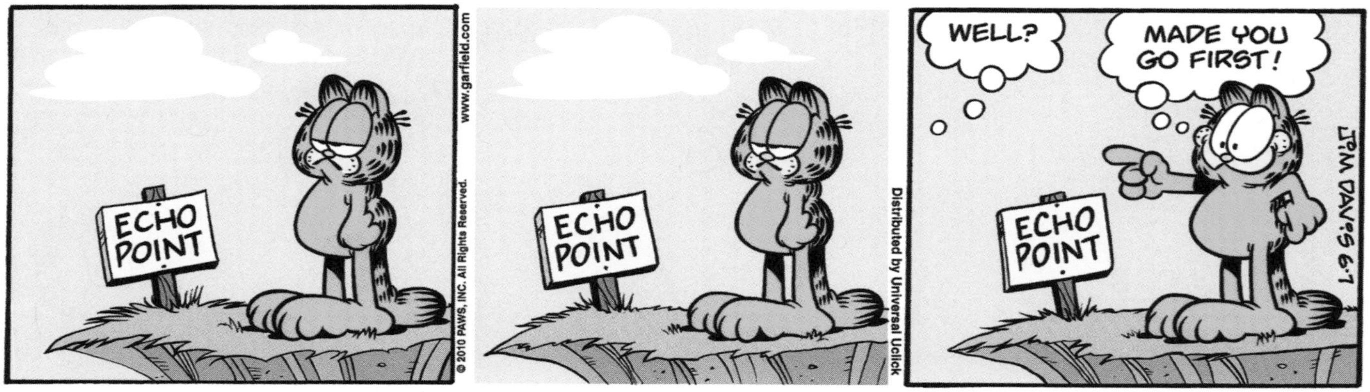
ECHO POINT
ECHO POINT
WELL?
ECHO POINT
MADE YOU GO FIRST!

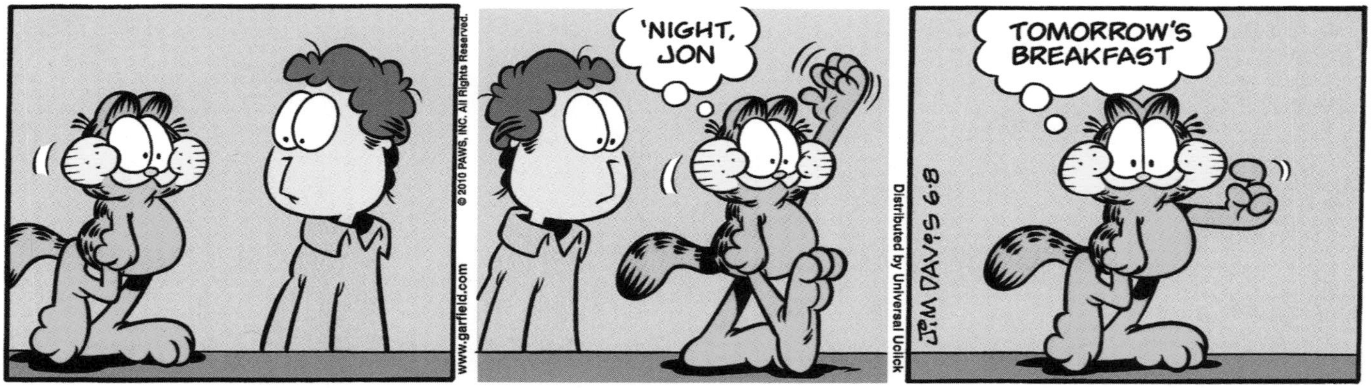
'NIGHT, JON
TOMORROW'S BREAKFAST

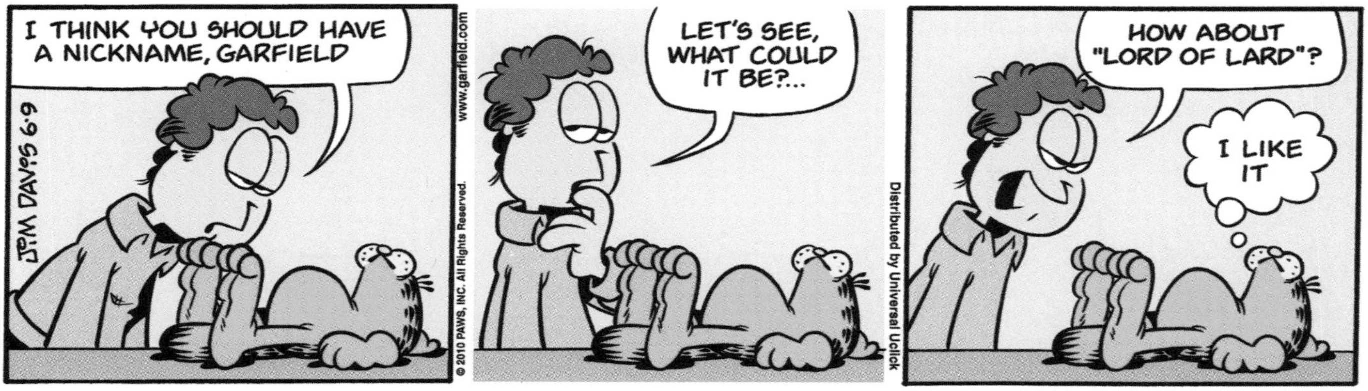
I THINK YOU SHOULD HAVE A NICKNAME, GARFIELD
LET'S SEE, WHAT COULD IT BE?...
HOW ABOUT "LORD OF LARD"?
I LIKE IT

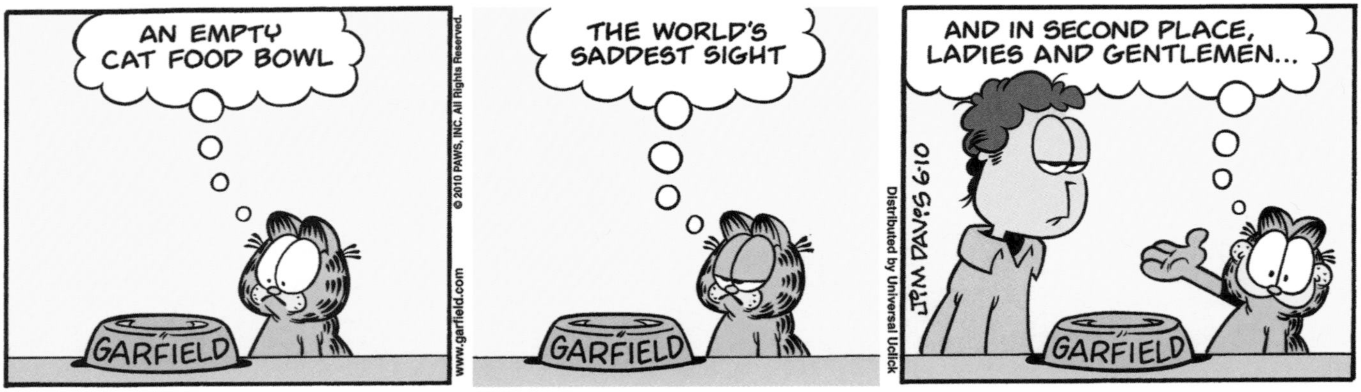
AN EMPTY CAT FOOD BOWL
GARFIELD
© 2010 PAWS, INC. All Rights Reserved.
www.garfield.com
THE WORLD'S SADDEST SIGHT
GARFIELD
Distributed by Universal Uclick
AND IN SECOND PLACE, LADIES AND GENTLEMEN...
JIM DAVIS 6-10
GARFIELD

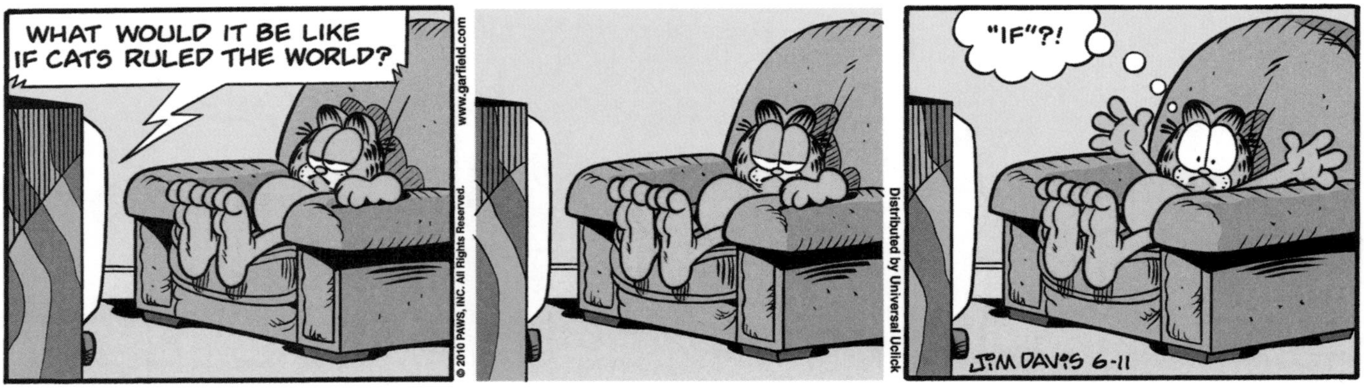
WHAT WOULD IT BE LIKE IF CATS RULED THE WORLD?
www.garfield.com
© 2010 PAWS, INC. All Rights Reserved.
Distributed by Universal Uclick
"IF"?!
JIM DAVIS 6-11

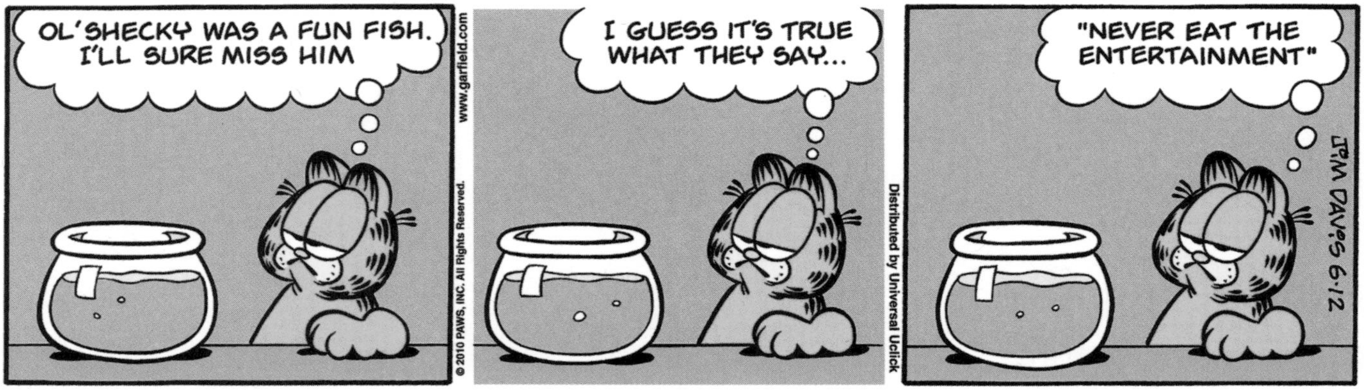
OL' SHECKY WAS A FUN FISH. I'LL SURE MISS HIM
www.garfield.com
© 2010 PAWS, INC. All Rights Reserved.
I GUESS IT'S TRUE WHAT THEY SAY...
Distributed by Universal Uclick
"NEVER EAT THE ENTERTAINMENT"
JIM DAVIS 6-12

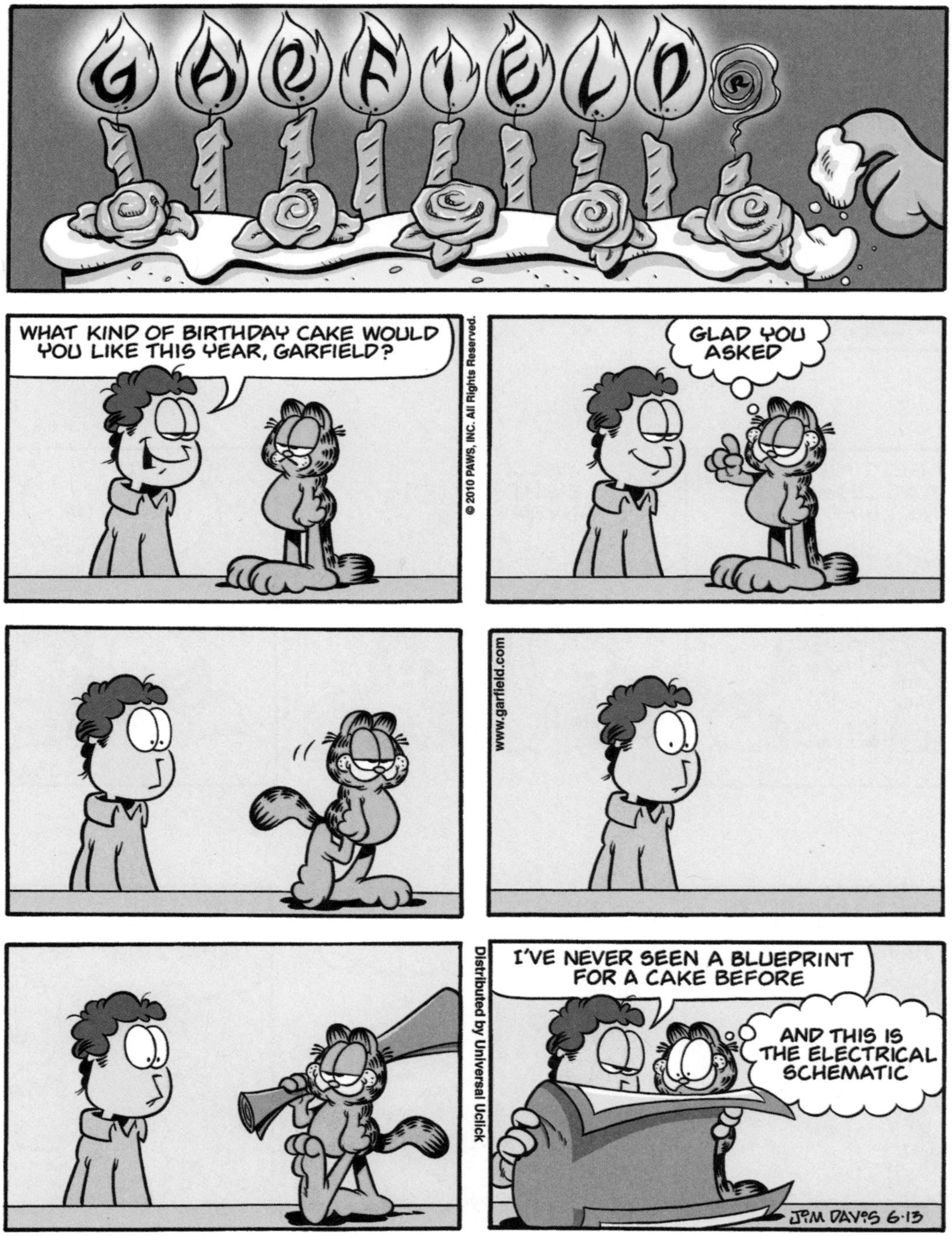
GARFIELD®
WHAT KIND OF BIRTHDAY CAKE WOULD YOU LIKE THIS YEAR, GARFIELD?
GLAD YOU ASKED
I'VE NEVER SEEN A BLUEPRINT FOR A CAKE BEFORE
AND THIS IS THE ELECTRICAL SCHEMATIC
JIM DAVIS 6·13
© 2010 PAWS, INC. All Rights Reserved.
www.garfield.com
Distributed by Universal Uclick

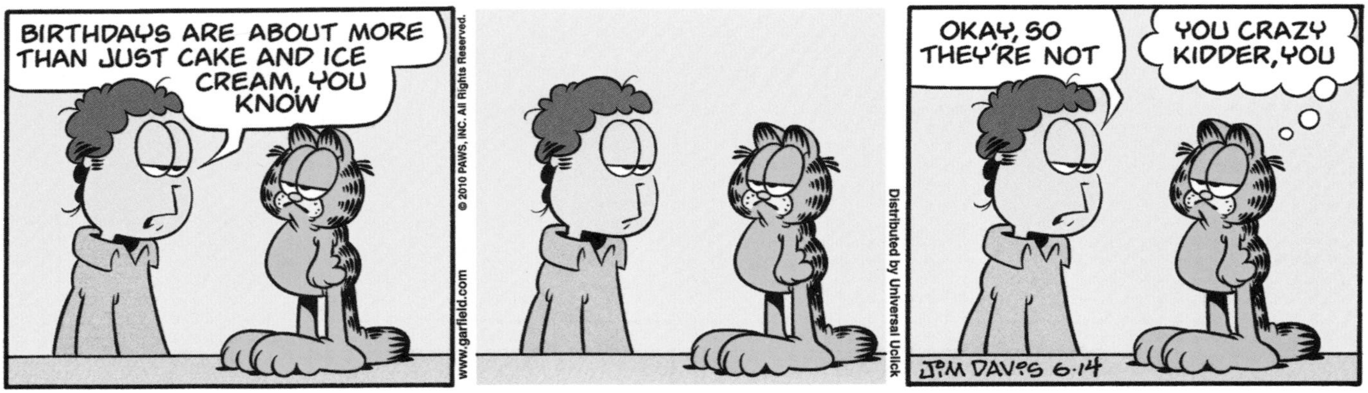
BIRTHDAYS ARE ABOUT MORE THAN JUST CAKE AND ICE CREAM, YOU KNOW
OKAY, SO THEY'RE NOT
YOU CRAZY KIDDER, YOU
JIM DAVIS 6-14

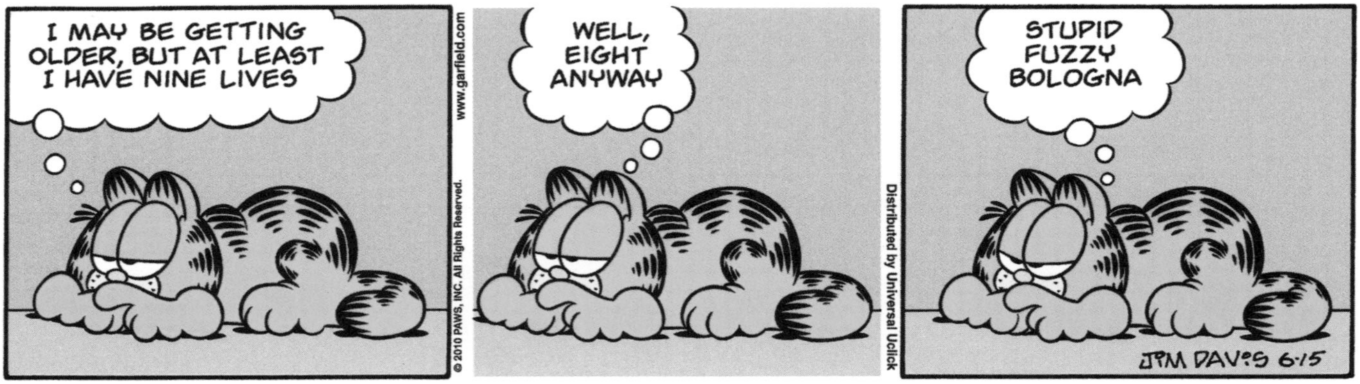
I MAY BE GETTING OLDER, BUT AT LEAST I HAVE NINE LIVES
WELL, EIGHT ANYWAY
STUPID FUZZY BOLOGNA
JIM DAVIS 6-15

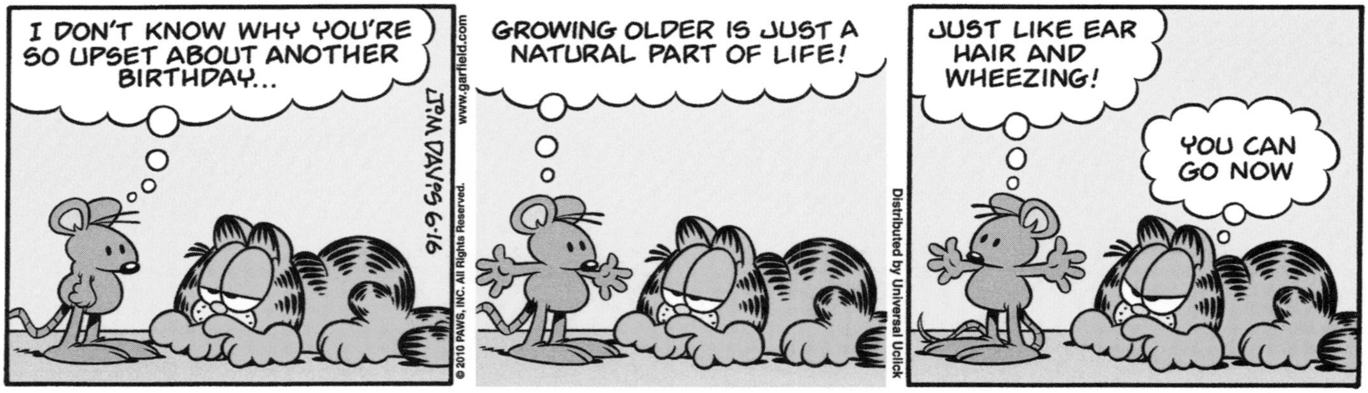
I DON'T KNOW WHY YOU'RE SO UPSET ABOUT ANOTHER BIRTHDAY...
GROWING OLDER IS JUST A NATURAL PART OF LIFE!
JUST LIKE EAR HAIR AND WHEEZING!
YOU CAN GO NOW
JIM DAVIS 6-16

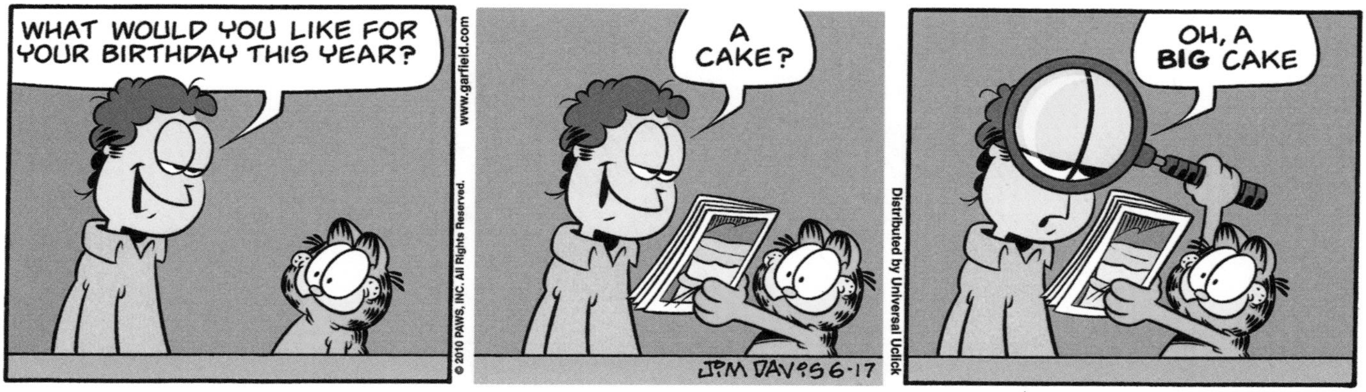
WHAT WOULD YOU LIKE FOR YOUR BIRTHDAY THIS YEAR?
A CAKE?
OH, A **BIG** CAKE
JIM DAVIS 6-17
© 2010 PAWS, INC. All Rights Reserved.
www.garfield.com
Distributed by Universal Uclick

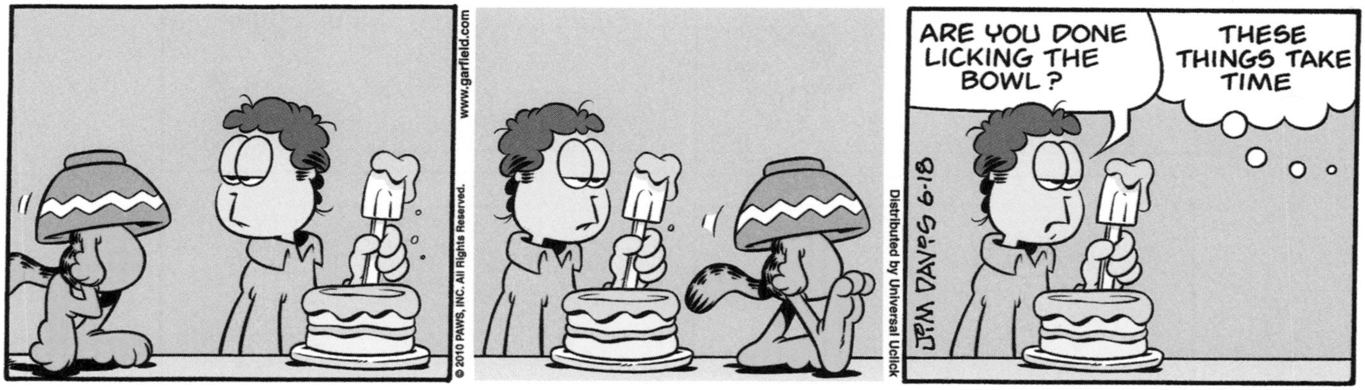
ARE YOU DONE LICKING THE BOWL?
THESE THINGS TAKE TIME
JIM DAVIS 6-18
© 2010 PAWS, INC. All Rights Reserved.
www.garfield.com
Distributed by Universal Uclick

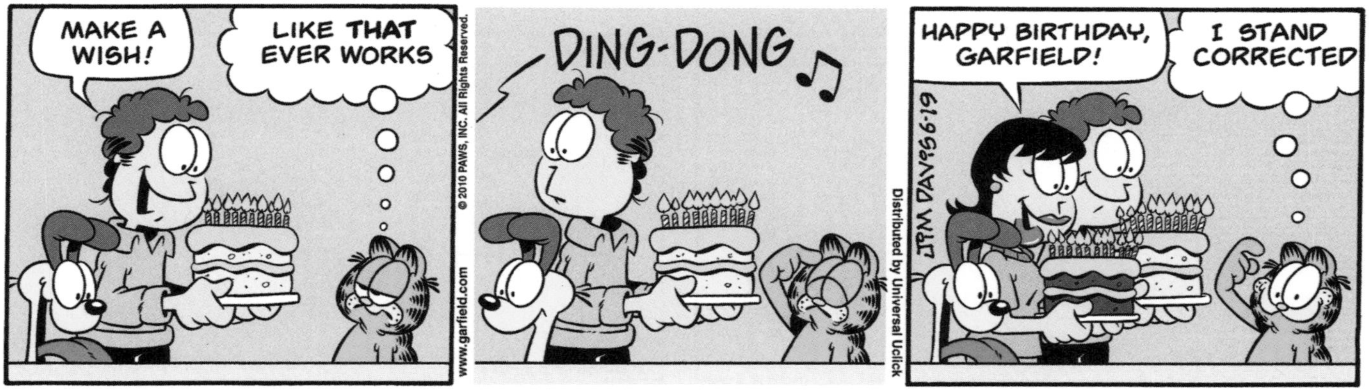
MAKE A WISH!
LIKE **THAT** EVER WORKS
DING-DONG
HAPPY BIRTHDAY, GARFIELD!
I STAND CORRECTED
JIM DAVIS 6-19
© 2010 PAWS, INC. All Rights Reserved.
www.garfield.com
Distributed by Universal Uclick

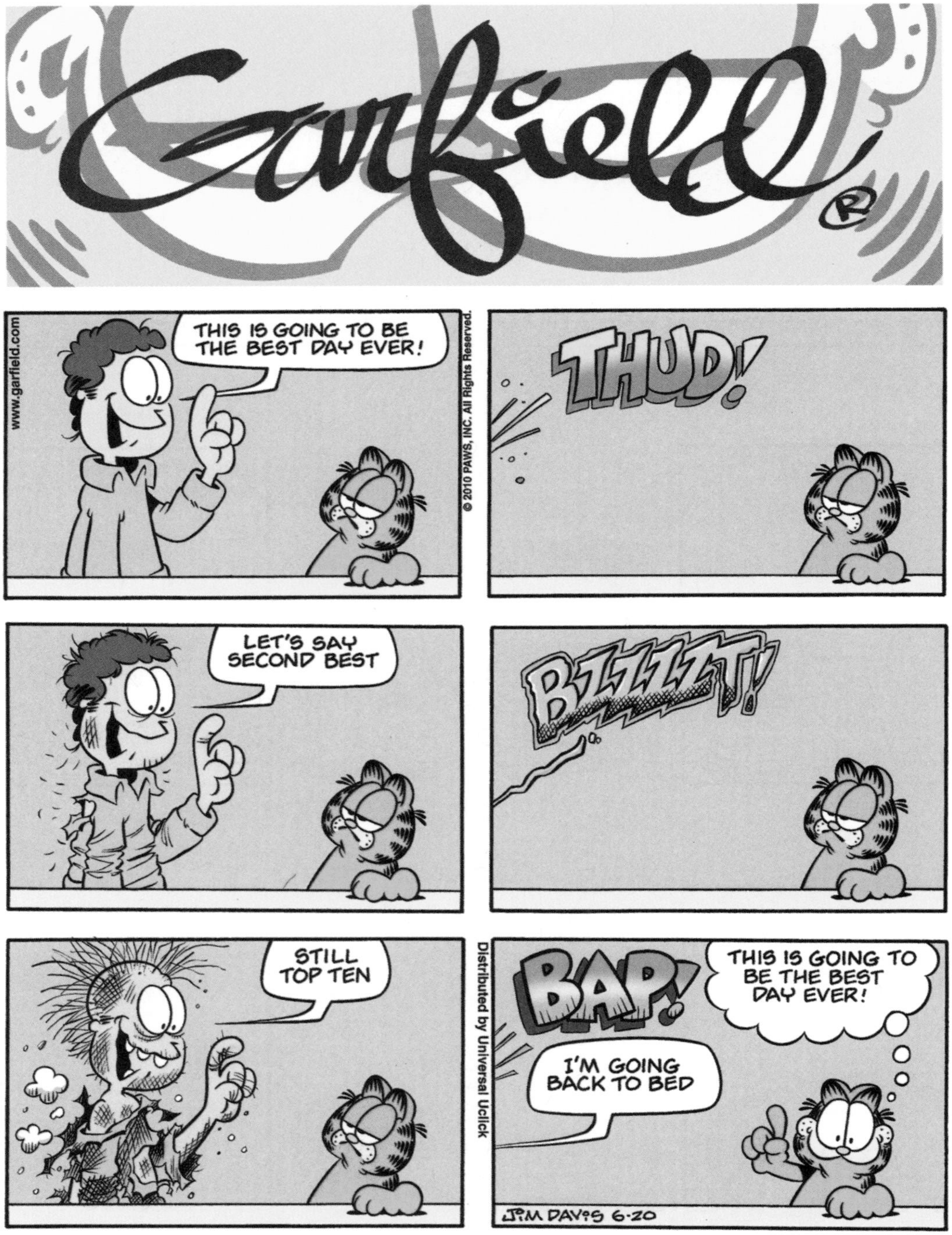
Garfield®
www.garfield.com
THIS IS GOING TO BE THE BEST DAY EVER!
© 2010 PAWS, INC. All Rights Reserved.
THUD!
LET'S SAY SECOND BEST
BZZZZT!
STILL TOP TEN
Distributed by Universal Uclick
BAP!
THIS IS GOING TO BE THE BEST DAY EVER!
I'M GOING BACK TO BED
JIM DAVIS 6-20

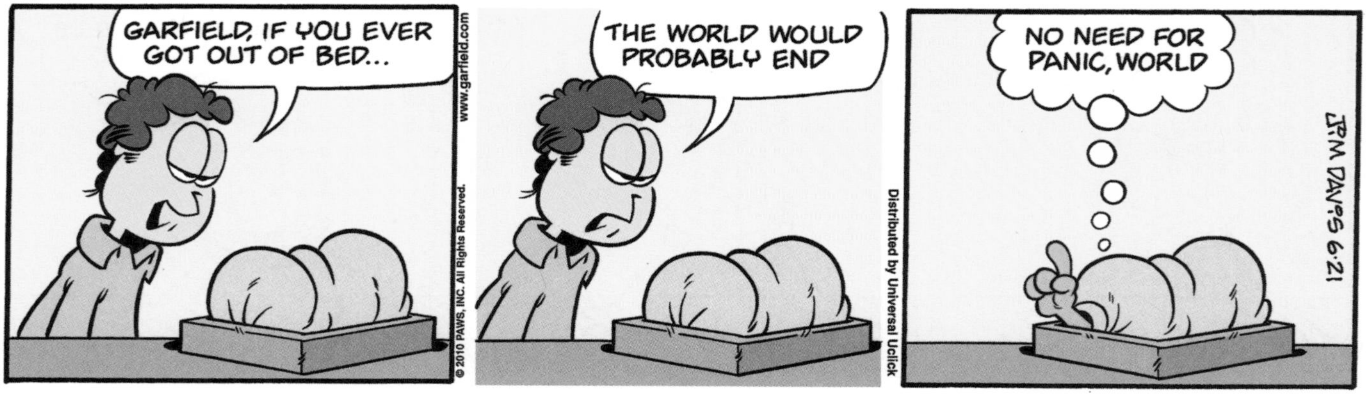
GARFIELD, IF YOU EVER GOT OUT OF BED...
THE WORLD WOULD PROBABLY END
NO NEED FOR PANIC, WORLD
JIM DAVIS 6·21
www.garfield.com
© 2010 PAWS, INC. All Rights Reserved.
Distributed by Universal Uclick

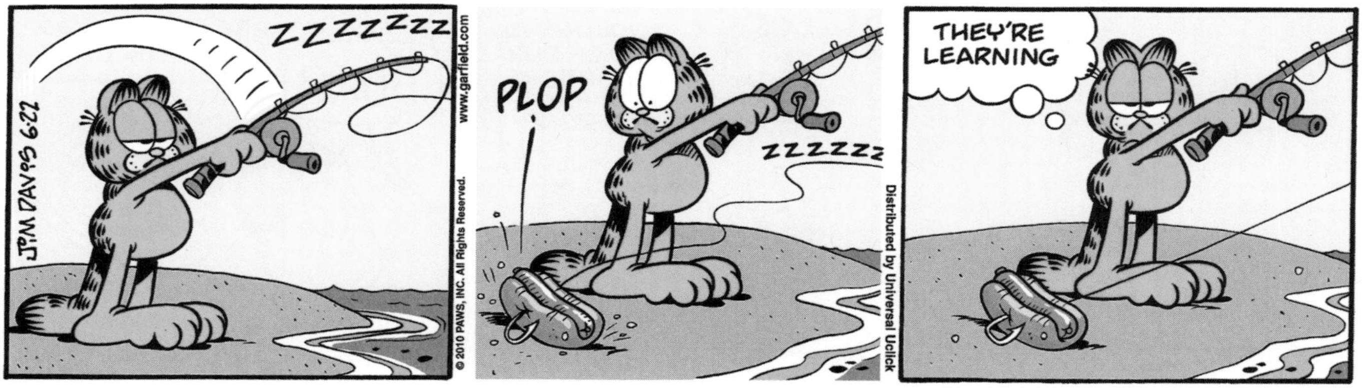
ZZZZZZZ
JIM DAVIS 6·22
PLOP
ZZZZZZ
THEY'RE LEARNING
www.garfield.com
© 2010 PAWS, INC. All Rights Reserved.
Distributed by Universal Uclick

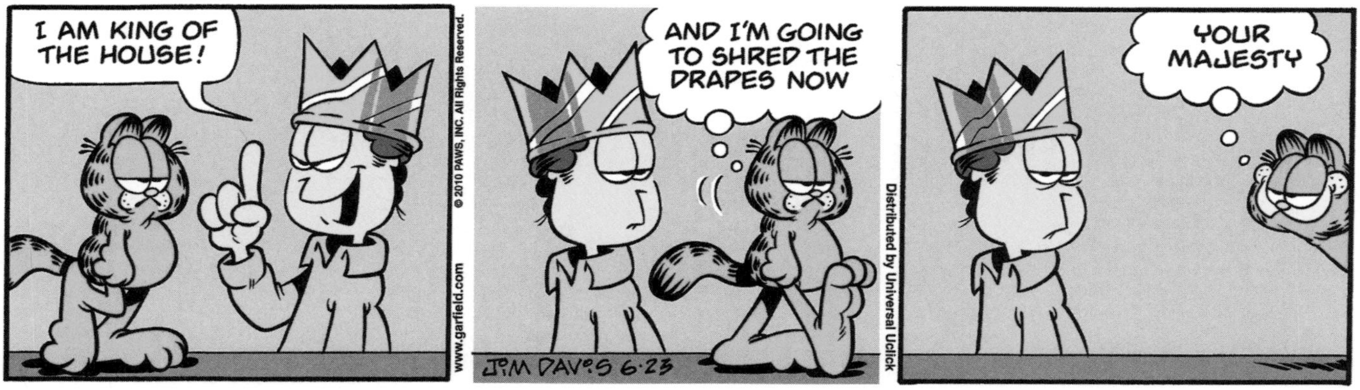
I AM KING OF THE HOUSE!
AND I'M GOING TO SHRED THE DRAPES NOW
YOUR MAJESTY
JIM DAVIS 6·23
www.garfield.com
© 2010 PAWS, INC. All Rights Reserved.
Distributed by Universal Uclick

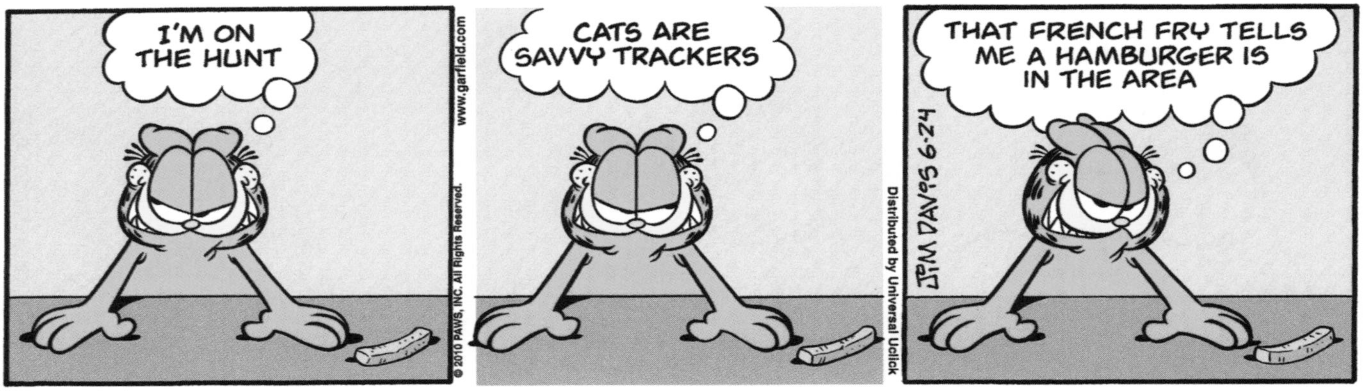
I'M ON THE HUNT
CATS ARE SAVVY TRACKERS
THAT FRENCH FRY TELLS ME A HAMBURGER IS IN THE AREA
JIM DAVIS 6·24
© 2010 PAWS, INC. All Rights Reserved.
www.garfield.com
Distributed by Universal Uclick

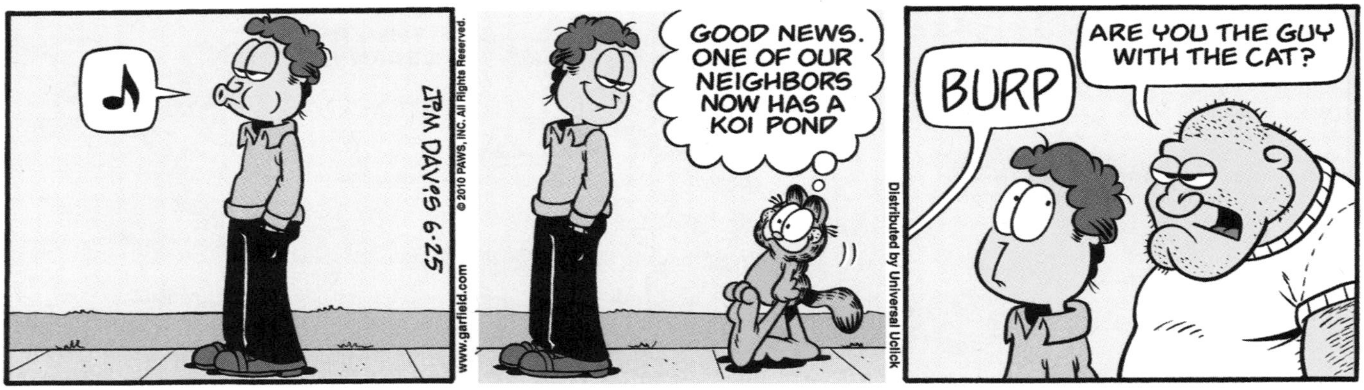
♪
JIM DAVIS 6·25
GOOD NEWS. ONE OF OUR NEIGHBORS NOW HAS A KOI POND
BURP
ARE YOU THE GUY WITH THE CAT?
© 2010 PAWS, INC. All Rights Reserved.
www.garfield.com
Distributed by Universal Uclick

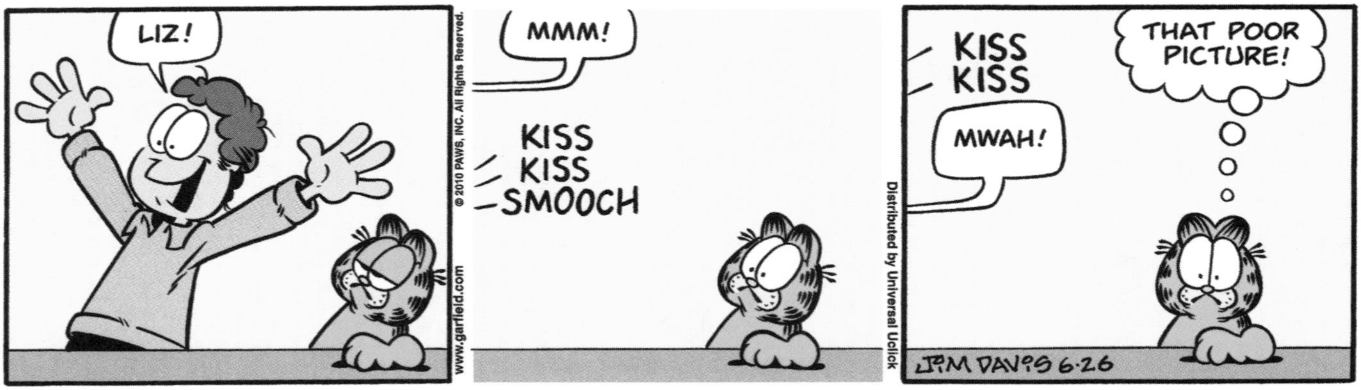
LIZ!
MMM!
KISS
KISS
SMOOCH
KISS
KISS
MWAH!
THAT POOR PICTURE!
JIM DAVIS 6·26
© 2010 PAWS, INC. All Rights Reserved.
www.garfield.com
Distributed by Universal Uclick

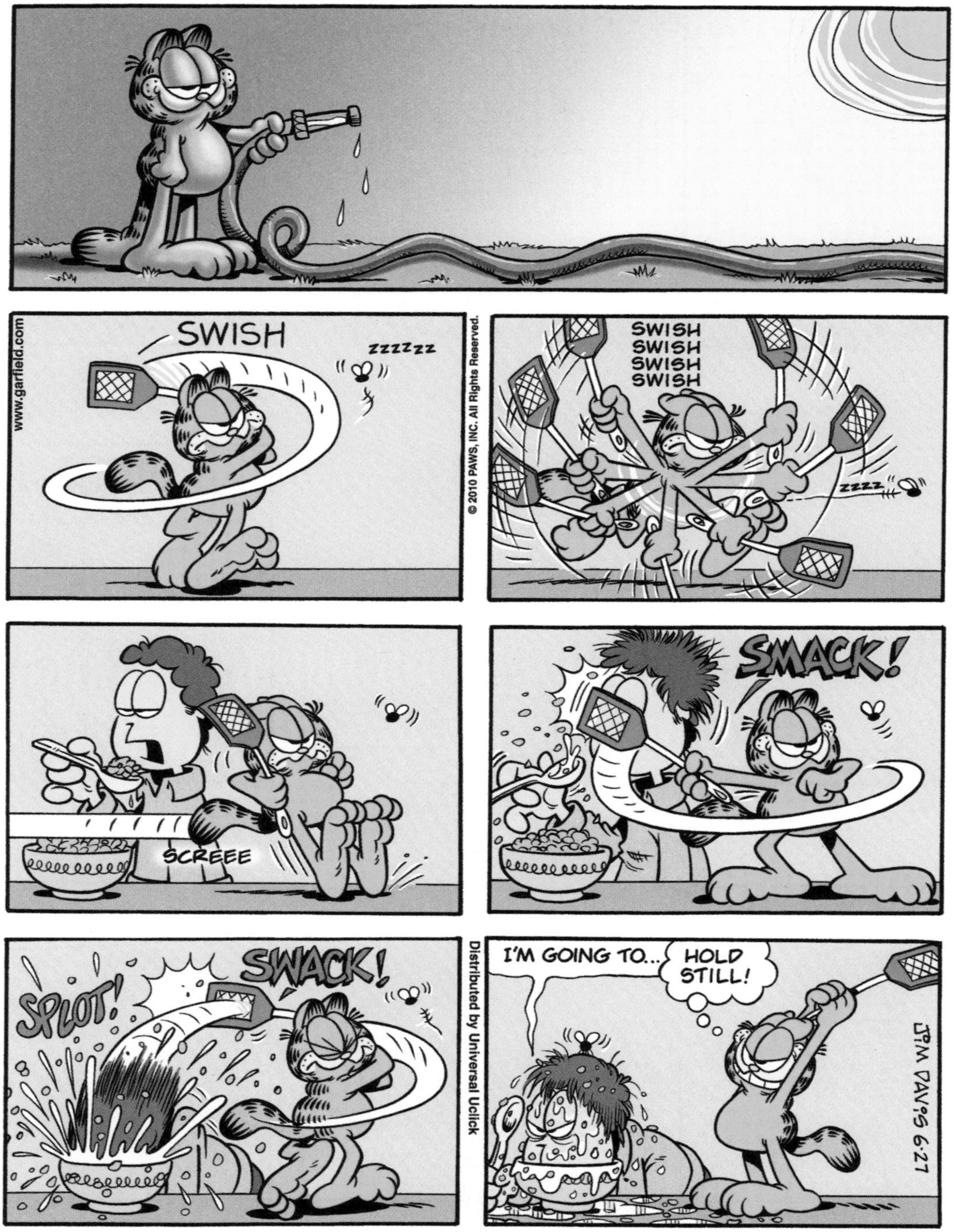

SWISH
zzzzzz
SWISH
SWISH
SWISH
SWISH
zzzz
SCREEE
SMACK!
SPLOT!
SWACK!
I'M GOING TO...
HOLD STILL!
JIM DAVIS 6-27

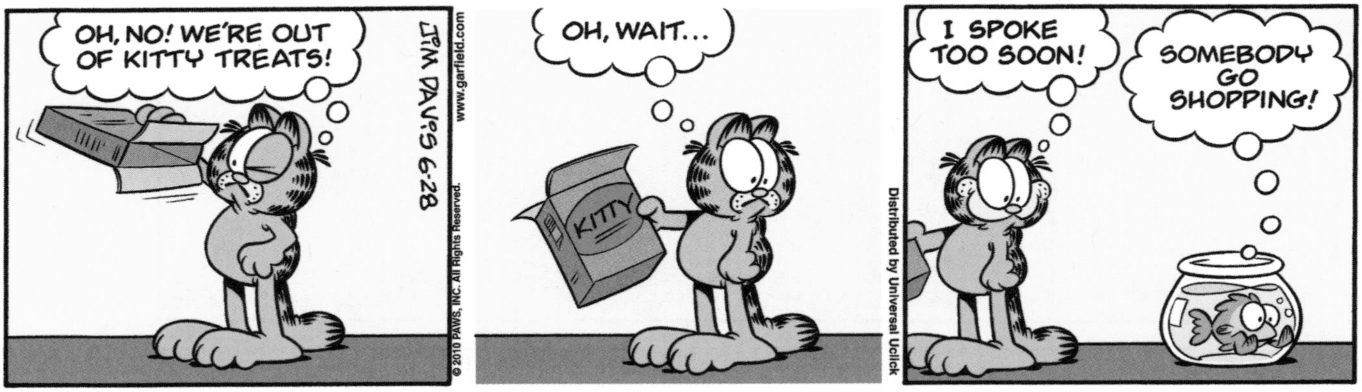
OH, NO! WE'RE OUT OF KITTY TREATS!
JIM DAVIS 6-28
© 2010 PAWS, INC. All Rights Reserved. www.garfield.com
OH, WAIT...
KITTY
Distributed by Universal Uclick
I SPOKE TOO SOON!
SOMEBODY GO SHOPPING!

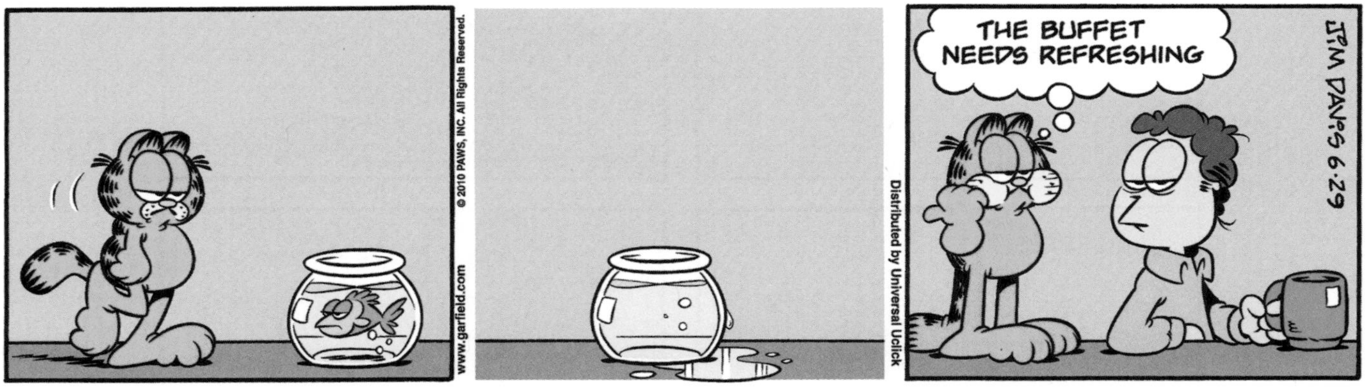
© 2010 PAWS, INC. All Rights Reserved. www.garfield.com
Distributed by Universal Uclick
THE BUFFET NEEDS REFRESHING
JIM DAVIS 6-29

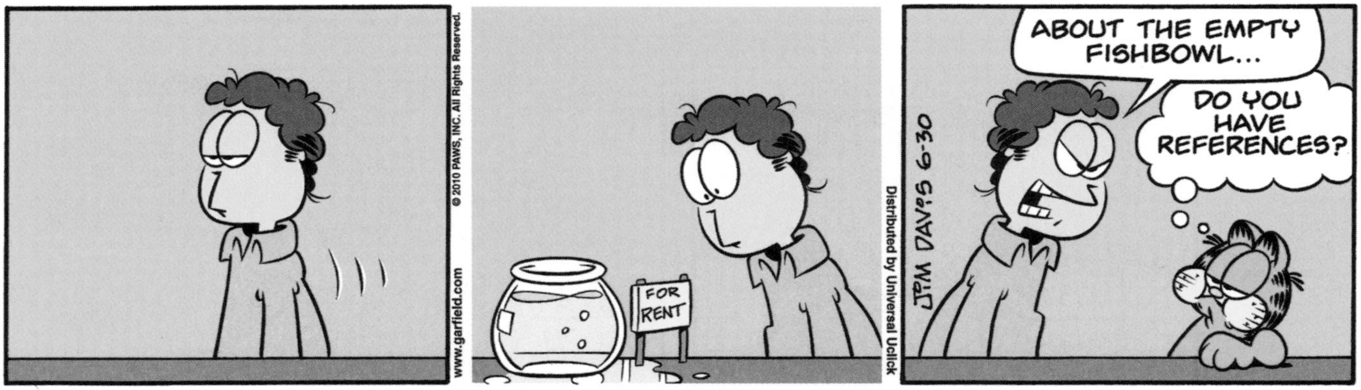
© 2010 PAWS, INC. All Rights Reserved. www.garfield.com
FOR RENT
Distributed by Universal Uclick
JIM DAVIS 6-30
ABOUT THE EMPTY FISHBOWL...
DO YOU HAVE REFERENCES?

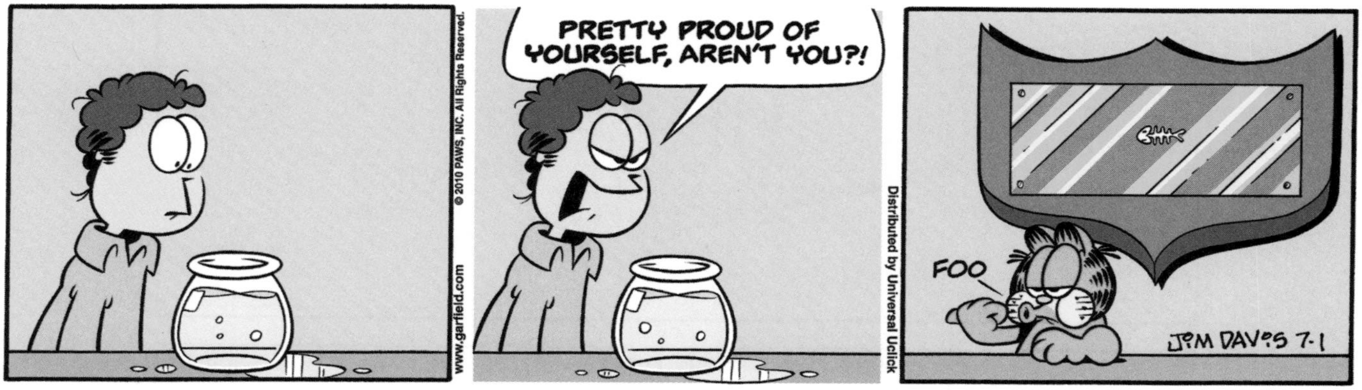
PRETTY PROUD OF YOURSELF, AREN'T YOU?!
FOO
JIM DAVIS 7-1
© 2010 PAWS, INC. All Rights Reserved.
www.garfield.com
Distributed by Universal Uclick

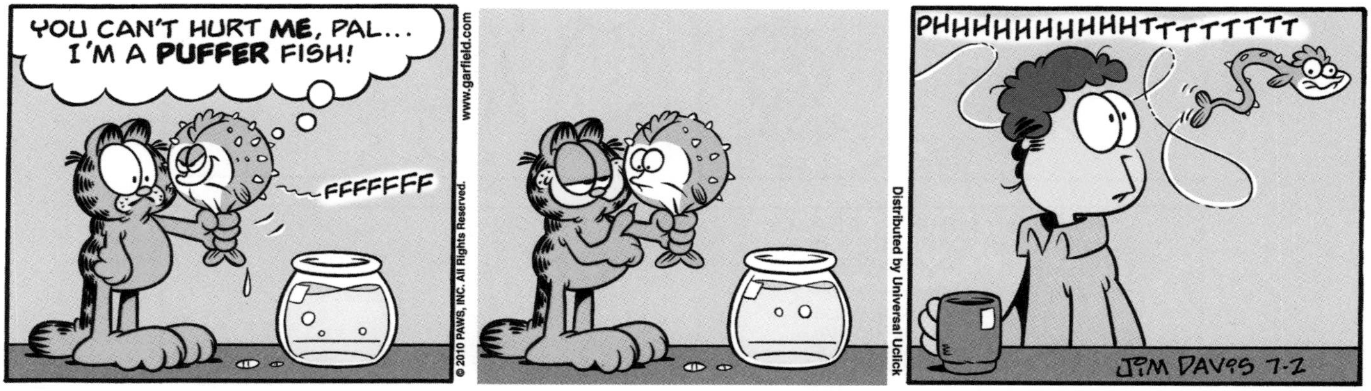
YOU CAN'T HURT **ME**, PAL... I'M A **PUFFER** FISH!
FFFFFFF
PHHHHHHHHHTTTTTTTT
JIM DAVIS 7-2
© 2010 PAWS, INC. All Rights Reserved.
www.garfield.com
Distributed by Universal Uclick

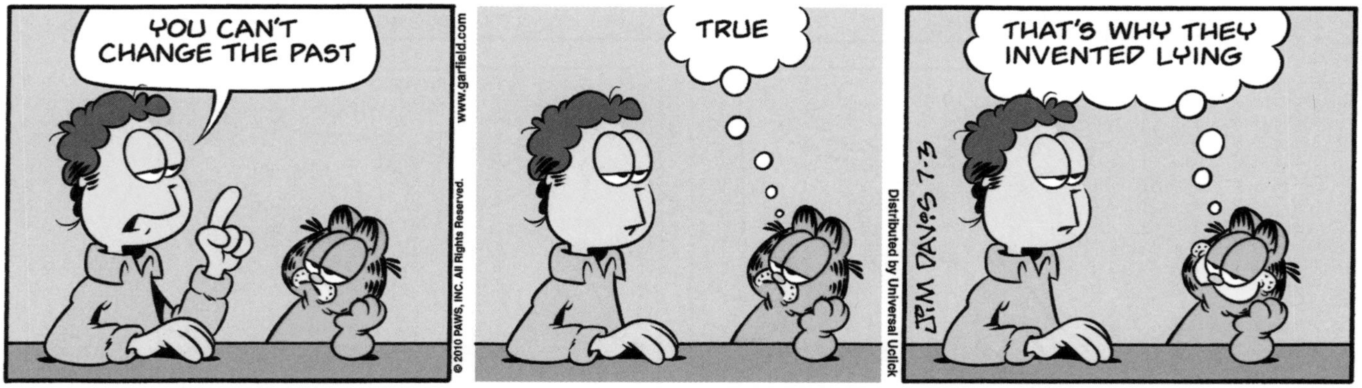
YOU CAN'T CHANGE THE PAST
TRUE
THAT'S WHY THEY INVENTED LYING
JIM DAVIS 7-3
© 2010 PAWS, INC. All Rights Reserved.
www.garfield.com
Distributed by Universal Uclick

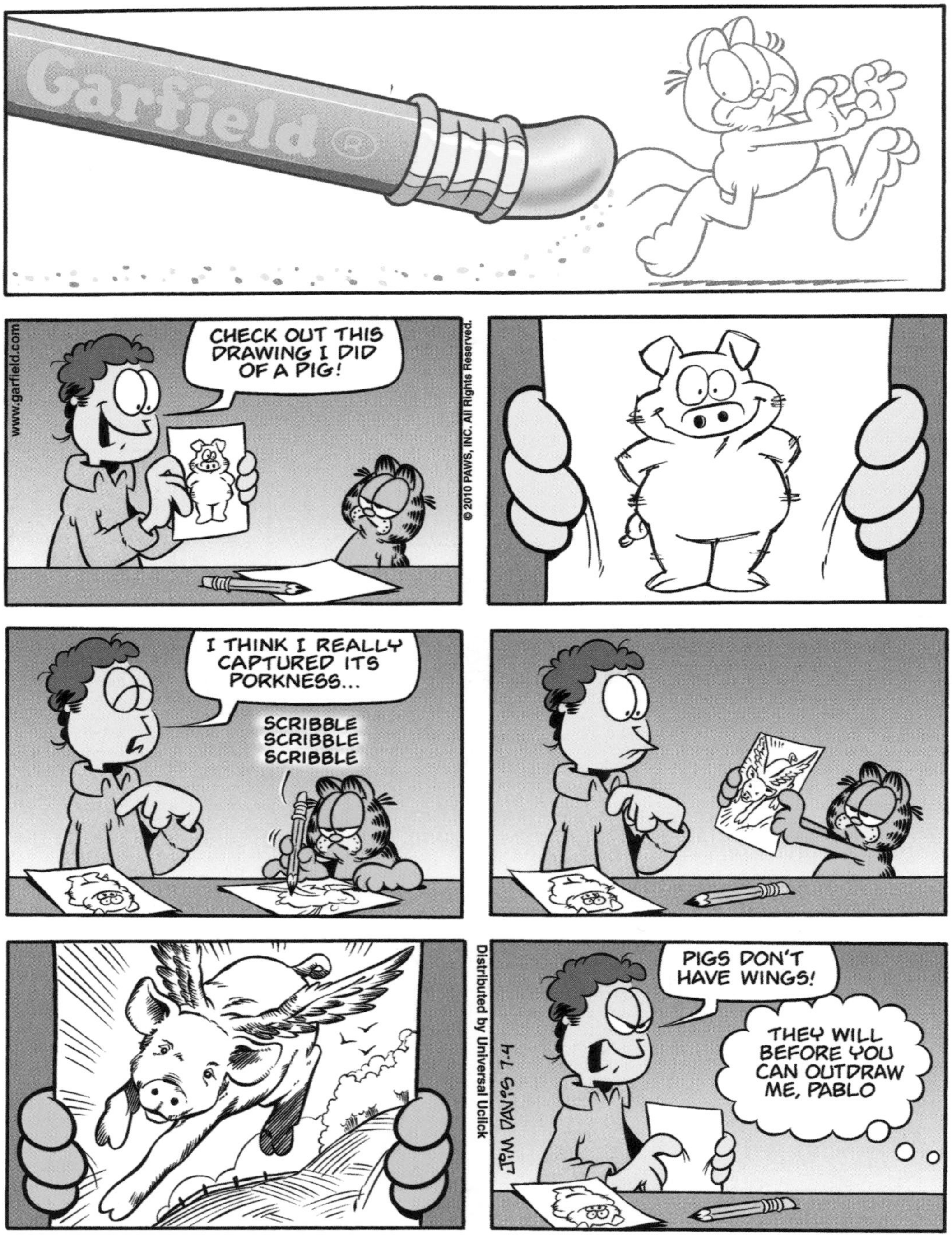
Garfield ®
www.garfield.com
CHECK OUT THIS DRAWING I DID OF A PIG!
© 2010 PAWS, INC. All Rights Reserved.
I THINK I REALLY CAPTURED ITS PORKNESS...
SCRIBBLE SCRIBBLE SCRIBBLE
Distributed by Universal Uclick
JPM DAVIS 7-4
PIGS DON'T HAVE WINGS!
THEY WILL BEFORE YOU CAN OUTDRAW ME, PABLO

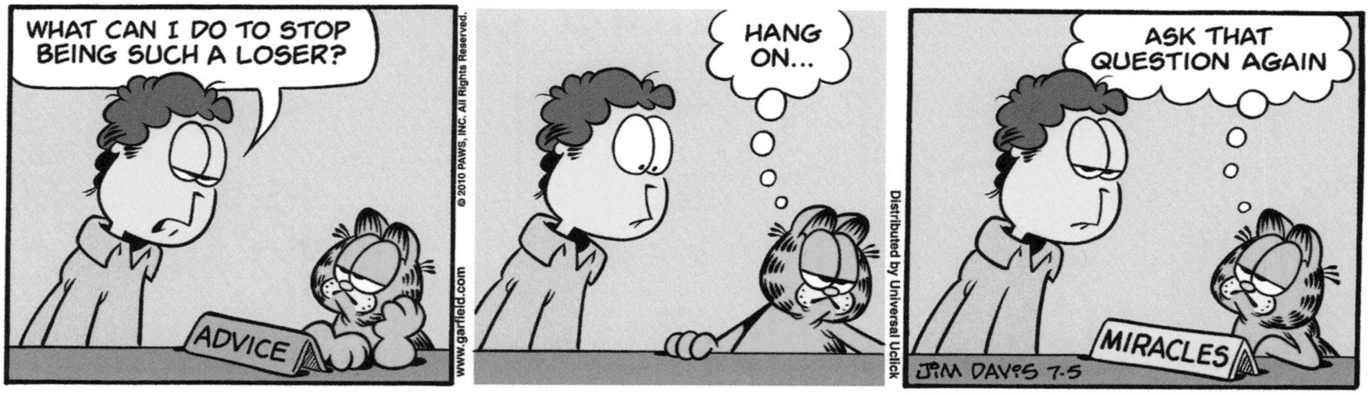
WHAT CAN I DO TO STOP BEING SUCH A LOSER?
ADVICE
HANG ON...
ASK THAT QUESTION AGAIN
MIRACLES
JIM DAVIS 7-5
© 2010 PAWS, INC. All Rights Reserved.
www.garfield.com
Distributed by Universal Uclick

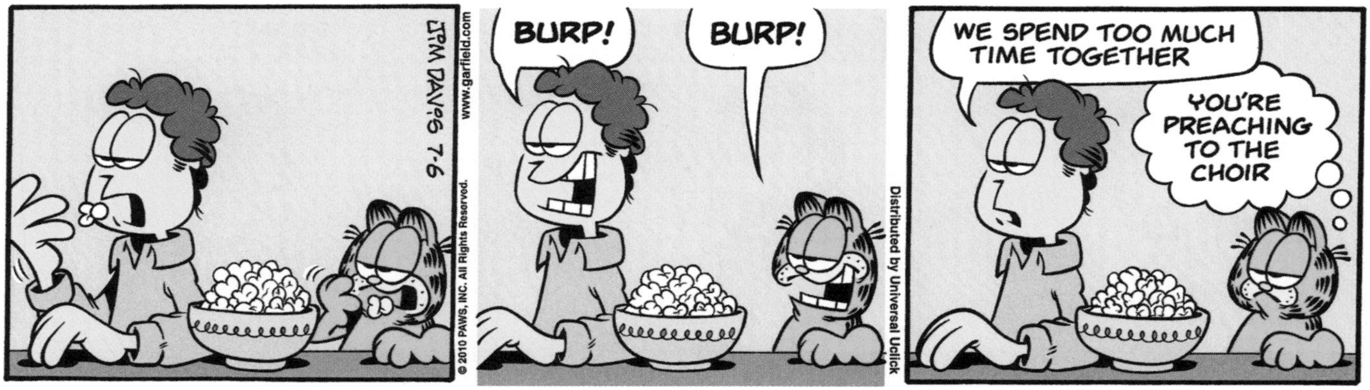
JIM DAVIS 7-6
BURP!
BURP!
WE SPEND TOO MUCH TIME TOGETHER
YOU'RE PREACHING TO THE CHOIR
www.garfield.com
© 2010 PAWS, INC. All Rights Reserved.
Distributed by Universal Uclick

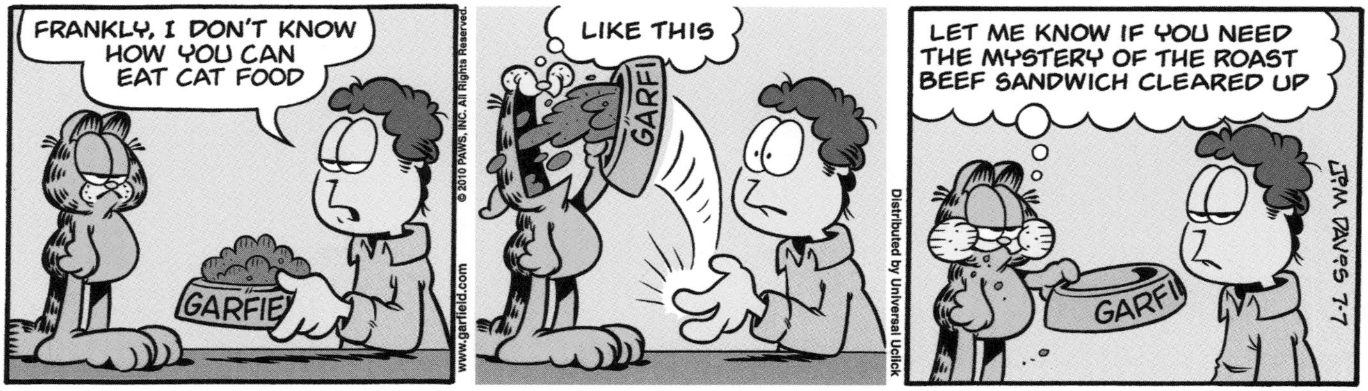
FRANKLY, I DON'T KNOW HOW YOU CAN EAT CAT FOOD
GARFIE
LIKE THIS
GARFI
LET ME KNOW IF YOU NEED THE MYSTERY OF THE ROAST BEEF SANDWICH CLEARED UP
GARFI
JIM DAVIS 7-7
© 2010 PAWS, INC. All Rights Reserved.
www.garfield.com
Distributed by Universal Uclick

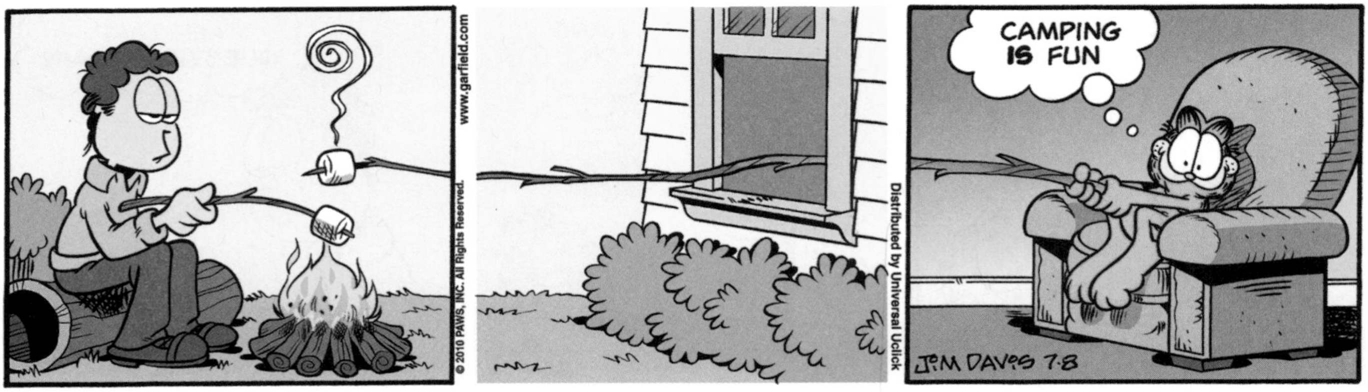
www.garfield.com
© 2010 PAWS, INC. All Rights Reserved.
Distributed by Universal Uclick
CAMPING IS FUN
JIM DAVIS 7-8

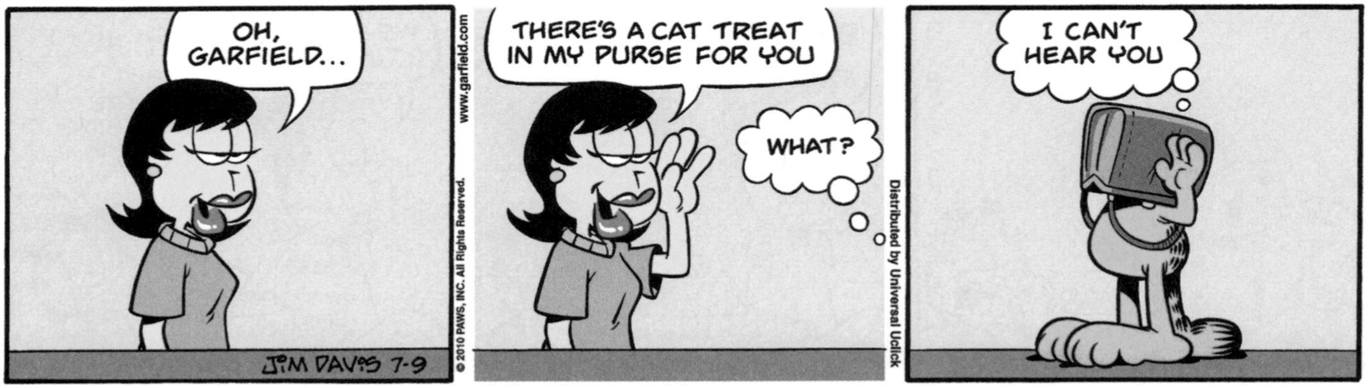
OH, GARFIELD...
JIM DAVIS 7-9
www.garfield.com
© 2010 PAWS, INC. All Rights Reserved.
THERE'S A CAT TREAT IN MY PURSE FOR YOU
WHAT?
Distributed by Universal Uclick
I CAN'T HEAR YOU

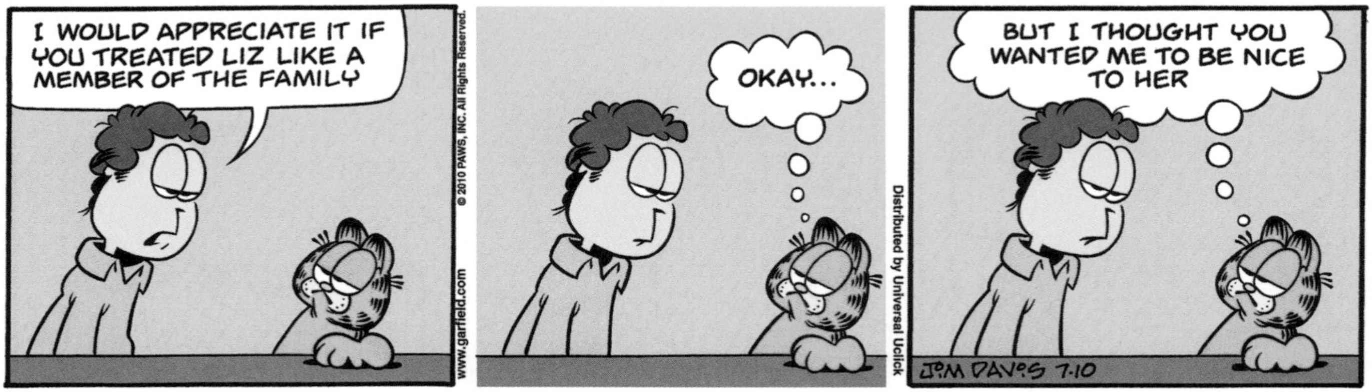
I WOULD APPRECIATE IT IF YOU TREATED LIZ LIKE A MEMBER OF THE FAMILY
www.garfield.com
© 2010 PAWS, INC. All Rights Reserved.
OKAY...
Distributed by Universal Uclick
BUT I THOUGHT YOU WANTED ME TO BE NICE TO HER
JIM DAVIS 7-10

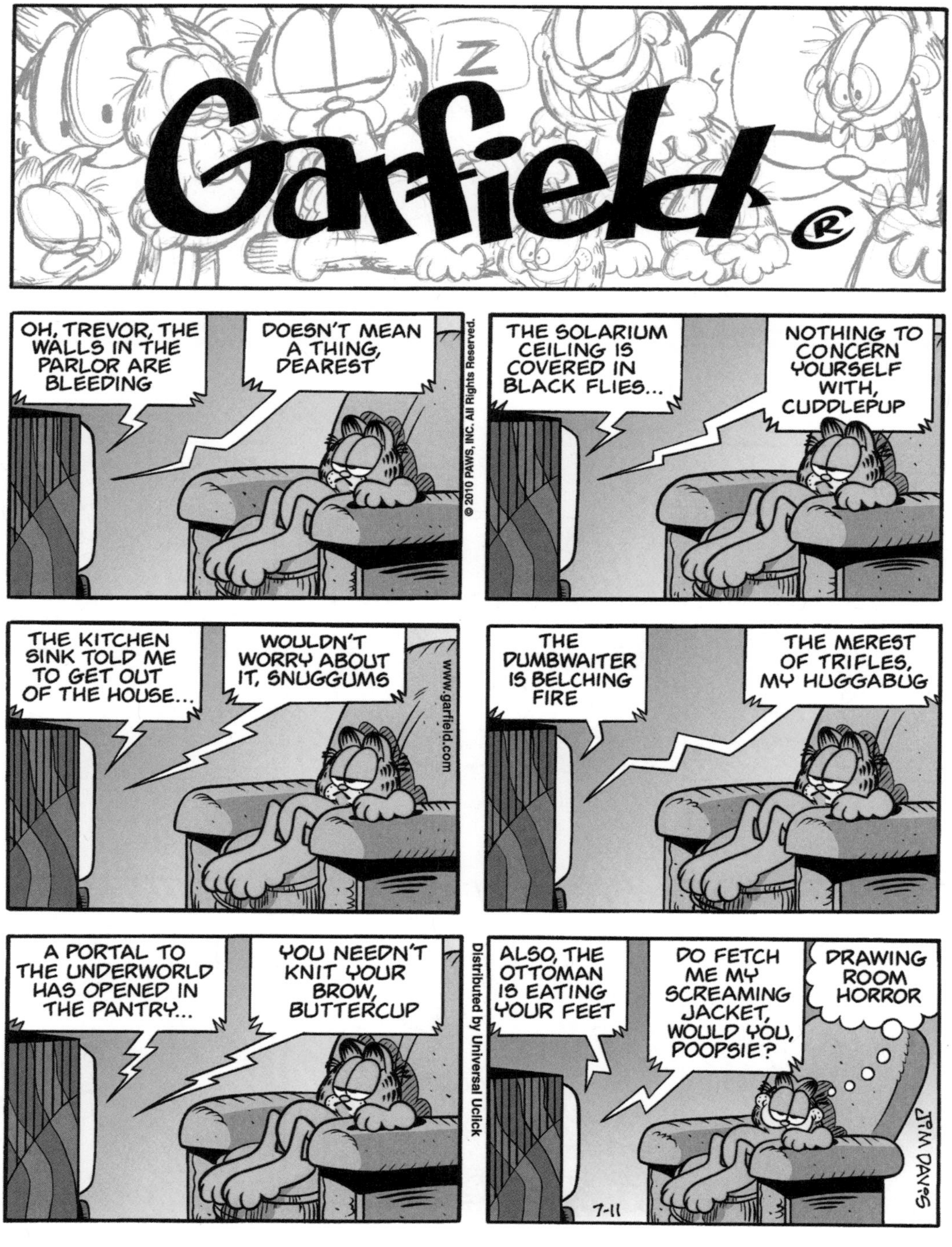
Garfield®
OH, TREVOR, THE WALLS IN THE PARLOR ARE BLEEDING
DOESN'T MEAN A THING, DEAREST
© 2010 PAWS, INC. All Rights Reserved.
THE SOLARIUM CEILING IS COVERED IN BLACK FLIES...
NOTHING TO CONCERN YOURSELF WITH, CUDDLEPUP
THE KITCHEN SINK TOLD ME TO GET OUT OF THE HOUSE...
WOULDN'T WORRY ABOUT IT, SNUGGUMS
www.garfield.com
THE DUMBWAITER IS BELCHING FIRE
THE MEREST OF TRIFLES, MY HUGGABUG
A PORTAL TO THE UNDERWORLD HAS OPENED IN THE PANTRY...
YOU NEEDN'T KNIT YOUR BROW, BUTTERCUP
Distributed by Universal Uclick
ALSO, THE OTTOMAN IS EATING YOUR FEET
DO FETCH ME MY SCREAMING JACKET, WOULD YOU, POOPSIE?
DRAWING ROOM HORROR
JIM DAVIS
7-11

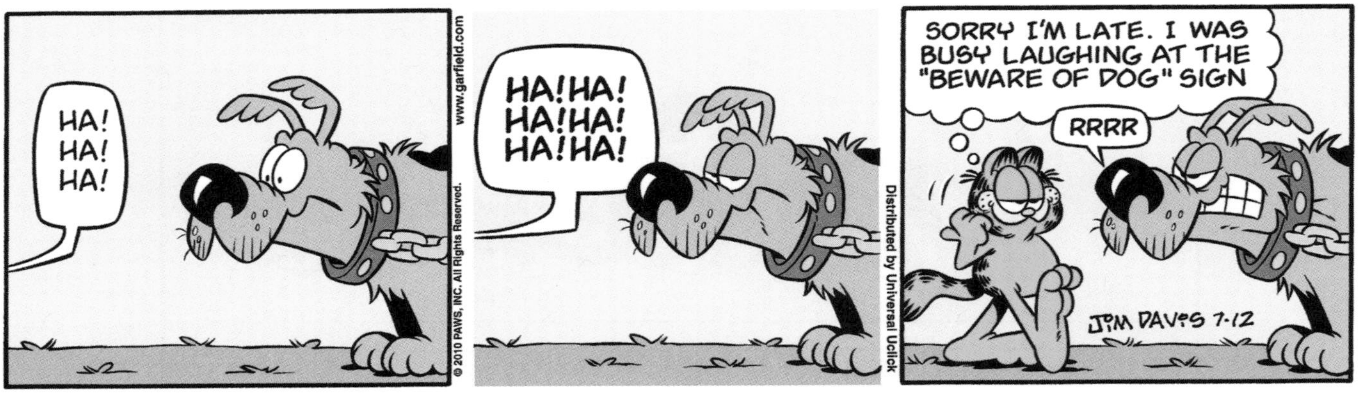
HA! HA! HA!
HA!HA! HA!HA! HA!HA!
SORRY I'M LATE. I WAS BUSY LAUGHING AT THE "BEWARE OF DOG" SIGN
RRRR
JIM DAVIS 7-12
© 2010 PAWS, INC. All Rights Reserved.
www.garfield.com
Distributed by Universal Uclick

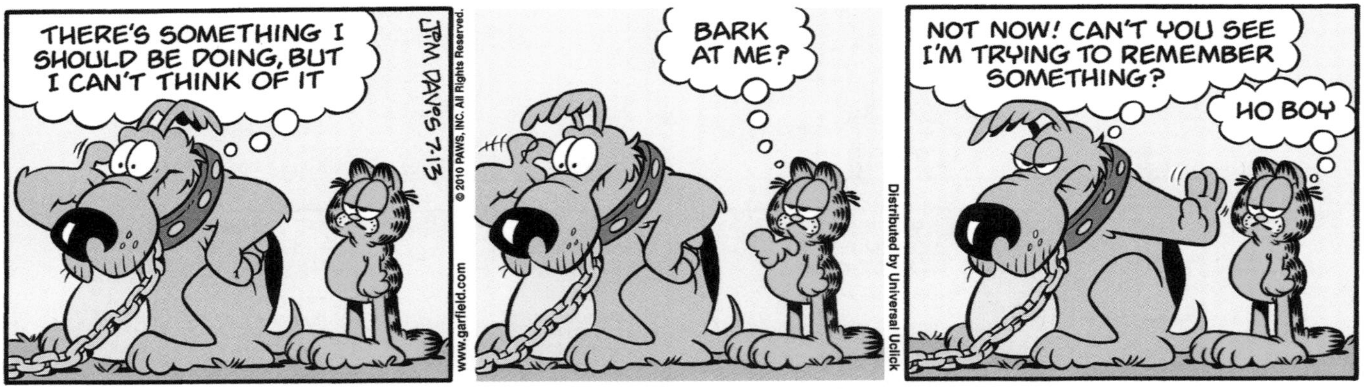
THERE'S SOMETHING I SHOULD BE DOING, BUT I CAN'T THINK OF IT
JIM DAVIS 7-13
© 2010 PAWS, INC. All Rights Reserved.
www.garfield.com
BARK AT ME?
NOT NOW! CAN'T YOU SEE I'M TRYING TO REMEMBER SOMETHING?
HO BOY
Distributed by Universal Uclick

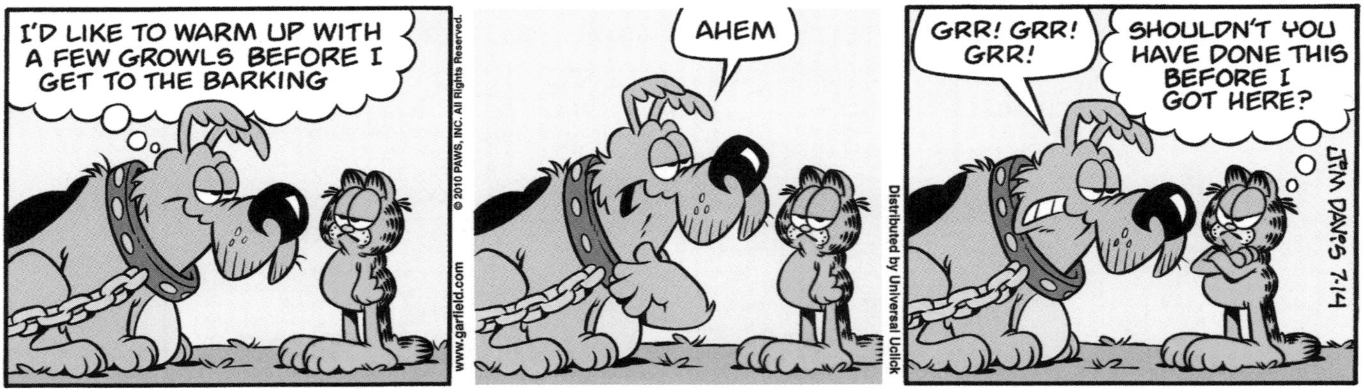
I'D LIKE TO WARM UP WITH A FEW GROWLS BEFORE I GET TO THE BARKING
© 2010 PAWS, INC. All Rights Reserved.
www.garfield.com
AHEM
GRR! GRR! GRR!
SHOULDN'T YOU HAVE DONE THIS BEFORE I GOT HERE?
JIM DAVIS 7-14
Distributed by Universal Uclick

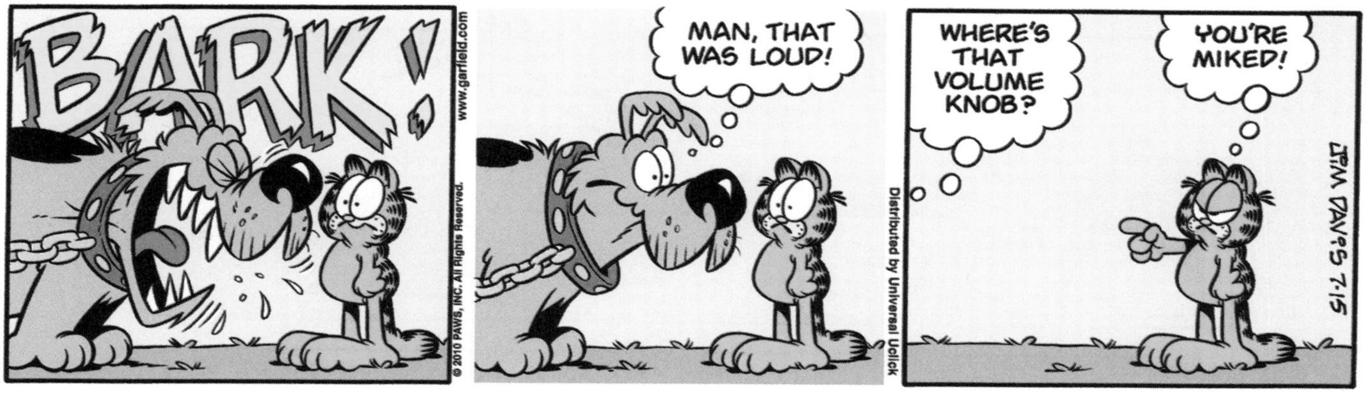
BARK!
MAN, THAT WAS LOUD!
WHERE'S THAT VOLUME KNOB?
YOU'RE MIKED!
JIM DAVIS 7-15
© 2010 PAWS, INC. All Rights Reserved.
www.garfield.com
Distributed by Universal Uclick

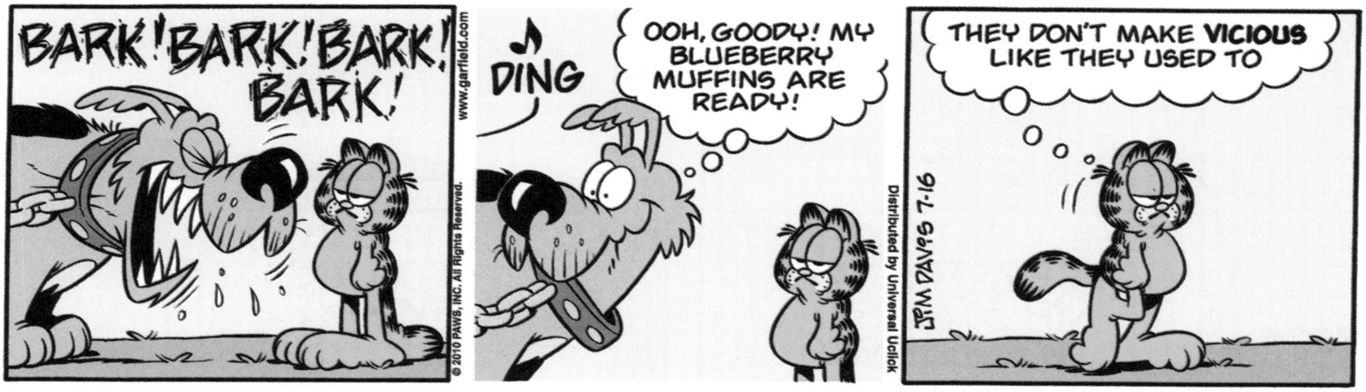
BARK! BARK! BARK! BARK!
DING
OOH, GOODY! MY BLUEBERRY MUFFINS ARE READY!
THEY DON'T MAKE **VICIOUS** LIKE THEY USED TO
JIM DAVIS 7-16
© 2010 PAWS, INC. All Rights Reserved.
www.garfield.com
Distributed by Universal Uclick

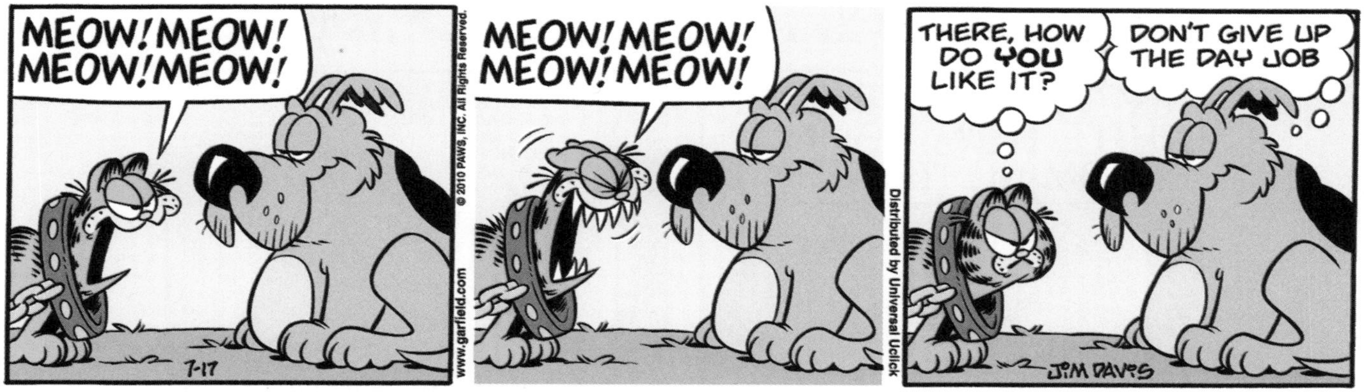
MEOW! MEOW! MEOW! MEOW!
MEOW! MEOW! MEOW! MEOW!
THERE, HOW DO **YOU** LIKE IT?
DON'T GIVE UP THE DAY JOB
7-17
JIM DAVIS
© 2010 PAWS, INC. All Rights Reserved.
www.garfield.com
Distributed by Universal Uclick

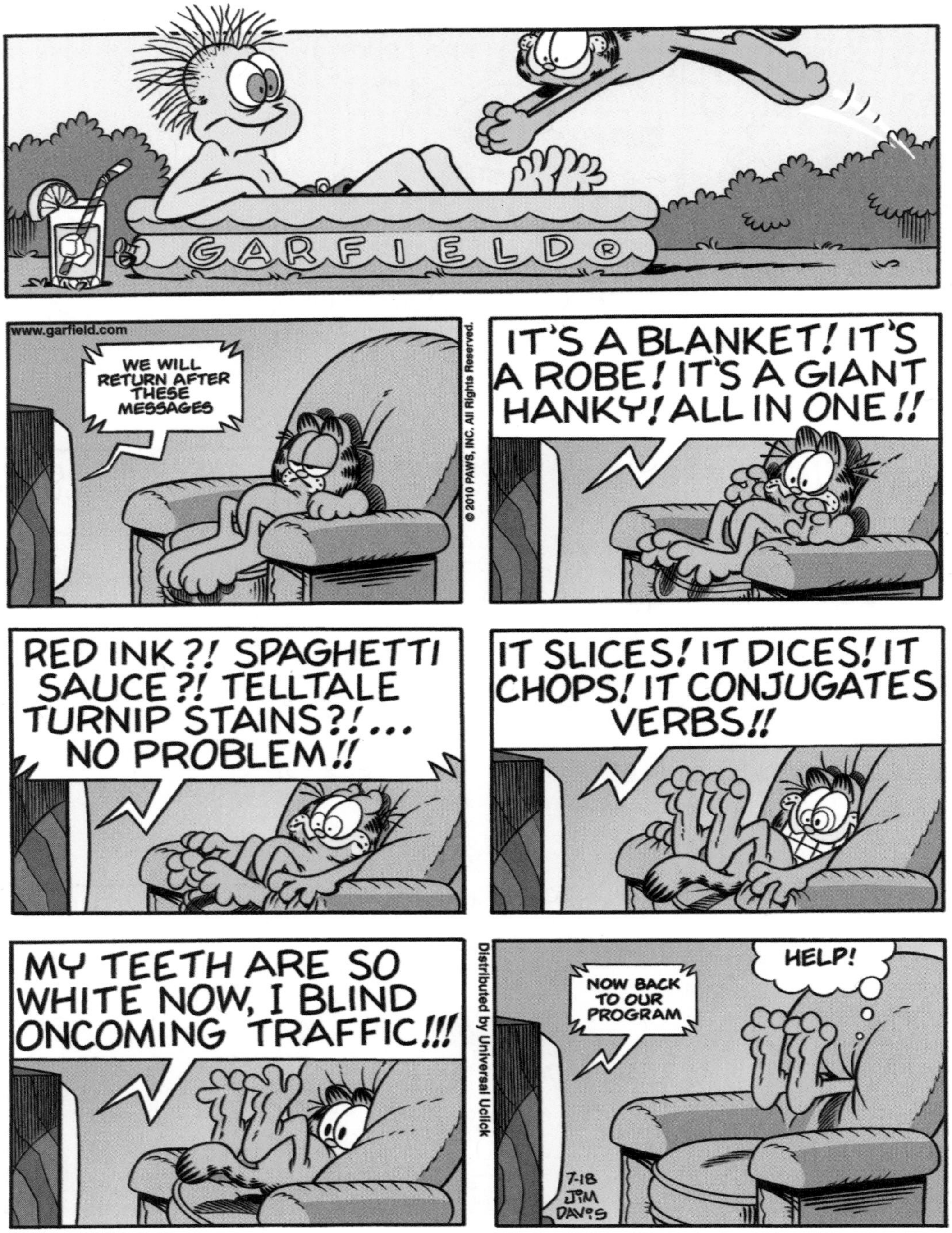

GARFIELD®
www.garfield.com
© 2010 PAWS, INC. All Rights Reserved.
WE WILL RETURN AFTER THESE MESSAGES
IT'S A BLANKET! IT'S A ROBE! IT'S A GIANT HANKY! ALL IN ONE!!
RED INK?! SPAGHETTI SAUCE?! TELLTALE TURNIP STAINS?!... NO PROBLEM!!
IT SLICES! IT DICES! IT CHOPS! IT CONJUGATES VERBS!!
MY TEETH ARE SO WHITE NOW, I BLIND ONCOMING TRAFFIC!!!
Distributed by Universal Uclick
NOW BACK TO OUR PROGRAM
HELP!
7-18 JIM DAVIS

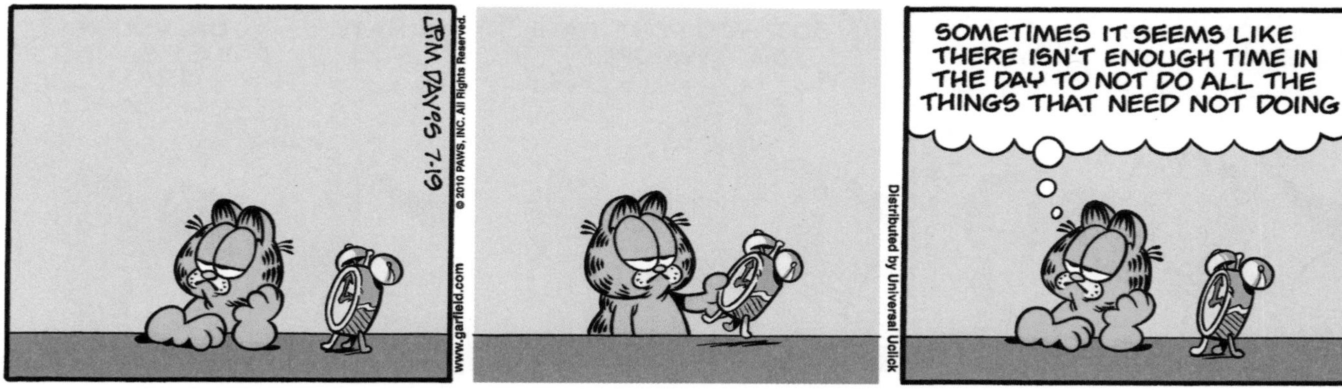
JIM DAVIS 7-19
SOMETIMES IT SEEMS LIKE THERE ISN'T ENOUGH TIME IN THE DAY TO NOT DO ALL THE THINGS THAT NEED NOT DOING

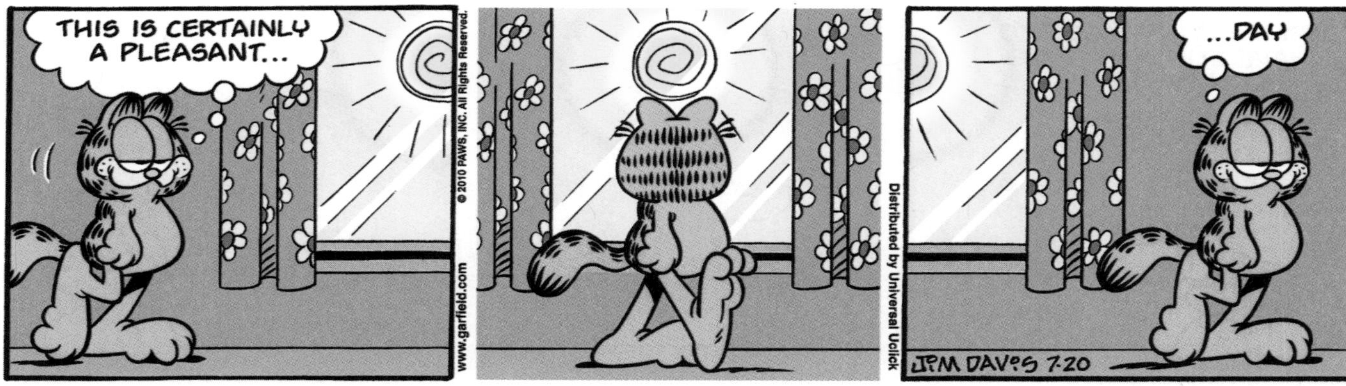
THIS IS CERTAINLY A PLEASANT...
...DAY
JIM DAVIS 7-20

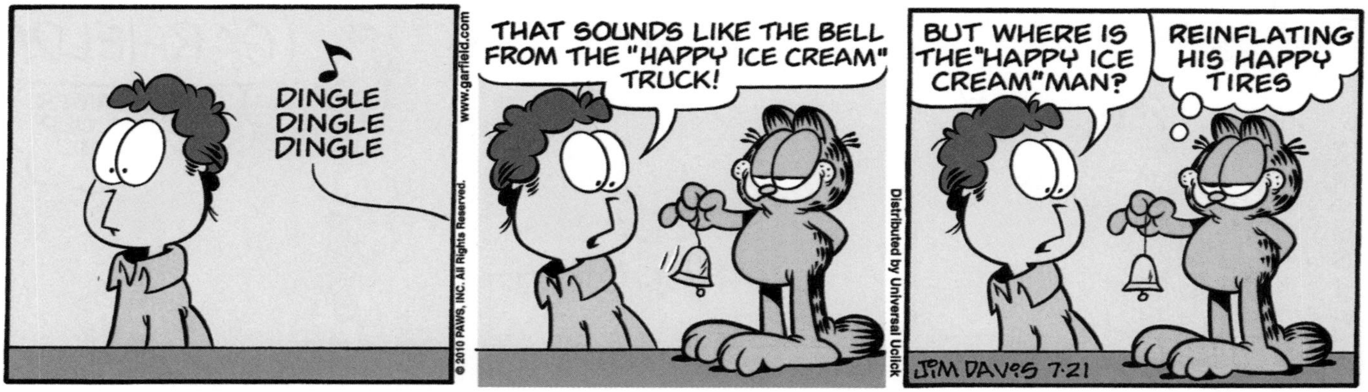
DINGLE DINGLE DINGLE
THAT SOUNDS LIKE THE BELL FROM THE "HAPPY ICE CREAM" TRUCK!
BUT WHERE IS THE "HAPPY ICE CREAM" MAN?
REINFLATING HIS HAPPY TIRES
JIM DAVIS 7-21

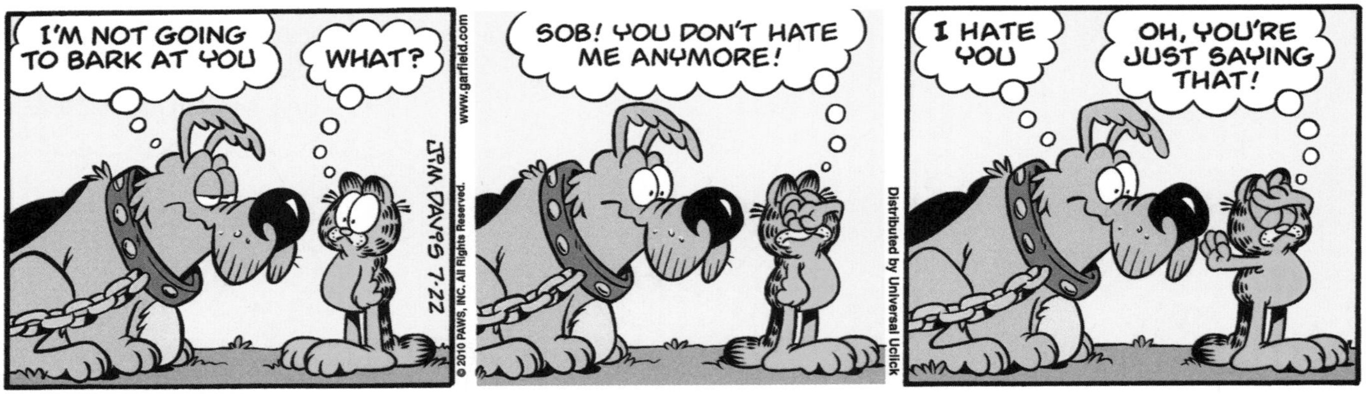
I'M NOT GOING TO BARK AT YOU
WHAT?
SOB! YOU DON'T HATE ME ANYMORE!
I HATE YOU
OH, YOU'RE JUST SAYING THAT!
JIM DAVIS 7-22
© 2010 PAWS, INC. All Rights Reserved. www.garfield.com
Distributed by Universal Uclick

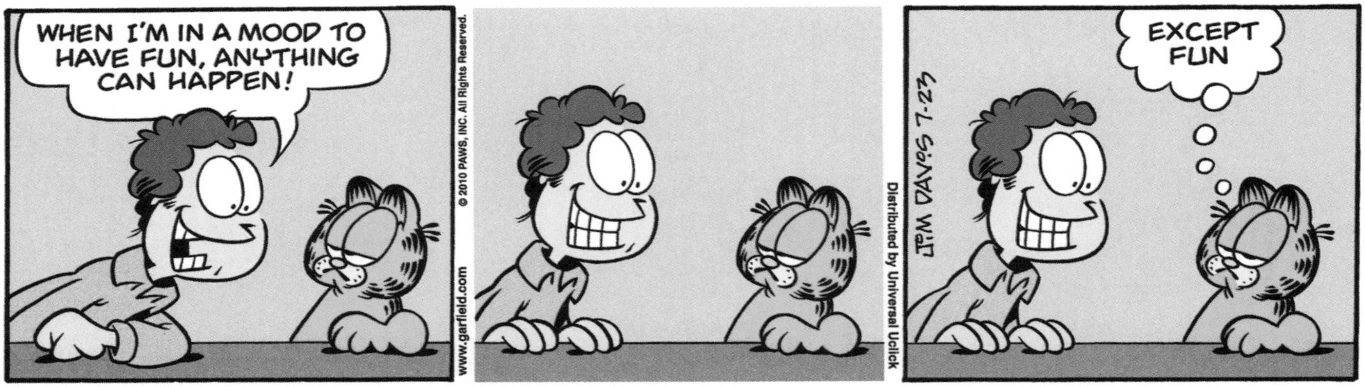
WHEN I'M IN A MOOD TO HAVE FUN, ANYTHING CAN HAPPEN!
EXCEPT FUN
JIM DAVIS 7-23
© 2010 PAWS, INC. All Rights Reserved. www.garfield.com
Distributed by Universal Uclick

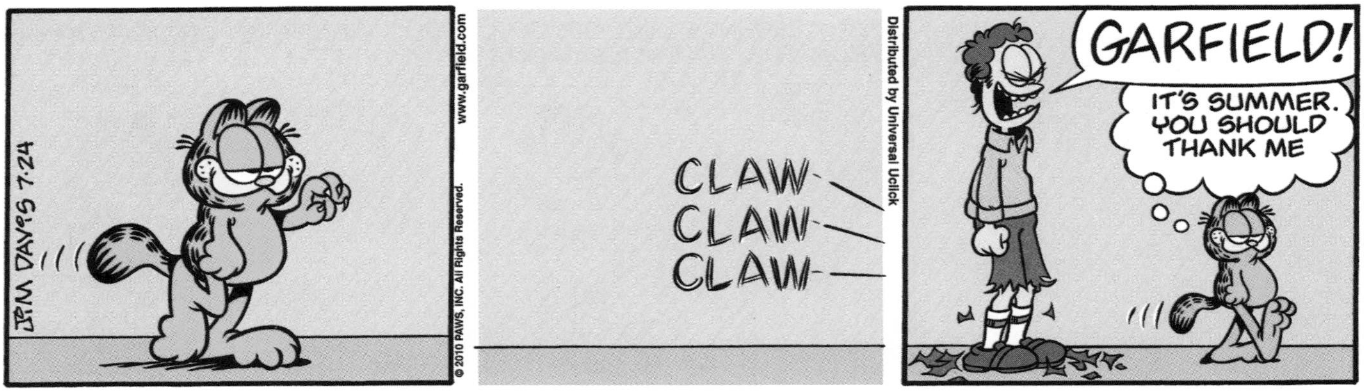
JIM DAVIS 7-24
CLAW
CLAW
CLAW
GARFIELD!
IT'S SUMMER. YOU SHOULD THANK ME
© 2010 PAWS, INC. All Rights Reserved. www.garfield.com
Distributed by Universal Uclick

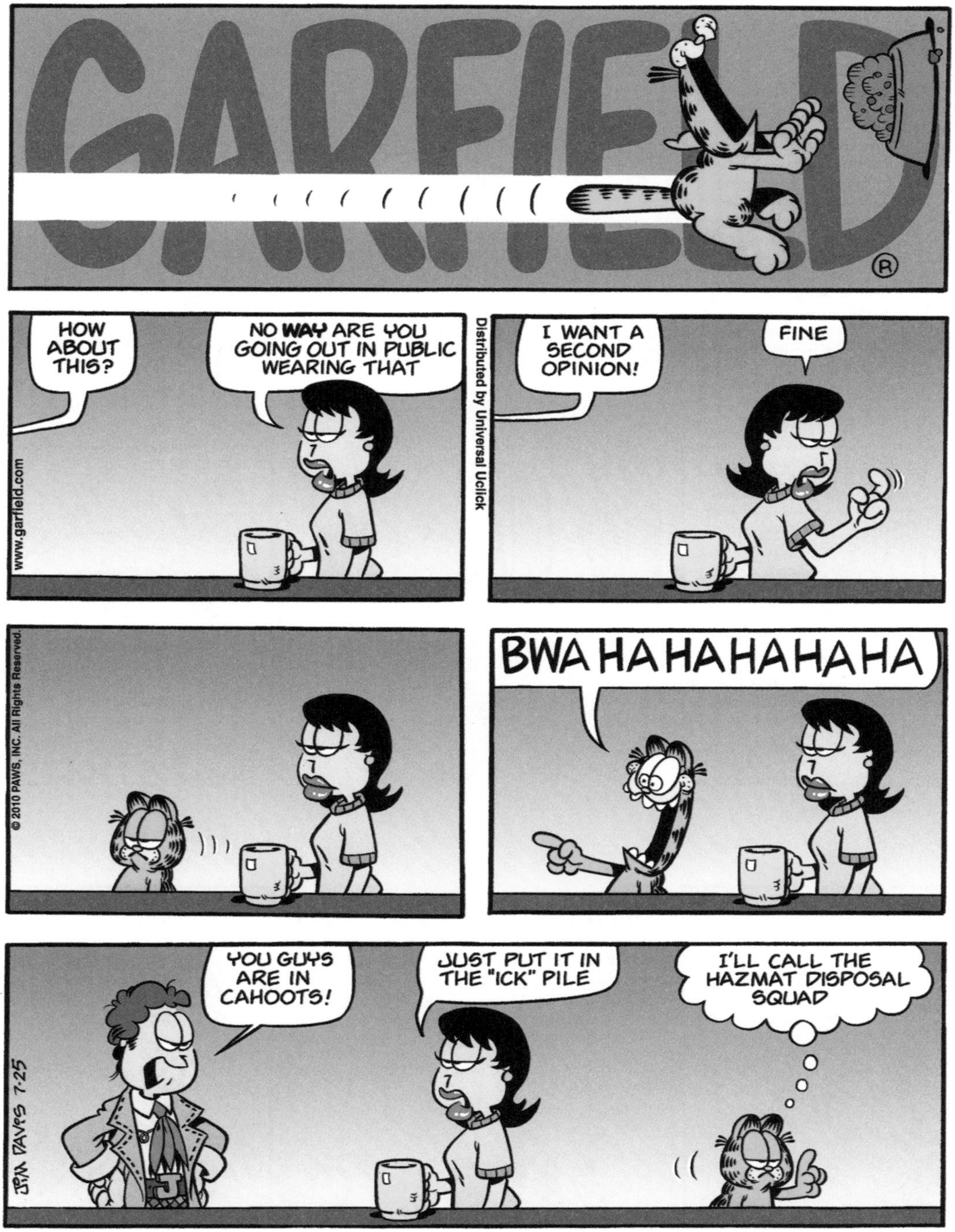
GARFIELD®
HOW ABOUT THIS?
NO WAY ARE YOU GOING OUT IN PUBLIC WEARING THAT
www.garfield.com
Distributed by Universal Uclick
I WANT A SECOND OPINION!
FINE
© 2010 PAWS, INC. All Rights Reserved.
BWA HAHAHAHAHAHA
JPM DAVPS 7-25
YOU GUYS ARE IN CAHOOTS!
JUST PUT IT IN THE "ICK" PILE
I'LL CALL THE HAZMAT DISPOSAL SQUAD

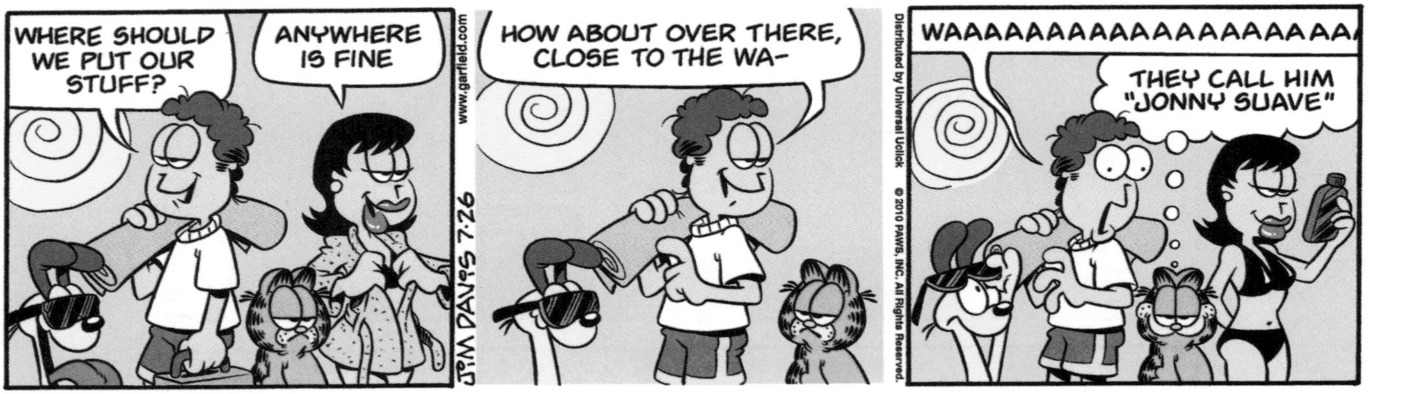
WHERE SHOULD WE PUT OUR STUFF?
ANYWHERE IS FINE
JPM DAVIS 7·26
www.garfield.com
HOW ABOUT OVER THERE, CLOSE TO THE WA-
Distributed by Universal Uclick
© 2010 PAWS, INC. All Rights Reserved.
WAAAAAAAAAAAAAAAAAAAA
THEY CALL HIM "JONNY SUAVE"

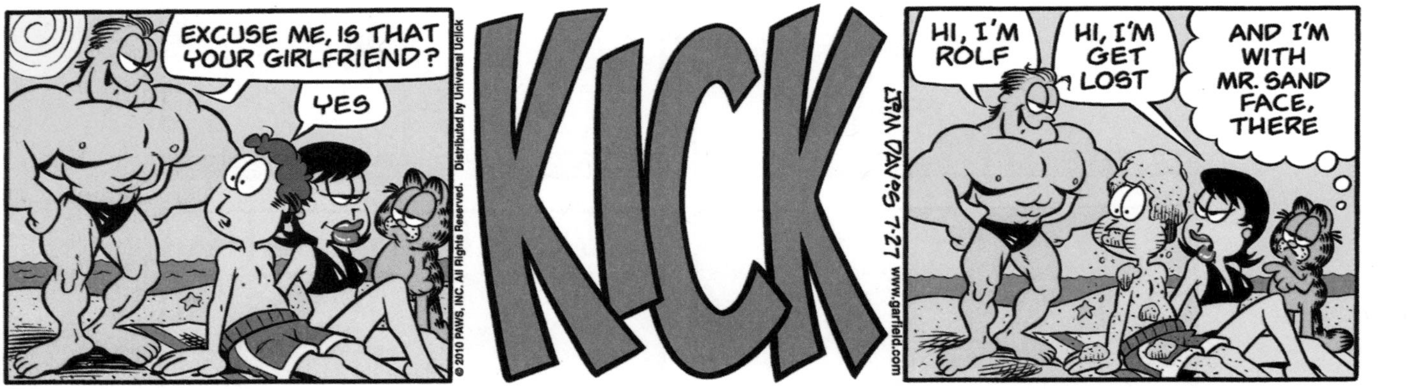
EXCUSE ME, IS THAT YOUR GIRLFRIEND?
YES
© 2010 PAWS, INC. All Rights Reserved. Distributed by Universal Uclick
KICK
JPM DAVIS 7·27
www.garfield.com
HI, I'M ROLF
HI, I'M GET LOST
AND I'M WITH MR. SAND FACE, THERE

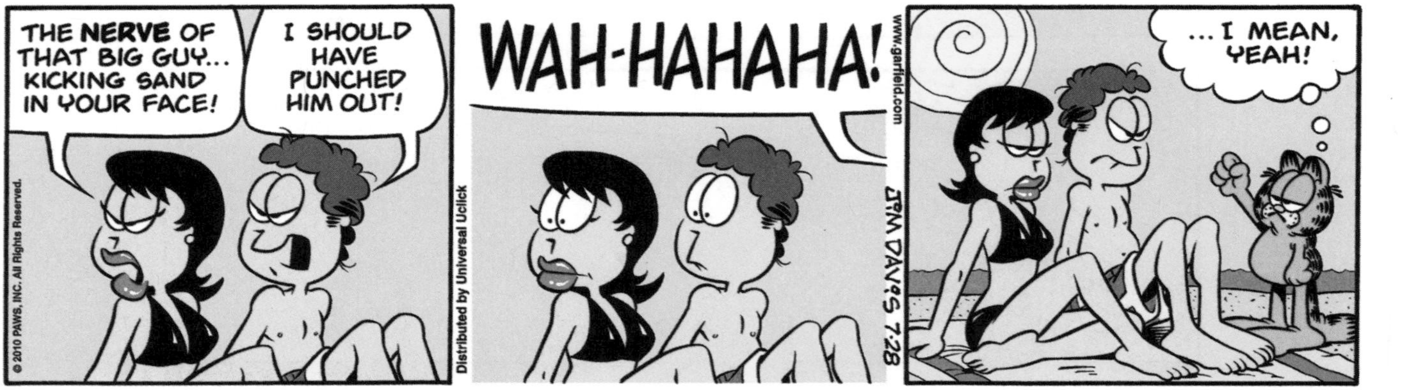
© 2010 PAWS, INC. All Rights Reserved.
THE NERVE OF THAT BIG GUY... KICKING SAND IN YOUR FACE!
I SHOULD HAVE PUNCHED HIM OUT!
Distributed by Universal Uclick
WAH-HAHAHA!
www.garfield.com
JPM DAVIS 7·28
... I MEAN, YEAH!

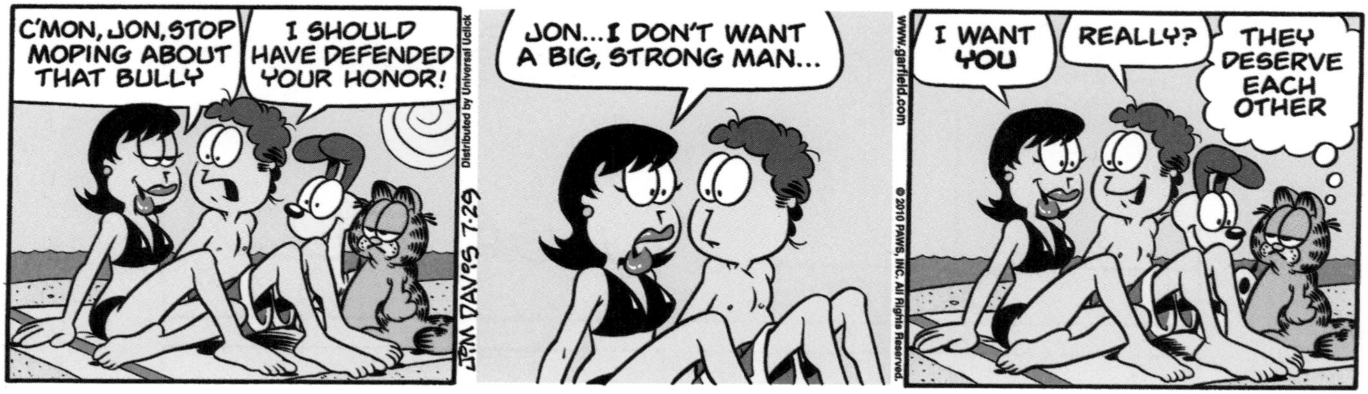
C'MON, JON, STOP MOPING ABOUT THAT BULLY
I SHOULD HAVE DEFENDED YOUR HONOR!
JIM DAVIS 7-29
Distributed by Universal Uclick
JON... I DON'T WANT A BIG, STRONG MAN...
www.garfield.com
© 2010 PAWS, INC. All Rights Reserved.
I WANT YOU
REALLY?
THEY DESERVE EACH OTHER

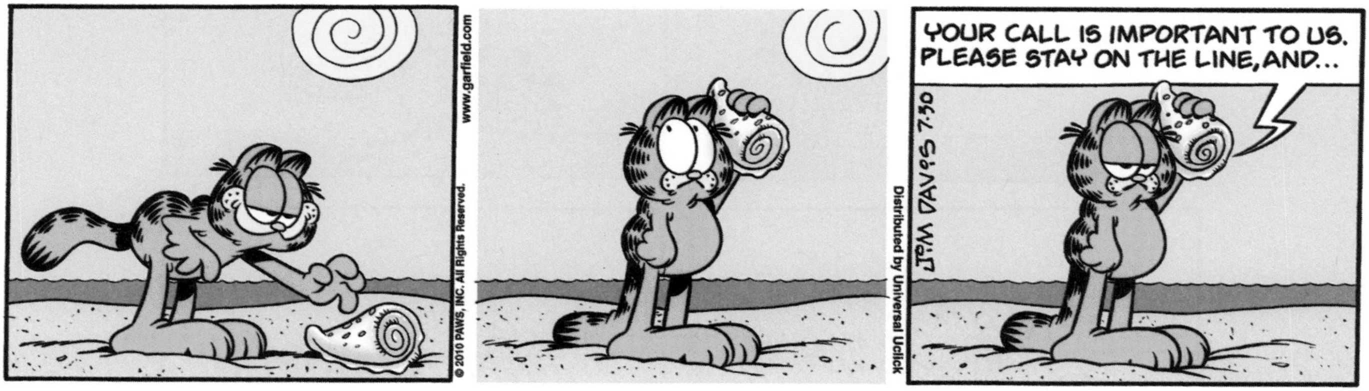
www.garfield.com
© 2010 PAWS, INC. All Rights Reserved.
Distributed by Universal Uclick
YOUR CALL IS IMPORTANT TO US. PLEASE STAY ON THE LINE, AND...
JIM DAVIS 7-30

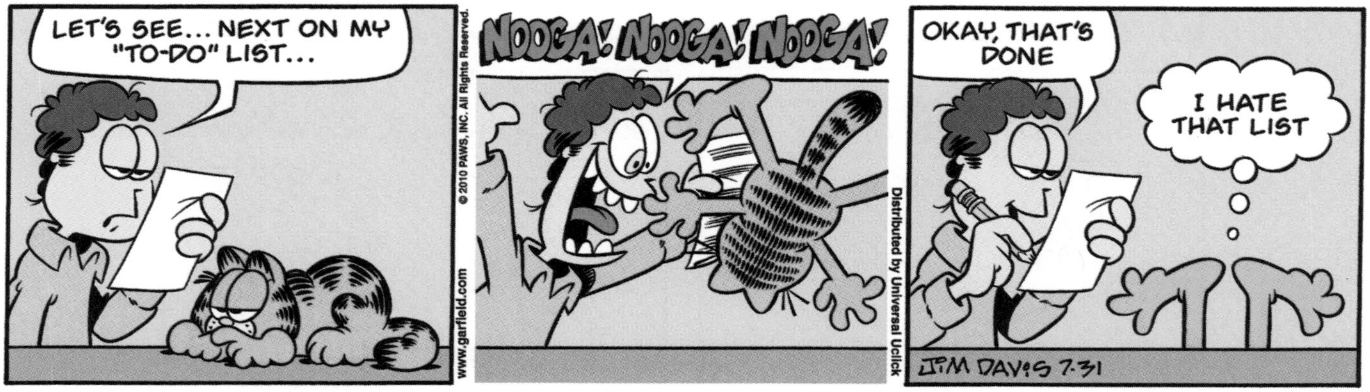
LET'S SEE... NEXT ON MY "TO-DO" LIST...
www.garfield.com
© 2010 PAWS, INC. All Rights Reserved.
NOOGA! NOOGA! NOOGA!
Distributed by Universal Uclick
OKAY, THAT'S DONE
I HATE THAT LIST
JIM DAVIS 7-31

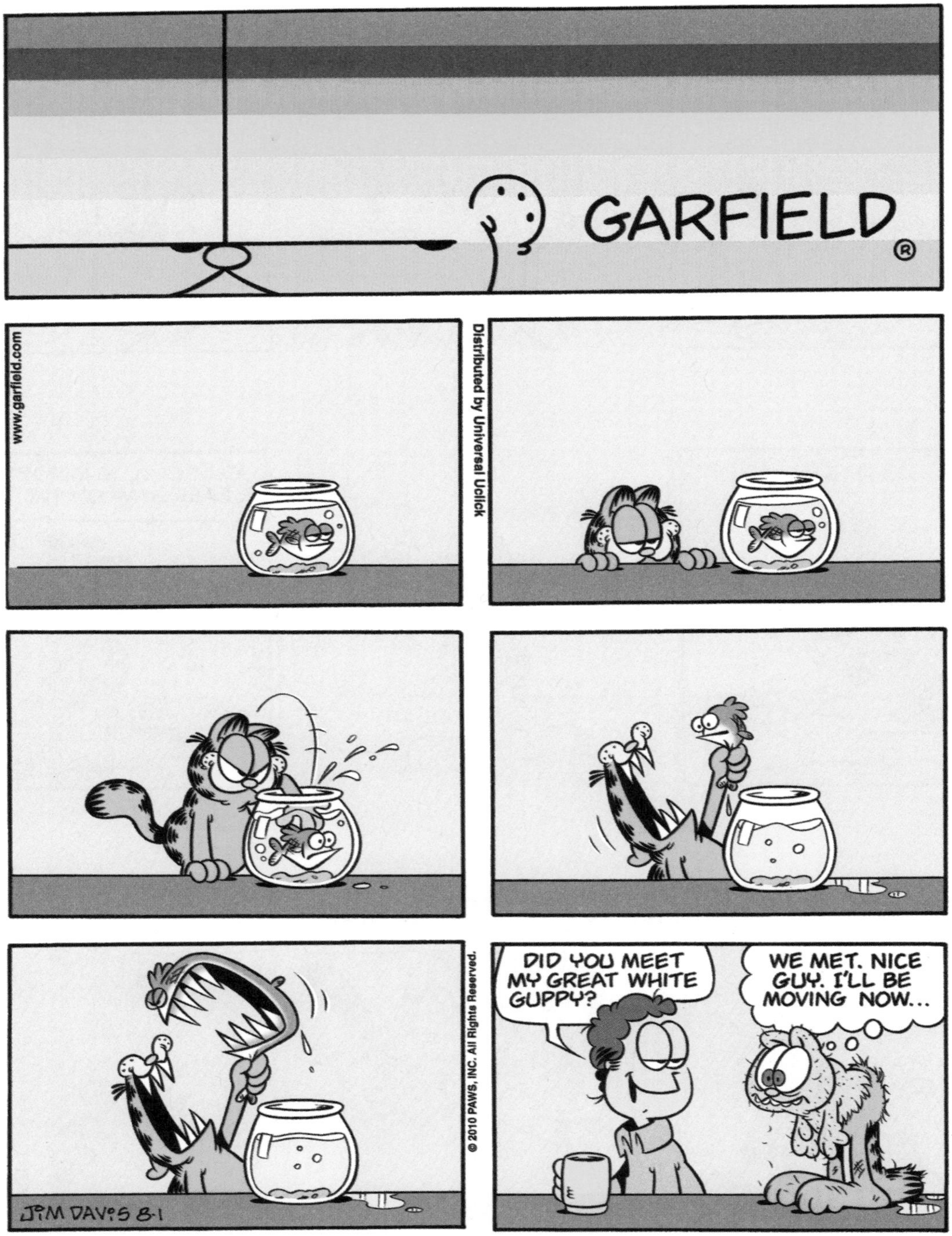
GARFIELD ®
www.garfield.com
Distributed by Universal Uclick
© 2010 PAWS, INC. All Rights Reserved.
JIM DAVIS 8-1
DID YOU MEET MY GREAT WHITE GUPPY?
WE MET. NICE GUY. I'LL BE MOVING NOW...

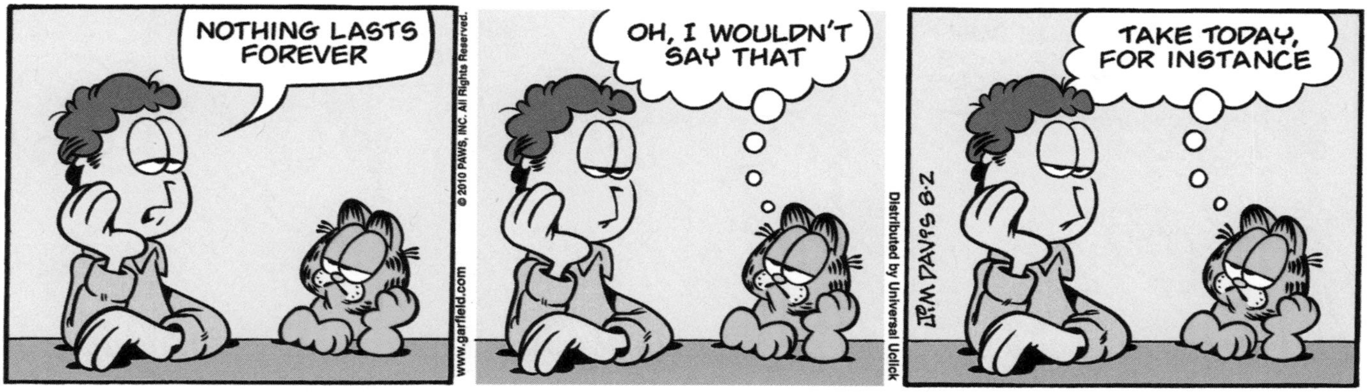
NOTHING LASTS FOREVER
© 2010 PAWS, INC. All Rights Reserved.
www.garfield.com
OH, I WOULDN'T SAY THAT
Distributed by Universal Uclick
TAKE TODAY, FOR INSTANCE
JIM DAVIS 8·2

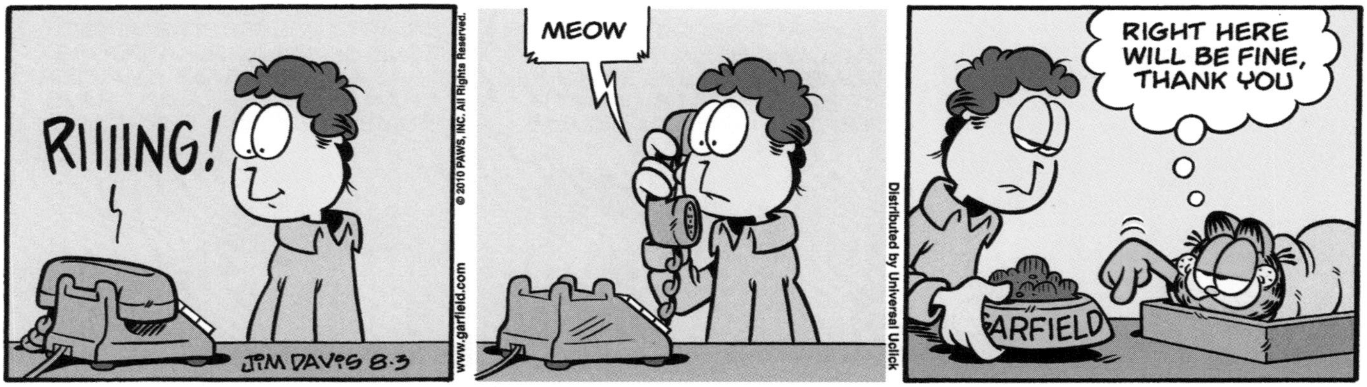
RIIIING!
JIM DAVIS 8·3
© 2010 PAWS, INC. All Rights Reserved.
www.garfield.com
MEOW
Distributed by Universal Uclick
RIGHT HERE WILL BE FINE, THANK YOU
GARFIELD

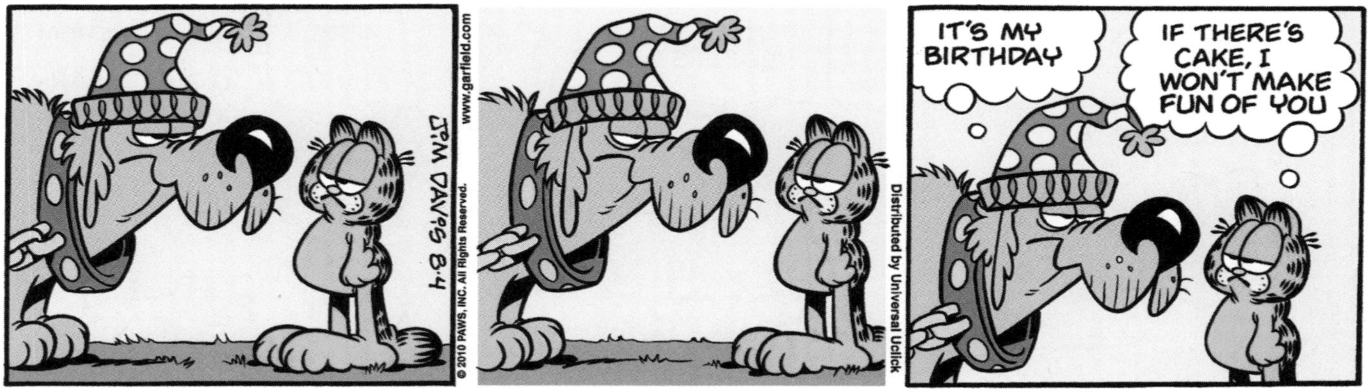
JIM DAVIS 8·4
www.garfield.com
© 2010 PAWS, INC. All Rights Reserved.
Distributed by Universal Uclick
IT'S MY BIRTHDAY
IF THERE'S CAKE, I WON'T MAKE FUN OF YOU

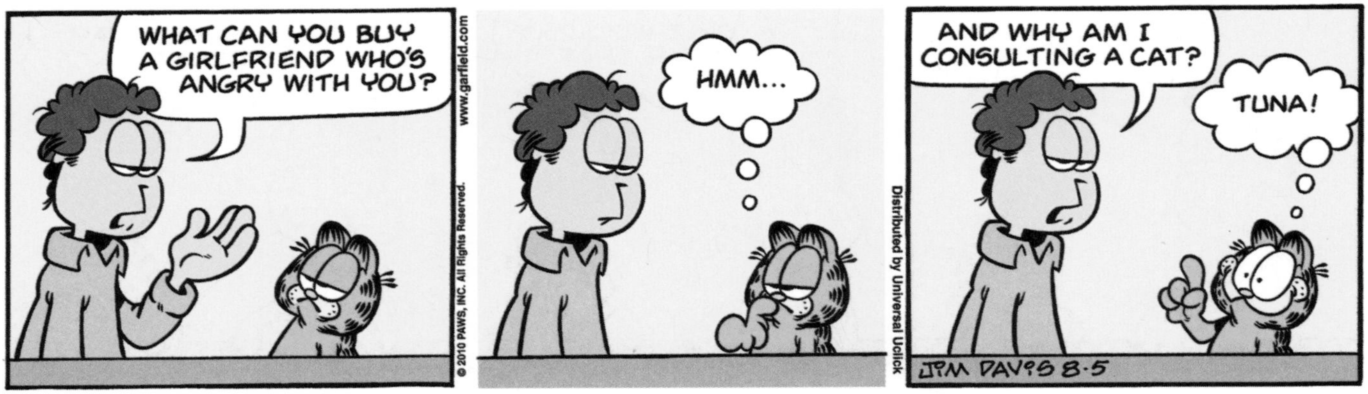
WHAT CAN YOU BUY A GIRLFRIEND WHO'S ANGRY WITH YOU?
© 2010 PAWS, INC. All Rights Reserved. www.garfield.com
HMM...
AND WHY AM I CONSULTING A CAT?
TUNA!
Distributed by Universal Uclick
JIM DAVIS 8-5

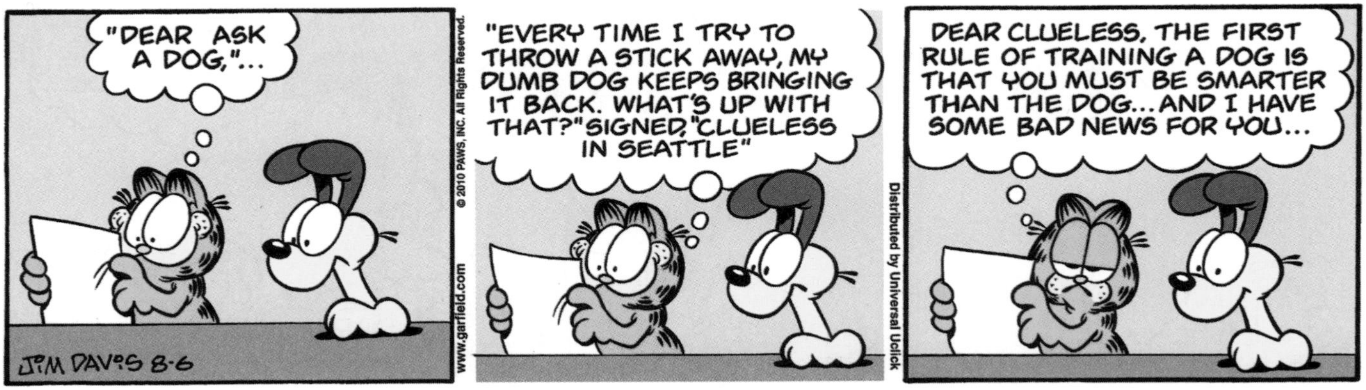
"DEAR ASK A DOG,"...
JIM DAVIS 8-6
© 2010 PAWS, INC. All Rights Reserved. www.garfield.com
"EVERY TIME I TRY TO THROW A STICK AWAY, MY DUMB DOG KEEPS BRINGING IT BACK. WHAT'S UP WITH THAT?" SIGNED, "CLUELESS IN SEATTLE"
Distributed by Universal Uclick
DEAR CLUELESS, THE FIRST RULE OF TRAINING A DOG IS THAT YOU MUST BE SMARTER THAN THE DOG... AND I HAVE SOME BAD NEWS FOR YOU...

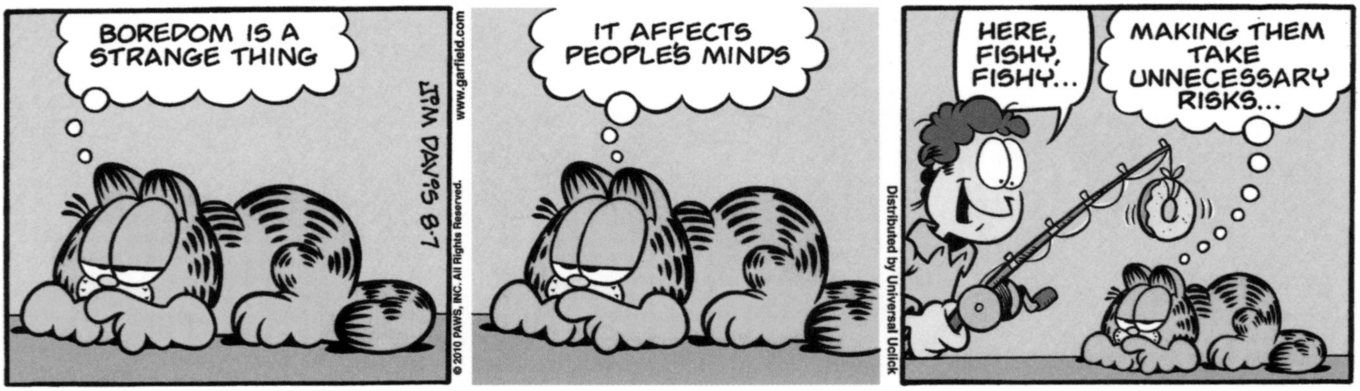
BOREDOM IS A STRANGE THING
JIM DAVIS 8-7
© 2010 PAWS, INC. All Rights Reserved. www.garfield.com
IT AFFECTS PEOPLE'S MINDS
Distributed by Universal Uclick
HERE, FISHY, FISHY...
MAKING THEM TAKE UNNECESSARY RISKS...

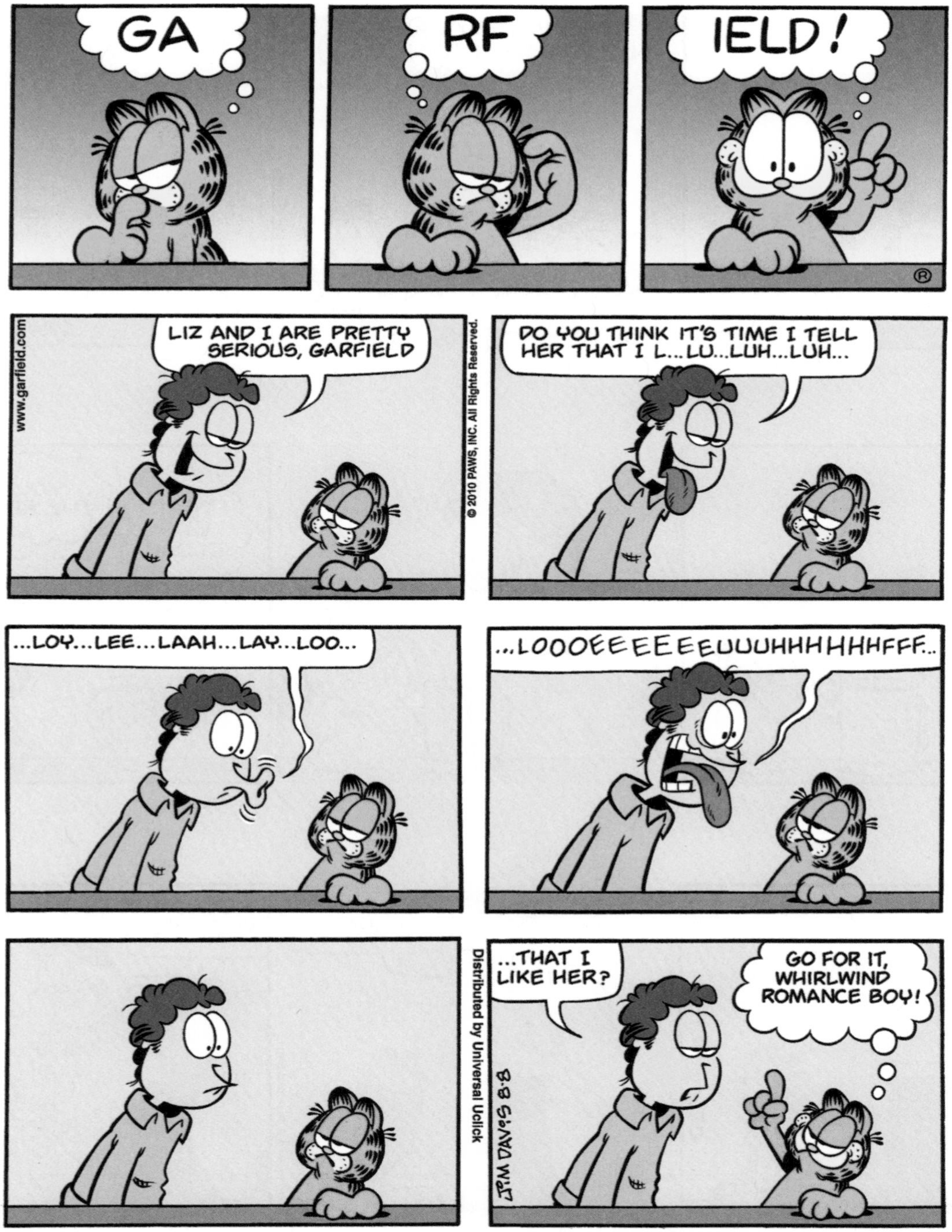
GA
RF
IELD!
www.garfield.com
LIZ AND I ARE PRETTY SERIOUS, GARFIELD
© 2010 PAWS, INC. All Rights Reserved.
DO YOU THINK IT'S TIME I TELL HER THAT I L...LU...LUH...LUH...
...LOY...LEE...LAAH...LAY...LOO...
...LOOOEEEEEEUUUHHHHHHFFF...
Distributed by Universal Uclick
...THAT I LIKE HER?
GO FOR IT, WHIRLWIND ROMANCE BOY!
JIM DAVIS 8-8

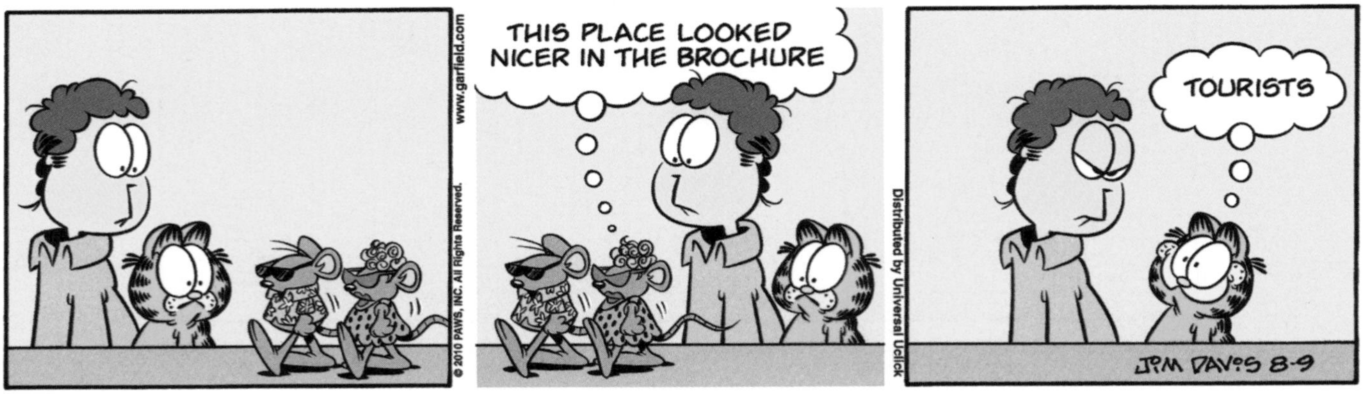
THIS PLACE LOOKED NICER IN THE BROCHURE
TOURISTS
© 2010 PAWS, INC. All Rights Reserved. www.garfield.com
Distributed by Universal Uclick
JIM DAVIS 8-9

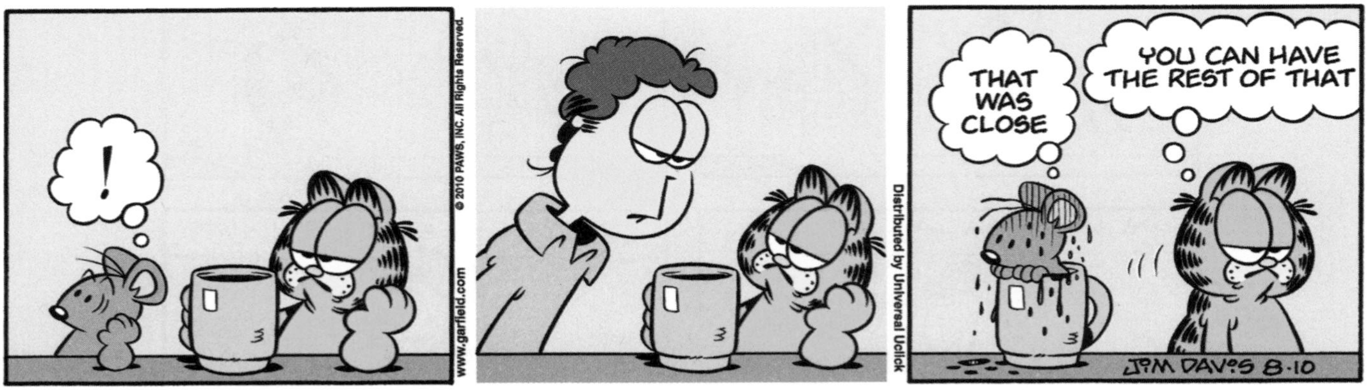
!
THAT WAS CLOSE
YOU CAN HAVE THE REST OF THAT
© 2010 PAWS, INC. All Rights Reserved. www.garfield.com
Distributed by Universal Uclick
JIM DAVIS 8-10

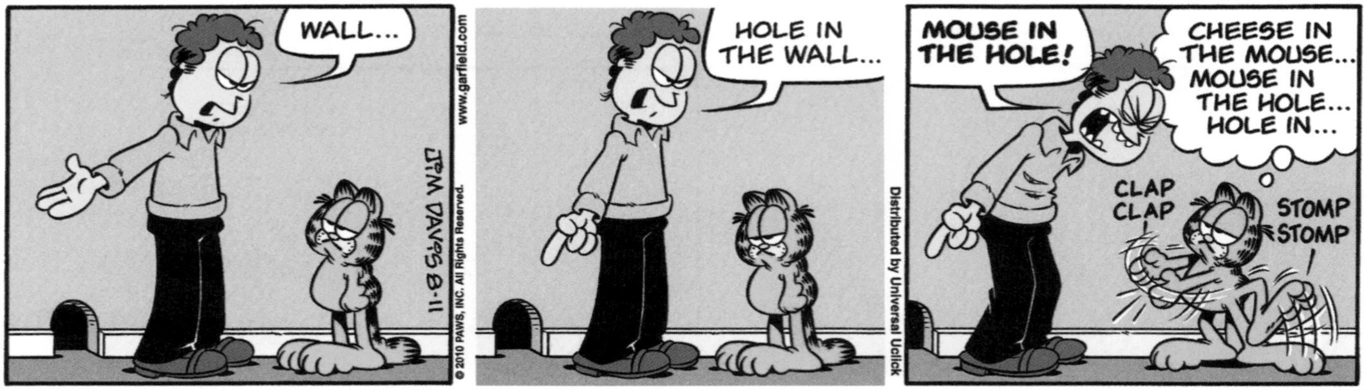
WALL...
HOLE IN THE WALL...
MOUSE IN THE HOLE!
CHEESE IN THE MOUSE... MOUSE IN THE HOLE... HOLE IN...
CLAP CLAP
STOMP STOMP
JIM DAVIS 8-11
© 2010 PAWS, INC. All Rights Reserved. www.garfield.com
Distributed by Universal Uclick

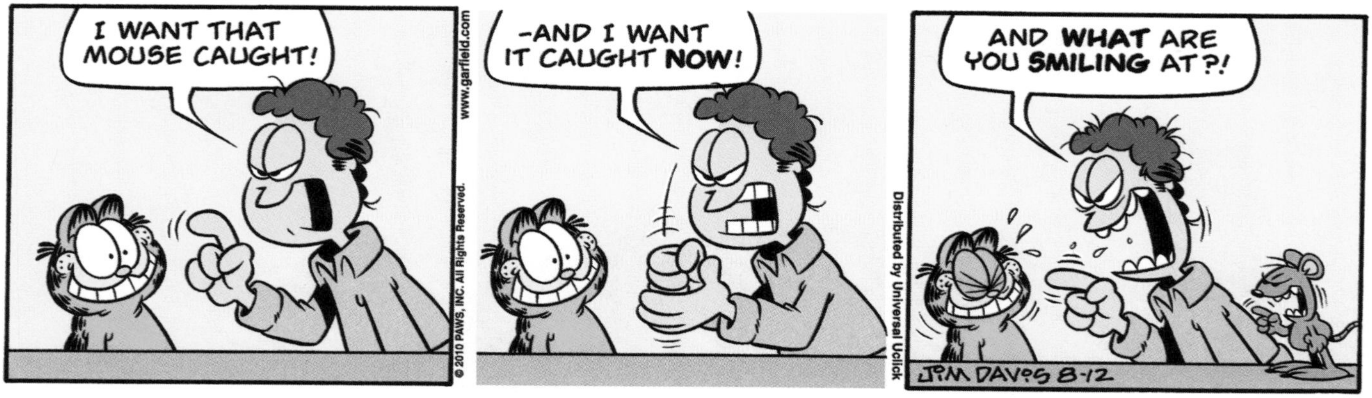
I WANT THAT MOUSE CAUGHT!
www.garfield.com
© 2010 PAWS, INC. All Rights Reserved.
-AND I WANT IT CAUGHT NOW!
Distributed by Universal Uclick
AND WHAT ARE YOU SMILING AT?!
JIM DAVIS 8-12

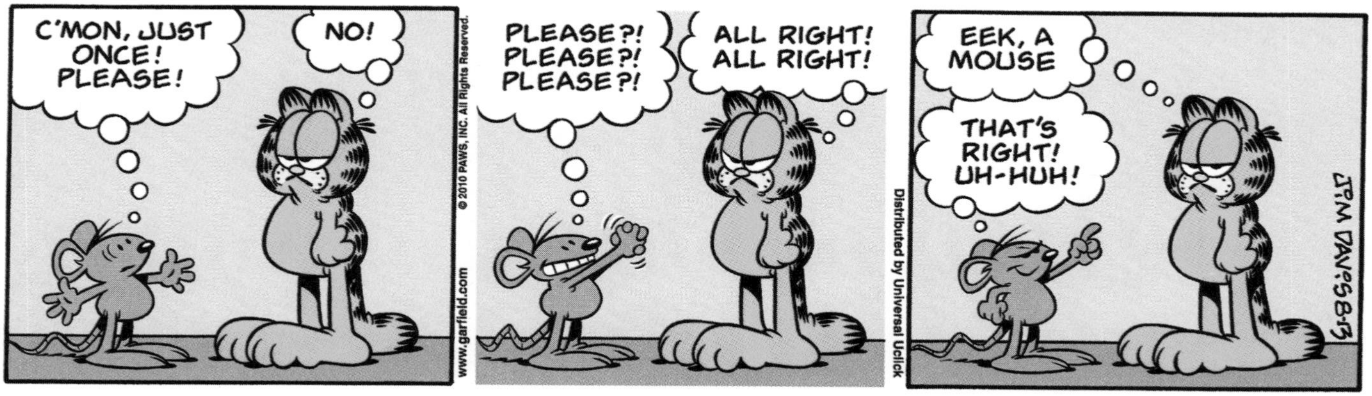
C'MON, JUST ONCE! PLEASE!
NO!
© 2010 PAWS, INC. All Rights Reserved.
www.garfield.com
PLEASE?! PLEASE?! PLEASE?!
ALL RIGHT! ALL RIGHT!
Distributed by Universal Uclick
EEK, A MOUSE
THAT'S RIGHT! UH-HUH!
JIM DAVIS 8-13

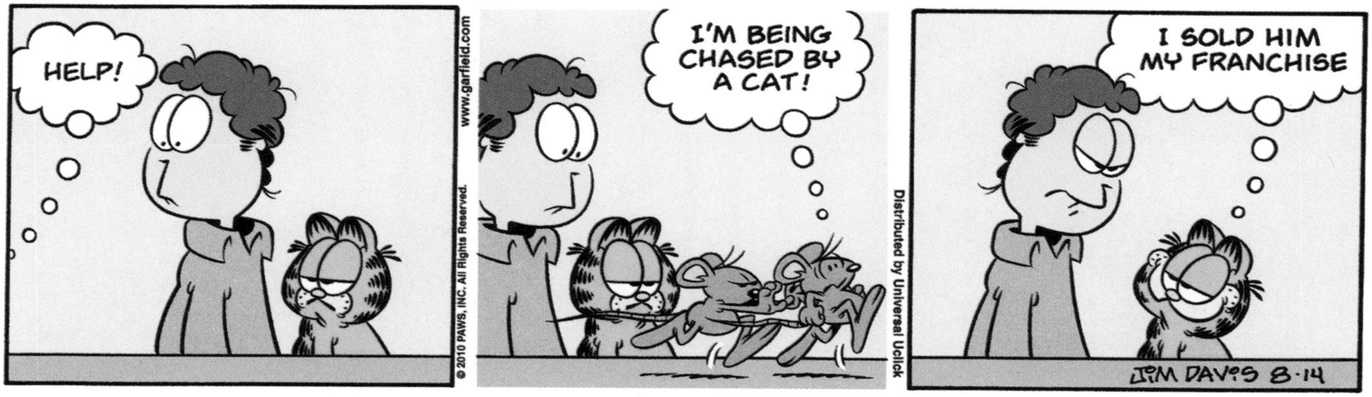
HELP!
www.garfield.com
© 2010 PAWS, INC. All Rights Reserved.
I'M BEING CHASED BY A CAT!
Distributed by Universal Uclick
I SOLD HIM MY FRANCHISE
JIM DAVIS 8-14

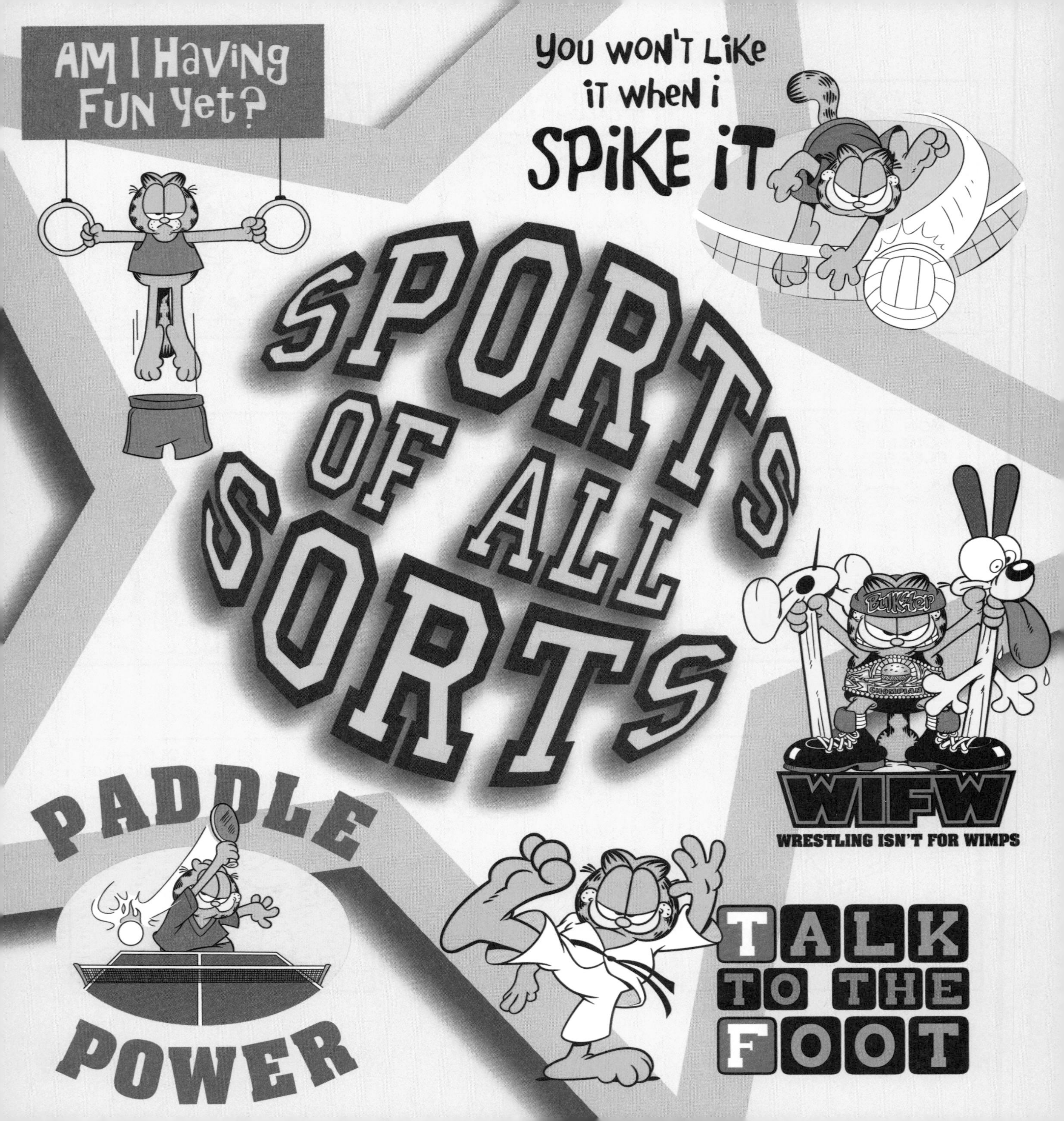
AM I Having FUN Yet?
YOU WON'T LIKE IT WHEN I SPIKE IT
SPORTS OF ALL SORTS
WIFW
WRESTLING ISN'T FOR WIMPS
PADDLE POWER
TALK TO THE FOOT